Work and Migration

One of the most common reasons for the migration of people is the search for a better livelihood. However, this remains one of the most under-researched and theorized area of migration studies.

This book aims to redress the balance, and shift focus away from the economic factors usually examined by scholars of migration. Mobile populations do not necessarily migrate to start a new life elsewhere, but rather to search out new opportunities that may allow them to enhance and diversify livelihoods practiced back home.

Using case studies of local people from across the world who have moved either transnationally or internally within their own country, international contributors offer various definitions of what it means to make a living on the move. Mobile livelihoods, which have emanated from the Caribbean, Latin America and East Africa and expanded to North America, Europe and Asia are analyzed to present a picture of multiple flows of lives and skills through migrating to work.

This book will appeal to researchers in migration studies, anthropology and development studies.

Ninna Nyberg Sørensen is Senior Researcher at the Centre for Development Research, Copenhagen. She has worked extensively on transnational migration in the Dominican Republic, the United States, Spain and Morocco, and internal migration in Peru.

Karen Fog Olwig is Senior Lecturer in Anthropology at the University of Copenhagen. She has published widely on the meaning of place, identity and movement in the Caribbean. Her recent publications include *Siting Culture: The Shifting Anthropological Object* (with Kirsten Hastrup) which is also published by Routledge.

Transnationalism
Edited by Steven Vertovec
University of Oxford

'Transnationalism' broadly refers to multiple ties and interactions linking people or institutions across the borders of nation-states. Today myriad systems of relationship, exchange and mobility function intensively and in real time while being spread across the world. New technologies, especially involving telecommunications, serve to connect such networks. Despite great distances and notwithstanding the presence of international borders (and all the laws, regulations and national narratives they represent), many forms of association have been globally intensified and now take place paradoxically in a planet-spanning yet common arena of activity. In some instances transnational forms and processes serve to speed up or exacerbate historical patterns of activity, in others they represent arguably new forms of human interaction. Transnational practices and their consequent configurations of power are shaping the world of the twenty-first century.

This book forms part of a series of volumes concerned with describing and analyzing a range of phenomena surrounding this field. Serving to ground theory and research on 'globalization', the Routledge book series on 'Transnationalism' offers the latest empirical studies and ground-breaking theoretical works on contemporary socio-economic, political and cultural processes which span international boundaries. Contributions to the series are drawn from Sociology, Economics, Anthropology, Politics, Geography, International Relations, Business Studies and Cultural Studies.

The series is associated with the Transnational Communities Research Programme of the Economic and Social Research Council (see http://www.transcomm.ox.ac.uk).

The series consists of two strands:

Transnationalism aims to address the need of students and teachers and these titles will be published in hardback and paperback. Titles include:

Culture and Politics in the Information Age
A new politics?
Edited by Frank Webster

Routledge Research in Transnationalism is a forum for innovative new research intended for a high-level specialist readership, and the titles will be available in hardback only. Titles include:

Work and Migration

Life and livelihoods in a
globalizing world

Edited by
Ninna Nyberg Sørensen
and
Karen Fog Olwig

London and New York

First published 2002
by Routledge
11 New Fetter Lane, London EC4P 4EE
Simultaneously published in the USA and Canada
by Routledge
29 West 35th Street, New York, NY 10001

Routledge is an imprint of the Taylor & Francis Group

Typeset in 10/12 pt Times by
Newgen Imaging Systems (P) Ltd, Chennai, India
Printed and bound in Great Britain by Biddles Ltd, Guildford and King's Lynn

British Library Cataloguing in Publication Data
A catalogue record for this book is available
from the British Library

Library of Congress Cataloguing in Publication Data
Sørensen, Nina Nyberg
   Work and migration: life and livelihoods in a globalizing world/
   Ninna Nyberg Sørensen and Karen Fog Olwig
      p. cm.
   Includes bibliographical references and index.
   ISBN 0-415-26372-7
      1. Alien labor. 2. Emigration and immigration – Economic aspects.
   3. Globalization – Economic aspects. I. Olwig, Karen Fog, 1948– II. Title.

HD6300 .S67 2002
331.6'2–dc21   2001052016

Contents

Tables

Contributors

Vered Amit is Associate Professor at the Department of Sociology and Anthropology, Concordia University, Montreal, Canada.

Jorge Duany is Professor of Anthropology at the Department of Sociology and Anthropology, University of Puerto Rico, Río Piedras, Puerto Rico.

Bodil Folke Frederiksen is Senior Lecturer in International Development Studies at Roskilde University Center, Denmark.

Carla Freeman is Associate Professor at the Department of Anthropology, Institute of Women's Studies, Emory University, USA.

Karen Fog Olwig is Senior Lecturer at the Institute of Anthropology, University of Copenhagen, Denmark.

Karsten Paerregaard is Senior Lecturer at the Institute of Anthropology, University of Copenhagen, Denmark.

Ninna Nyberg Sørensen is Senior Researcher at the Centre for Development Research, Gammel Kongevej 5, DK-1610 Copenhagen V, Denmark.

Finn Stepputat is Senior Researcher at the Centre for Development Research in Copenhagen, Denmark.

Carla Tamagno is completing her PhD at the Department of Sociology's Development Studies Section, University of Wageningen, The Netherlands.

Elizabeth Thomas-Hope is Professor of Environmental Management in the Department of Geography and Geology at the University of the West Indies, Mona, Jamaica.

Mobile livelihoods

Making a living in the world[1]

Karen Fog Olwig and Ninna Nyberg Sørensen

A basic assumption in migration studies is that the search for a better livelihood is a main cause of migratory movements. Nevertheless, such studies rarely take in-depth research into specific livelihoods as their point of departure. This sort of approach would focus on the ways in which making a livelihood links up with larger-scale patterns of population movement, the range and variation in mobility that such movements involve, the social institutions and networks facilitating and sustaining mobile livelihoods, and the social and spatial practices of mobile populations.

It is the contention of this book that a focus on mobile livelihoods can offer a point of departure in migration research that resolves some of the field's definitional and conceptual problems. These problems concern, first and foremost, the habit of viewing migration primarily as a recent historical phenomenon linked to the globalization of capitalism and involving one-way movements between nation states that entail ruptures with former livelihoods. As the empirical case studies in this volume show, contemporary migration movements, whether internal or international, often have historical antecedents. In addition, the case studies demonstrate that mobile populations do not necessarily migrate to start a new life elsewhere, but rather to search out new opportunities that may allow them to enhance and diversify livelihoods practised and valued back home.

Migration research, once a fairly small and specialized subfield within the social sciences, acquired a central place in academia during the last decades of the twentieth century. An important result of this new focus on migration has been that there is now much greater awareness of the significance of movement and the formation and sustaining of long-distance ties in human life and society. This has led to the emergence of new concepts, such as globalization, de/reterritorialization, diaspora and transnationalism, that seek to capture the mobile and spatially ruptured, yet socio-culturally interconnected nature of human life. Within the field of migration research, the concept of transnationalism moved centre stage during the 1990s and figures as a key term in a number of publications from this decade (see, e.g. Featherstone 1990; Rouse 1991, 1995; Appadurai 1991; Glick Schiller *et al.* 1992; Basch *et al.* 1994; Kearney 1991, 1995, 1998; Mahler 1995, 1998; Guarnizo 1997; Smith and Guarnizo 1998; Vertovec and Cohen 1999). This literature, which is mainly based on immigration to the United States, suggests that contemporary migrants develop transnational identities that challenge the notion of migration as involving settled populations crossing political borders in order to establish a new home in a new nation state. Proponents of transnationalism thus argue that migrants often interact and identify with multiple nations, states, and/or communities, and that their identifications and practices contribute to the development of transnational communities or a new type of transnational social space (Rouse 1991; Fletcher 1999).

In the wake of the sudden prominence given to transnationalism, some scholars have expressed concern about the term's increasing ambiguity, and recently it has been criticized on empirical as well as theoretical grounds (Smith and Guanizo 1998). This book examines two related issues that have emerged in recent discussions of transnationalism. One concerns the need for the further specification and refinement of the concept of transnationalism, which has been used to describe a broad range of movements and networks of interrelations spanning disparate places (various contributions in Smith and Guarnizo 1998; Ong 1999; Glick Schiller 1999; Portes *et al.* 1999). The other is motivated by the fear that the very diffuseness of the notion of transnationalism may narrow the field of investigation to movements and networks of relations that involve the bodily crossing of nation state boundaries, because this is the only explicitly and clearly defined feature of transnationalism (Olwig 1997; Sørensen 2000). The present volume seeks to resolve some of these issues by redirecting migration research away from the narrow focus on international population movements and the concomitant emergence of cross-border networks of relations, calling instead for a broader investigation of mobile livelihoods and the fluid fields of social, economic and political relations and cultural values that these livelihoods imply. We thus advocate shifting the analytical focus from place to mobility, and from 'place of origin' and 'place of destination' to the movements involved in sustaining a livelihood. It is our hope that the shift in focus that characterizes this collection of chapters will contribute towards an understanding of the importance of mobility to the relationship between people, place, identity and belonging.

Notions of livelihood

Livelihood, at least implicitly, is a central concept in migration research. Researchers, and often migrants themselves, explain migration movements in terms of economic factors that imply a notion of livelihood. Researchers have pointed to the role of world capitalism in creating unequal economic relations. They have examined the push/pull factors that lead people in economically less developed areas to migrate to economic centres, and have pointed to the improved means of communication and transportation that have enabled such movements to escalate in number and intensity in recent decades (for a discussion, see Glick Schiller *et al.* 1992: 8–9; Castles and Miller 1993; Skeldon 1997; Van Hear 1998). When asked why they migrate, migrants will often reply that they are moving for 'better opportunities' elsewhere. Yet, there is often no clear correlation between economic changes and migration movements, and it is difficult to preserve the image of the migrant as a 'homo oeconomicus' who is making decisions about migration on the basis of informed economic calculations. As Hvidt notes (1975: 35), writing of migrants from Europe to America, one 'cannot help sighing a little at the firm, sometimes even heavy-handed and generalizing way in which [. . .] individual human lives have been dragged in and out of diagrams and tables, and have had motives for their momentous decision ascribed to them which they themselves very likely would have regarded without much understanding.' Ideas of 'better (economic) opportunities' and the ways in which they are viewed and acted upon through migration movement therefore need further examination. We believe that the notion of mobile livelihoods will provide a useful concept in this endeavour.

Generally, 'livelihood' tends to be thought of in economic terms. *The Oxford English Dictionary* of 1971 defines the term as a 'means of living, maintenance, sustenance; especially to earn, gain, get, make, seek a livelihood.' This definition, however, leaves open the question of what kinds of 'means' are deemed necessary to secure a desirable 'living, maintenance, sustenance' and the means by which people attempt to achieve this. This aspect of livelihood is brought out in an older notion of livelihood found in *The Oxford English Dictionary*, which refers to 'course of life, life time, kind or manner of life.' This points to a historical shift in the definition of livelihood from an emphasis on the cultural and social to a stress on the more economic, material aspects of livelihood.

The anthropological literature suggests that, while livelihood, at its basis, may involve the control of nature in order to 'wrest a living from it,' the 'working relationship between man and nature is never unembroidered' (Wallman 1979: 1). In his study of patterns of livelihood activities, Gudeman (1986: vii–viii) elucidates several different 'models of livelihood' and argues that the 'activities of livelihood are enacted through a symbolic scheme which is drawn from known features of the social world.' Knowledge of the social world is therefore necessary to understand 'what is being modeled concerning gaining a livelihood' (ibid.: 39). Furthermore, these social worlds are not necessarily confined to local communities but may be informed by global relations with, for example, former colonial empires. This notion of livelihood is apparent in Parkin's ethnographic study of 'work' in coastal Kenya (1979), which demonstrates that wage employment, with its regular provision of income, may be perceived as offering a greater control of resources than fishing or farming, which provide a higher but more irregular income. Parkin relates this to distinctions and value judgements concerning 'good' and 'bad' domestic labour introduced by colonial governments and maintained in the post-colonial society. This, in turn, may lead to migration for a type of work not readily available locally (Parkin 1979: 332; see also Murray 1979).

In a discussion of rural livelihood diversification, Ellis (1998) argues that a livelihood encompasses income (in both cash and kind), as well as the social institutions (kin, family, compound, village, etc.), gender relations, and the property rights required to support and sustain a certain standard of living. Social and kinship networks become particularly important in facilitating and sustaining diversified livelihoods that involve a range of spatially extended social and economic activities. Any study of livelihood therefore requires an awareness of the wider spatial context of the unit of analysis (whether individual, household, village or nation). For this reason, the notion of livelihood offers a particularly useful concept in analysing the ways in which actors deal with the varying and complex local and global interrelations in which human life is embedded today. Following a similar line of thought, Long argues (2000: 196) that the livelihood concept 'best expresses the idea of individuals and groups striving to make a living, attempting to meet their various consumption and economic necessities, coping with uncertainties, responding to new opportunities, and choosing between different value positions.' He adds that livelihood strategies may be organized in a variety of different contexts – some spanning great geographical as well as social distances – and that it is therefore necessary to identify 'relevant social units and fields of activity' in studies of livelihoods (ibid.: 196–7). Furthermore, these strategies concern 'value choice, status issues, identification with or distantiation from other modes of living and types of social persons' (ibid.: 197) that involve changes as well as continuities through time.

We suggest that migration be conceptualized in relation to an analytical framework concerning the practice of particular livelihoods. This research agenda takes its point of departure in studies of livelihood practices and thus avoids problems of having to define a priori the topical units and forms of movement that comprise the constitutive units within migration research. Rather, it examines various forms of livelihood as practised, and conceived, by specific social actors in particular ethnographic and historical contexts, and the local, regional and more distant spheres of activity that these livelihoods imply. From this point of view, places emerge as sites of particular importance, as people, in the course of practising their livelihoods, develop social and economic relations and cultural values in relation to, and spanning, particular localities under varying historical, social and personal circumstances. In other words, our concern with the ways people make a living puts an equal emphasis on habitus and habitat, on mobile livelihood practices connecting different localities. By studying movement from the point of view of mobile livelihoods that both define and cut across a range of social, economic and cultural boundaries, it is possible to explore critically the topical units and forms of movement that may be of relevance in migratory movements. This approach raises questions about the tradition in migration research which has tended to examine population movements only in relation to formal administrative units, in particular the nation state. The following discussion of some of the constitutive elements in migration research will clarify, and substantiate, this assertion.

Migration as movement between places

In the 1990s, the *Merriam-Webster Collegiate Dictionary* was still offering a definition of migration as the act of 'moving from one country, place, or locality to another'. Though few may quibble with this definition, most would probably agree that it is deceptively simple, begging more questions than it answers. It is, for example, apparent that many 'moves' are not final in the sense that they do not involve complete 'changes of residence or location' so that one 'residence' or 'location' is abandoned in favour of another. Indeed, a host of recent migration studies have documented an increasing tendency for migrants to engage in repeated moves and to maintain a strong presence in more than one locality through active engagement in fields of socio-economic relations that span more than one locality. Moves, in other words, often do not involve displacement, but rather multi-placement, that is, an expansion of the space for personal or familial livelihood practices to two or more localities (Georges 1990; Olwig 1993; Gardner 1995). Furthermore, migrants' deep involvement in geographically extensive yet socio-economically close-knit fields of relations has led to the very notions of place or locality being questioned. Thus, it is difficult to define clearly demarcated and unambiguous topical units when they are embedded in social and cultural contexts of life that are not confined to particular spots on the geographic map (Appadurai 1995; Olwig and Hastrup 1997). The only spatial units that have a clear, formal demarcation are legal, administrative units, in the sense that they are well defined and governed by a body of laws and regulations. Some of these units have played a central role in the regulation of population movements, and movement in relation to these units has therefore been relatively well documented. This is particularly the case as far as nation states are concerned, and this may be an important reason why population movements between nation states have figured so prominently in migration research.[2]

Place as the legal-administrative unit of the nation state

The role of the nation state in controlling population movements has changed a great deal through time. In Europe, the end of feudalism and the growing influence of the market economy, accompanied by the increasing significance of towns and townspeople, marked the beginning of mass migrations from the rural countryside to nascent cities. Until 1800, European states placed severe restrictions on inhabitants' movements within and particularly out of the country. The state regarded the loss of people through emigration as a serious loss of its resources (Hvidt 1975: 15). After the Napoleonic Wars and the French Revolution, however, the right of citizens to move out of the country was codified in the constitutions of a number of European countries (ibid.: 17). The nineteenth century was generally characterized by substantial population movements within and out of Europe, as well as from Europe to countries in other continents, especially North America. Approximately 2.5 million people migrated from Scandinavia to 'America' in 1850–1930 alone – a third of Scandinavia's mid-nineteenth century population. While these migrations have generally been explained by large population increases in Europe – from 1750 to 1850 the population increased 83 per cent, from 145 million to 265 million – Oivind Fuglerud (2001) points to factors such as rural-urban migrants' inclination to seek livelihoods further away, as well as the importance of networks of information established in private correspondence and commercial advertising.

Thus, historical analyses offer many points of resemblance with contemporary transnational theorizing (see also Hvidt 1975).

The relatively free mobility of people between Europe and North America in the nineteenth century was brought to an abrupt halt with the introduction of immigration quotas in the United States in 1921. This led to a new situation in which nation states began to protect their borders against immigration rather than emigration (Hvidt 1975: 19). The quota system was instituted after mass migration from Europe had peaked (ibid.: 12).[3] The restrictions on migration therefore became targeted primarily at potential immigrants from other parts of the world who had begun to emigrate in increasing numbers. In the course of the twentieth century, most countries have instituted restrictions on immigration. In the developed Western countries, these restrictions were first applied primarily against the inhabitants of former European colonies. Thus, whereas the subjects of, for example, the British colonies were in theory able to move freely to Great Britain, progressively greater restrictions were placed on all immigrants after the 1950s. As former imperial structures have been broken up into smaller units of politically independent nation states, population movements have become further checked by an increasing number of controls within the developing world.[4] However, these restrictions against crossing borders do not seem to have led to a decrease in international migration. Quite the contrary, migration across political borders seems more prevalent than ever, though much of this migration is spurred by increasing political and economic instability in developing countries leading to forced displacements and undocumented entries for those who do not 'qualify' as asylum seekers or refugees (Van Hear 1998).

Due to the emphasis on the gate-keeping function of the political borders of nation states, there has been a long tradition of collecting data on cross-border movements. Though the data gathered often lacks consistency, this means that a large body of information on international migration has been available for statistical analyses of various aspects of this particular form of migration. Much of the early research on international migration has therefore had a rather quantitative orientation and has focused on the demographic and economic implications of migration between different nation states (Hvidt 1975: 32–5; Yans-McLaughlin 1990: 258–9). In Europe, the main research interest concerned the effects of migration out of Europe until well into the latter half of the twentieth century. This changed, however, when considerable migration to Europe began and the focus shifted to the impact of immigration into Europe. In North America, a central topic of investigation has been the effects of immigration on the receiving country, as reflected in the strong tradition of doing research on the integration of immigrants into American or Canadian society.[5] This research is primarily concerned with the creation of, for example, new American citizens and the future development of American society, and only secondarily with the phenomenon of migration itself (see also Olwig 2001). This North American research tradition has had, and continues to have, a major impact on migration studies, even after conceptualizations and understandings of migration changed direction in the last decades of the twentieth century.[6]

In recent decades, as international migration has become subject to greater control and increasing numbers of international migrants travel and live in undocumented ways, researchers have also begun to focus on the ability of migrants to negotiate the legal, social and economic barriers they encounter because of their precarious legal status. This has perhaps been most thoroughly investigated in studies of undocumented migration between Mexico and other Central American countries and the United States (see, e.g. Chavez 1991; Kearney 1991; Smith 1994; Hagan 1994; Fitzgerald 2000; Kyle 2000). In Europe, the Strait of Gibraltar serves the function of separating the European Union from unwanted migration from Africa. Only recently have studies of the effects of heightened migration controls on undocumented migration begun to emerge (Driessen 1998; Harding 2000; Sørensen 2000).

The strong focus on international migration has had the unfortunate result that other kinds of population movement have received less attention. Yet, migration is hardly confined to movements that involve the crossing of international borders. Indeed, the number of people who have migrated within the borders of nation states may be much larger. It is, for example, noticeable that the historical relocation of African-Americans from the South to other parts of the United States – a movement that involved more than five million people – as well as more contemporary massive displacements within developing countries, have not been incorporated into the mainstream of migration research because of its international focus. The historical split between migration and refugee studies partly accounts for this.[7] In this disciplinary partitioning of fields, internal displacement is allocated to 'refugee-studies'. That this split, and the concomitant split categorization of mobile populations into migrants, refugees and internally displaced populations, is problematic to maintain for analytical purposes is argued by Stepputat, Tamagno and Sørensen (this volume).

The strong interest in the relationship between international migration and the development of nation states may be related to the fact that most researchers on migration are located in major Western countries and thus influenced by social, economic and political concerns in these countries. In recent years, these concerns have tended to revolve around the negative and positive impact of foreigners on the receiving societies. In stating this, we do not mean to imply that migration researchers have served the interests of the state. Indeed, a great deal of research has sought to document the adverse effects of migration policies on migrants in Western states. We are instead suggesting that the phenomenon of migration has been defined in the light of issues that are accorded significance in the receiving Western countries, where most researchers live and work, rather than from the vantage point of the migrants themselves or from the sending countries. To the extent that a sending country perspective has been included, Third World migrants have often been viewed through the prism of concern about the migration problems they pose for the Western world due to rapid population growth, poverty and conflict in the source countries (for exceptions, see Georges 1990; Gardner 1995; Wilson 1999; Kyle 2000). Less attention has been paid to how migration and its causes are structured and articulated within the overall pattern of global, political and economic relations. Even less attention has been paid to the specificities of particular regions, for example differences between the Americas, Africa, Asia and Europe (but see Castles and Miller 1993; Skeldon 1997; Weiner 1997; Rogers 2000). The significance of the dominant though unspecified Western point of view in migration studies is perhaps most apparent in studies of the cultural and social aspects of migration.

Place and the socio-cultural construction of the nation state

While modern nation states have functioned as central administrative entities in the regulation of global migration movements, citizens of such political units do not see their country merely as a bureaucratic unit. Indeed, modern nation states are predicated on the nationalist ideology that nations correspond to specific socio-cultural 'communities' that constitute natural places of belonging and dwelling for their citizens (Anderson 1983). According to this way of thinking, therefore, international migration involves much more than simply crossing a political border protected by a large legal and administrative apparatus – it also means leaving a native country and culture in order to settle in 'foreign' lands with an 'unknown' culture. Migration therefore comes to implicate a rupture and break with former modes of life and, eventually, integration into new ways of living. Yet, as several anthropologists have noted, this '*National Geographic*' approach, which maintains that a nation state corresponds to a particular culture, is not tenable because it ignores both the considerable cultural variation that exists within the borders of a nation state and the cultural continuities that may obtain across political borders (Gupta and Ferguson 1992; Malkki 1992; Hannerz 1992; Lavie and Swedenburg 1996; Olwig and Hastrup 1997). As Smith notes, there is a need to understand the social construction of place beyond essentialist assumptions about the equivalence of locality and culture. He asks, 'just what makes a place a place like no other place ... what about a place persists and what changes over time ... who changes what in alternative representations of any place's future, and how do these changes selectively appropriate or reject particular elements of any place's historical past?' (Smith 2001: 115). Yi-Fu Tuan suggests (1974) that the primary meaning of place refers to one's place in society, and that the term only secondarily refers to locality. In this social sense, one's place in society is tied to one's livelihood.

In light of the critique of the one nation–one culture equation, migrants' place in receiving societies has been the subject of considerable debate in recent years, leading to the emergence of two major critical perspectives. Recognizing the pluralism of North American society, one perspective has raised the question of whether all migrants are integrated into mainstream America, suggesting that some may undergo a kind of segmented integration (Waters 1994, 1999). In the European case, authors such as Stolcke (1993) and Hintjens (1992) have argued that segregation and assimilation are conceptual opposites and that there may be an urgent need for a revitalized notion of assimilationist policy in the light of the increasing marginalization of immigrants in West European countries.

The other critical approach to the incorporation paradigm argues that migration does not mean abandoning one place for another because migrants maintain ties with their country of origin. As they settle more or less permanently into the societies of destination, migrants become part of transnational socio-cultural systems that transcend the political border between the receiving and sending countries. Or, in another theoretical paradigm, migrants form diasporas that cultivate affective-expressive links with past migration histories (Cohen 1997), implying multiple attachments (Clifford 1994) or several 'homelands' (Shuval 2000). In the work of foremost proponents of the transnational approach, such as Glick Schiller, Basch and Blanc (Glick Schiller *et al.* 1992; Basch *et al.* 1994), such systems are interpreted as counterforces to the American hegemonic structures of race, ethnicity and nationalism (Glick Schiller *et al.* 1992: 13). They thus view these systems as allowing migrants to live in 'a new social and cultural space which calls forth a new awareness of who they [migrants] are, a new consciousness, and new identities' (ibid.: 14).

Both these new approaches to migration research question the close relationship between place and culture, arguing that nationalist, racial and ethnic structures may prevent certain people from becoming, or from wishing to become, fully part of the dominant culture and society of the place to which they have migrated. This in turn means that the receiving country, as a place, does not correspond to a single culture and society. Rather, the migrants' culture, which is originally associated with their place of origin, may become extended to the receiving country in the form of a new non-local socio-cultural system. These approaches therefore challenge migration researchers to pay closer attention to what is outside the well-integrated mainstream society and culture of the nation state, which has been the primary unit of analysis in migration research.[8] Whereas these new approaches to the study of migration posit a critical stance toward the one nation – one culture equation, they do this primarily as a critique of the Western nation states' migration policies and the scholarly understandings of integration fostered by Western academia.

Given that most migration is neither international nor directed towards Western countries, we contend that it will be difficult to develop a broad, cross-cultural analytical framework for the analysis of migration as long as migration is seen as movement between places, and as long as such places can only be defined in terms of formal administrative units such as nation states.

Places and the practice of mobile livelihoods

We suggest that migration be conceptualized in relation to an analytical framework concerning the practice of particular livelihoods. Based on the assumption that one of the basic features of human life is mobility, the concept of mobile livelihoods explores the various practices involved in 'making a living', as well as the social relations used to make a living possible, in the different contexts where they take place. This approach makes it possible to delineate changes in mobility patterns through time in the form of, for example, retractions and extensions of livelihood practices, and the various factors that may have caused these changes to take place. In this way, it becomes possible to examine population movements, and the negotiation of social, economic, cultural and political boundaries that such movements may entail, from a new vantage point.

Central to our notion of mobile livelihoods is the great scope for variation and differentiated experiences that it entails. Mobile livelihoods may be practised over short or long distances, within states and within localities, and/or across national borders. Depending on the context, the study of mobile livelihoods may thus require a local, translocal or transnational perspective. When practised within the borders of a particular nation state, mobile livelihoods may be influenced by transnational processes, as demonstrated in the contributions by Frederiksen, Stepputat and Sørensen in this volume. When practised across national borders, transnationalism as a new and distinct form of identification or practice may or may not develop. But, as the contributions by Duany, Freeman, Olwig and Paerregaard suggest, extensive networks of transnational ties may have developed well before the recent upsurge in mass migration from particular places. Such patterns may vary according to gender (see Freeman, Paerregaard and Tamagno this volume) and class (see Amit, Olwig and Thomas-Hope, this volume). As Paerregaard and Tamagno suggest, they may also be premised on already existing internal migration patterns, whether voluntary or forced.

An important aspect of people's livelihood strategies is the social relationships and cultural values that various strategies involve, the communities of belonging they circumscribe, and the kinds of movement in time and space they make possible or necessitate. It is therefore possible to develop a framework of study where movement can be viewed as an integral aspect of the life trajectories of individuals and groups of people, and not as an abnormal interruption to normal stationary life, depending on the particular circumstances of the livelihoods of the persons studied. In this way, place or locality may be defined in terms of livelihood practices and the communities of socio-economic relations and cultural values with which they are associated. This suggests that 'home' is where one has one's livelihood (Shuval 2000) and that there are many different ways in which people perceive themselves to be 'at home' – as well as homeless – in today's world (Rapport and Dawson 1998).

The contributions

Contemporary mobile livelihoods may be distinguished by their extreme diversification in terms of the many types, labels or categories used to describe the moving subjects (Van Hear 1998; Stepputat and Sørensen 2000). At the outset we do not distinguish between rural–urban migrants and internally displaced populations, political refugees and transmigrants, alien residents, expellees, guest workers, ethnic and racial minorities, expatriate communities, ethnic and racial minorities expatriate communities, and border traders and suitcase peddlers, primarily because many of these categories crosscut one another and because people may shift between them over time. By including case studies concerned with various types of migration, forced as well as voluntary, intra-national as well as inter-or transnational, this volume seeks to challenge those studies of transnational migration that confine the field of investigation to 'transnationalism'. While this view, which has mainly been put forward by US scholars (first and foremost Glick Schiller *et al.* 1992; Basch *et al.* 1994; Glick Schiller 1999), has added valuable insight to our understanding of the nation state and the shifting meaning of nation-hood at the turn of the twentieth century, other aspects of transnational processes, such as the introduction and use/abuse of concepts of human rights and the 'inter-nally displaced', or the development of pan-African diasporic cultural practices, have received less attention. To help bridge the spatial and conceptual gap between scales of analysis, this volume seeks to develop a broader and more encompassing approach to the study of migration by locating it in the context of the pursuit of livelihood and the sort of places and fields of relations that it circumscribes.

The individual contributions included in the volume consist of a number of case studies that detail different forms of mobile livelihoods emanating from the Caribbean, Central America and the Central Andes, which, in some instances, have expanded to North America, Europe and Asia. In addition, the volume includes cases from urban East Africa and middle-class North America that situate the discussion of mobile livelihood practices within regional and social contexts that have not usually been studied from a transnational point of view and hence allow for further development of the concept.

The first part, 'Mobile livelihoods: Regional and historical perspectives', exam-ines instances of mobile livelihood practices in South America, East Africa and the Caribbean. The three contributions explore how livelihood practices have evolved over time in light of social, economic, political and cultural changes at the local, regional and global levels that have facilitated or impeded mobility. It also looks at how, in various ethnographic contexts, certain livelihoods attain particular cultural meaning associated with gender and class relations. The historical perspective reveals that, whereas there may be long traditions of mobile livelihoods involving spatially extended lives, the political framework of such mobile livelihoods may shift dramatically through time, placing different structural constraints on them. Ninna Nyberg Sørensen's chapter, 'Representing the local: Mobile livelihood prac-tices in the Peruvian Central Sierra,' documents a long tradition of highly mobile and complexly interwoven livelihood strategies that have led, in certain cases, to the establishment of multiple residence practices since the 1950s. During the vio-lent and unstable 1980s, the conflict between Sendero Luminoso and the Peruvian armed forces disrupted this pattern of livelihood and forced many to give up their mobile livelihood practices. When the state began to sponsor re-population in the mid-1990s, transnationally established distinctions between 'internally displaced persons' and 'migrants' influenced persons' ability to relocate in their areas of ori-gin. Such technical categories might have a limited bearing on the life situation of the persons involved when examined from the vantage point of their mobile liveli-hood strategies. Nevertheless, the categories were used, and abused, by differently situated actors struggling to re-establish their livelihoods and the 'community' of belonging associated with them.

Another example of historically rooted mobile livelihood strategies is found in Bodil Folke Frederiksen's chapter, 'Mobile minds, socio-economic barriers: Livelihoods and African/American identifications among youth in Nairobi'. East Africa is an area of extremely mobile livelihood practices associated with the region's past of slavery, wandering, trade, rural–urban migration and internal displacement, following ethnic clashes and flights across borders. The relatively well-educated young people who have grown up in ethnically mixed Nairobi therefore view mobile livelihoods in the region with considerable ambiguity, and desire either work in Nairobi commensurate with their educational level or employment opportunities beyond East Africa. Due to the collapse of local social and economic systems, neither possibility is realistic, so they pursue various 'business strategies' inspired by the popular culture of pan-African and African diasporic origin to which they have been exposed through global mass media and popular culture.

In the last chapter of Part I, 'Mobility, rootedness and the Caribbean higgler: Production, consumption and transnational livelihoods', Carla Freeman discusses the Caribbean higgler or market intermediary in 'her' historical as well as contemporary form. In this case, the long history of mobile livelihood is associated with particular gender and class identities. The historical perspective shows that this activity has developed from fairly localized marketing practices during slavery to more regional activities after emancipation, and, within the last few decades, to transnational travels that display an intricate relationship between formal and informal economies, production and consumption, work and leisure. This study of female higglers from Barbados suggests that these women are multiple territorialized subjects whose sense of place and self is closely defined by their travels as higglers and by the relationships engendered by them.

The second part, 'Livelihoods extended', examines what happens when people extend their livelihood practices to explore opportunities in distant geographical areas. Important themes are the interrelationship between individual and/or family-based livelihood strategies and the wider legal and economic structural frameworks within which these strategies are played out; the articulation of particular socio-cultural contexts of life with social and cultural systems associated with wider national and international spheres of life; and the range of movements and networks of relationships found among persons on the move with respect to the categorization and homogenization to which they are subjected.

Karen Fog Olwig's contribution, 'A "Respectable" livelihood: Mobility and identity in a Caribbean family', presents a micro-study of a family of professionals originating in the Caribbean nation state of Dominica. She details the family's roots in the educated middle class that emerged during the British colonial period as an integral part of the imperial structure. After World War II, with the opening of educational opportunities in Europe and North America, this family, along with others in the middle class, sought further education abroad and settled as professionals, either in various metropolitan societies or in the newly independent republic of Dominica. Despite the apparently metropolitan middle-class orientation of individuals, the family remains firmly grounded in, and maintains its cohesion through, adherence to the ideal of a 'respectable' livelihood associated with cultural values and social relations of the traditional Caribbean middle class. This ideal has a strong impact on perceptions of the Caribbean 'homeland' within the global family network.

In ' "You must win their affection . . .": Migrants' social and cultural practices between Peru and Italy', Carla Tamagno also focuses on family relationships and their articulation into mobile, wider-ranging socio-cultural and socio-economic relations. In her study of a poor urban neighbourhood in Huancayo, Peru, she finds that family relations are characterized by the notion of 'gaining love'. This means 'sharing' and, at the same time, 'fearing envy and jealousy' from people whose love has not been gained. It is difficult to unite these conflicting values within the small-scale communities of local life in Peru, where livelihoods have become precarious, due to poverty, instability and violence, with the consequence that work abroad becomes an attractive proposition for many Peruvian families. In a rich ethnography of a female-centered Peruvian family, Carla Tamagno goes on to analyse the social relations, cultural values and religious belief systems that underline family relations extending between family members located in Peru and Italy.

Karsten Paerregaard's chapter, 'Business as usual: Livelihood strategies and migration practice in the Peruvian diaspora', expands the analytical perspective on Peruvian migration. Through case studies of Peruvian migrants working in the US, Spain and Japan, Paerregaard argues that the migrant networks and transnational connections stemming from these seemingly distinct migration processes grow out of former rural-urban mobile livelihood strategies. However, these migration movements do not just involve extensions of long-term livelihood traditions in Peru, they are also the outcome of historical processes. In these processes, shifting economic and political interests have prompted the movement of Peruvians to geographical locations which have a high demand for migrant workers through labour recruitment and exploitation practices that link specific livelihood skills (e.g. shepherding or domestic work) to particular forms of migration.

In her chapter, 'The moving "Expert": A study of mobile professionals in the Cayman Islands and North America', Vered Amit concerns herself with the 'moving experts', a well-educated group of North Americans not usually studied by migration scholars. However, Amit argues that knowledge workers are subject to many of the same structural problems that other classes of workers face in the post-Fordist regime of flexible labour. When questioned about their work, many express a desire to escape the 'staleness' of settled life through individual travel and adventure. Yet others acknowledge the difficulty of making a home in countries where one is regarded as a transient guest only, and not granted permanent residents' rights. Amit suggests that the perception of knowledge as a 'context-free and highly valued resource', and the prestige and high status associated with work in information technology, may conceal the structural problems associated with it. She ends by warning against the normalization of mobility and flexibility that seems to have occurred in connection with the growing transnational traffic of knowledge workers.

In the last chapter of part II, '*Irse pa' fuera*: The mobile livelihoods of circular migrants between Puerto Rico and the United States', Jorge Duany notes the presence of the strong US hegemony in the Hispanic Caribbean since the end of the nineteenth century that led major segments of the population to travel to the United States in search of a livelihood. Well before the recent wave of migration and globalization, extensive networks of transnational ties had therefore emerged between the Spanish-speaking Caribbean and the United States. This does not mean that there is a single Hispanic transnational community; rather, Hispanic Caribbeans have entered the United States under quite disparate political, economic and social conditions, particularly in recent decades. The Spanish-speaking transnational population in the United States therefore presents an extremely differentiated group of people in terms of settlement patterns, occupational patterns and ties with their country of origin.

The chapters in the final part, 'Livelihoods and the transnational return', discuss how returnees draw on life experiences and resources gained abroad when returning to their place of origin. They therefore do not return to the same place they left behind when they migrated, but rather to the place of origin that they have constructed abroad as migrants. Furthermore, the social, economic and legal constraints on livelihood that they experienced abroad may follow them when they return, because of the globalization of economic, legal and political structures. In her chapter 'Transnational livelihoods and identities in return migration to the Caribbean: The case of skilled returnees to Jamaica', Elizabeth Thomas-Hope documents the return of a group of highly skilled persons who have moved back to Jamaica under a government programme. During their stay abroad, they developed livelihood expectations that cannot easily be met in their country of origin and therefore maintain close economic and social links with their former country of residence. Many returnees maintain a foreign or 'high-status' citizenship, indicating that this 'return' may not be the final move in the migration cycle.

Finn Stepputat's 'The final move? – Displaced livelihoods and collective returns in Peru and Guatemala' compares Guatemalan refugees returning from Mexico to Guatemala with internally displaced Peruvians returning from cities to rural villages. He argues that the legal categorization of people into migrants, displaced persons and refugees does not correspond to the perception of the persons involved. They see their experiences as overlapping considerably in terms of offering some social and economic opportunities in a different environment that can enhance their livelihood upon their return. However, international notions of human rights and the international agencies that work for these rights structure this return. For many, therefore, the ability to acquire a return status that will grant access to the best social and economic resources becomes an important precondition of a successful return.

The case studies in the book shed light on the many ways people sustain mobile livelihoods in different parts of the world. Several common themes have emerged which point the way toward a more encompassing understanding of migration. A future agenda for migration research can therefore benefit from a broader exploration of mobile livelihoods within and across borders.

Notes

1 This book is the outcome of a workshop: 'Migration and Transnational Theory Re-Examined: Place, Generation and Identity', held in Santo Domingo, The Dominican Republic, in 1999. We would like to thank the Research Programme 'Livelihood, Identity and Organisation in Situations of Instability', partly financed by the Danish Council for Development Research, for providing funds for the workshop as well as a fruitful research environment. We are indebted to Annette Smedegaard Christiansen for her expert assistance in preparing the final manuscript, and to Nicholas Van Hear and Kenneth Olwig for their helpful comments on this introductory chapter.

2 But, as Donnan and Haller (2000) recently argue, the ways in which, for example, local developments in border regions impact on national centres of power and hegemony are less well understood. Thus, life and livelihoods on the margins of the nation state can simultaneously result from and transcend political borders, as well as produce, reproduce and/or subvert a sense of (national) belonging – even without crossing the border.

3 There were two major periods of migration from Europe: 'the first from western Europe, which began about 1845, and the second from eastern Europe, which began about 1890, outdistanced the figures for western Europe in 1896, and culminated between 1906 and 1914' (Hvidt 1975: 12).

4 For some dependencies of former colonial powers, however, political independence brought about an increase in immigration quotas to the United States. This was the case, for example, when the former British West Indian dependencies became independent nation states (see, e.g. Olwig 1993).

5 The integrationist approach suggests that migration research has been concerned not just with population movements, but more significantly with the construction of nation states, with particular pre-defined identities, through population movements. The focus on the creation of the nation state is apparent in a recent special issue of the American journal *International Migration Review*, which re-examines the integration paradigm in migration research, where DeWind and Kasinitz suggest that the central questions are: 'What sort of Americans will they [immigrants] be, and what sort of America is being created in the interaction of immigrants and natives?' (DeWind and Kasinitz 1997: 1096).

6 For a critical historical point of view see Tilly 1990. It is only since the 1950s, when immigration to Europe became significant, that European scholars have become interested in integration research. On the specific representation of immigrants and discourses of integration in Denmark, see Schwartz 1985 and Sørensen 1995.

7 Perhaps colonial studies is another example where the phenomenon of movement has been split into different fields of study. The forced migration of Africans to the New World from around 1500 to the 1880s and the movements of indentured labourers primarily from Asia to the New World during the nineteenth century organized by governments or employers have been examined primarily as part of colonial history or the history of the American South. This is also true of the movement of European colonizers from the Old to the New World, even though the motives for, for example, Spanish settlement in Latin America and the Caribbean were in many ways spurred by the colonizer's search for social mobility and equality that could not be found within an Iberian peninsula obsessed with the Inquisition and the expulsion of the Moors and Sephardic Jews (Weismantel and Eisenman 1998; Sørensen 2000).

8 A similar point is made by Lavie and Swedenburg (1996: 16), who point to the importance of studying 'third time-spaces' that avoid 'the dual axes of migration between the distinct territorial entities.' The authors note that these spaces are difficult to describe, or even imagine, because they are 'fleeting, shifting, and emergent', but they seem firm enough with regard to their 'attempt to frustrate frontierization and to throw the Euro-center's policing energy back upon itself, to make the figures between identity and place unmendable' (ibid.: 16–17).

References

Anderson, Benedict (1983) *Imagined Communities*, London: Verso.

Appadurai, Arjun (1991) 'Global ethnoscapes: Notes and queries for a transnational anthropology', in R. Fox (ed.) *Recapturing Anthropology: Working in the Present*, Santa Fe, NM: School of American Research Press, pp. 191–210.

Appadurai, Arjun (1995) 'The production of locality', in R. Fardon (ed.) *Counterworks: Managing the Diversity of Knowledge*, London: Routledge, pp. 204–25.

Basch, Linda, Nina Glick Schiller and Cristina Szanton-Blanc (1994) *Nations Unbound: Transnational Projects and the Deterritorialized Nation State*, Langhorne, PA: Gordon and Breach.

Castles, Stephen and Mark J. Miller (1993) *The Age of Migration: International Population Movements in the Modern World*, Houndsmills: Macmillan.

Chavez, Leo R. (1991) 'Outside the imagined community: Undocumented settlers and experiences of incorporation', *American Ethnologist* 18(2): 257–78.

Clifford, James (1994) 'Diasporas', *Current Anthropology* 9(3): 302–38.

Cohen, Robin (1997) *Global Diasporas: An Introduction*, London: UCL Press.

DeWind, Josh and Philip Kasinitz (1997) 'Everything old is new again? Processes and theories of immigrant incorporation', *International Migration Review* 31(4): 1096–111.q

Donnan, Hastings and Dieter Haller (2000) 'Liminal no more: The relevance of borderland studies', *Ethnologia Europaea* 30(2): 7–22.

Driessen, Henk (1998) 'The new immigration and the transformation of the European-African frontier', in Thomas M. Wilson. and Hastings Donnan (eds) *Border Identities: Nation and State at International Frontiers*, Cambridge: Cambridge University Press.

Ellis, Frank (1998) 'Household strategies and rural livelihood diversification', *Journal of Development Studies* 35(1): 1–38.

Featherstone, Michael (ed.) (1990) *Global Culture: Nationalism, Globalization and Modernity*, London: Sage.

Fitzgerald, David (2000) *Negotiating Extra-Territorial Citizenship: Mexican Migration and the Transnational Politics of Community*, CCIS, University of California, San Diego: Monograph Series No. 2.

Fletcher, Rei L. (1999) *La Casa de Mis Sueños: Dreams of Home in a Transnational Migrant Community*, Boulder, CO: Westview Press.

Fuglerud, Oivind (2001) *Migrasjonsforståelse: flytteprocesser, racisme og globalisering*, Oslo: Universitetsforlaget.

Gardner, Katy (1995) *Global Migrants, Local Lives: Travel and Transformation in Rural Bangladesh*, Oxford: Clarendon Press.

Georges, Eugenia (1990) *The Making of a Transnational Community: Migration, Development, and Cultural Change in the Dominican Republic*, New York: Columbia University Press.

Glick Schiller, Nina (1999) 'Transmigrants and nation states: Something old and something new in the U.S. immigrant experience', in *The Handbook of International Migration*, New York: The Russell Sage Foundation.

Glick Schiller, Nina, Linda Basch and Cristina Szanton Blanc (eds) (1992) *Transnational Perspective on Migration: Race, Class, Ethnicity, and Nationalism Reconsidered*, New York: Annals of the New York Academy of Sciences 645.

Guarnizo, Luis E. (1997) 'The emergence of a transnational social formation and the mirage of return migration among Dominican transmigrants', *Identities* 4: 281–322.

Gudeman, Stephen (1986) *Economics and Culture: Models and Metaphors of Livelihood*, London: Routledge & Kegan Paul.

Gupta, Akhil and James Ferguson (1992) 'Beyond "Culture": Space, identity, and the politics of difference', *Cultural Anthropology* 7: 6–23.

Hagan, Jacqueline M. (1994) *Deciding to be Legal: A Maya Community in Houston*, Philadelphia: Temple University Press.

Hannerz, Ulf (1992) *Cultural Complexity: Studies in the Social Organization of Meaning*, New York: Columbia University Press.

Harding, Jeremy (2000) *The Uninvited: Refugees at the Rich Man's Gate*, London, Profile Books.

Hintjens, H. M. (1992) 'Immigration and citizenship debates: Reflections on ten common themes', *International Migration Review* 30(1): 5–17.

Hvidt, Kristian (1975) *Flight to America: The Social Background of 300,000 Danish Emigrants*, New York: Academic Press.

Kearney, Michael (1991) 'Borders and boundaries of state and self at the end of empire', *Journal of Historical Sociology* 4(1): 52–74.

Kearney, Michael (1995) 'The local and the global: The anthropology of globalization and transnationalism', *Annual Review of Anthropology* 24: 547–65.

Kearney, Michael (1998) 'Transnationalism in California and Mexico at the end of empire', in Thomas Wilson and Hastings Donnan (eds) *Border Identities: Nation and State at International Frontiers*, Cambridge: Cambridge University Press.

Kyle, David (2000) *Transnational Peasants: Migration, Networks, and Ethnicity in Andean Ecuador*, Baltimore: The Johns Hopkins University Press.

Lavie, Smadar and Ted Swedenburg (1996) 'Introduction: Displacement, diaspora, and geographies of identity', in *Displacement, Diaspora, and Geographies of Identity*, Durham: Duke University Press, pp. 1–25.

Long, Norman (2000) 'Exploring local/global transformations: A view from anthropology', in A. Arce and N. Long (eds) *Anthropology, Development and Modernities: Exploring Discourses, Counter-tendencies and Violence*, London: Routledge, pp. 184–201.

Mahler, Sarah J. (1995) *American Dreaming: Immigrant Life on the Margins*, Princeton, New Jersey: Princeton University Press.

Mahler, Sarah J. (1998) 'Theoretical and empirical contributions towards a research agenda for transnationalism', in Smith and Guarnizo (eds) *Transnationalism from Below*, New Brunswick: Transaction Publishers, pp. 64–100.

Malkki, Liisa (1992) 'National geographic: The rooting of peoples and the territorialization of national identity among scholars and refugees', *Cultural Anthropology* 7: 24–44.

Murray, Colin (1979) 'The work of men, women and the ancestors: Social reproduction in the periphery of Southern Africa', in Sandra Wallman (ed.) *Social Anthropology of Work*, ASA Monograph 19, London: Academic Press, pp. 337–65.

Olwig, Karen Fog (1993) *Global Culture, Island Identity: Continuity and Change in the Afro-Caribbean Community of Nevis*, Reading: Harwood Academic Press.

Olwig, Karen Fog (1997) 'Toward a reconceptualization of migration and transnationalism', in Bodil Folke Frederiksen and Fiona Wilson (eds), *Livelihood, Identity and Instability. Papers from an International Workshop*, Copenhagen, CDR.

Olwig, Karen Fog (2001) 'New York as a locality in a global family network', in Nancy Foner (ed.) *Islands in the City: West Indian Migration to New York*, Berkeley: University of California Press.

Olwig, Karen Fog and Kirsten Hastrup (eds) (1997) *Siting Culture: The Shifting Anthropological Object*, London: Routledge.

Ong, Aihwa (1999) *Flexible Citizenship: The Cultural Logics of Transnationality*, Durham: Duke University Press.

Parkin, David (1979) 'The categorization of work: Cases from coastal Kenya', in Sandra Wallman (ed.) *Social Anthropology of Work*, ASA Monograph 19, London: Academic Press, pp. 317–36.

Portes, Alejandro, Luís Guarnizo and Patricia Landolt (1999) 'Introduction: Pitfalls and promise of an emergent research field', *Ethnic and Racial Studies* 22(2): 217–37.

Rapport, Nigel and Andrew Dawson (1998) *Migrants of Identity: Perceptions of Home in a World of Movement*, Oxford: Berg.

Rogers, Alisdair (2000) *A European Space for Transnationalism?* Transnational Communities Working Paper Series, WPTC-2K-07. Available HTTP: http.//www.transcomm.ox.ac.uk

Rouse, Roger (1991) 'Mexican migration and the social space of postmodernism', *Diaspora* 1(1): 8–23.

Rouse, Roger (1995) 'Questions of identity: Personhood and collectivity in transnational migration to the United States', *Critique of Anthropology* 144: 351–80.

Schwartz, Jonathan M. (1985) *Reluctant Hosts: Denmark's Perception of Guest Workers*, Copenhagen: Academic Publishers.

Shuval, Judith T. (2000) 'Diaspora migration: Definitorial ambiguities and a theoretical paradigm', *International Migration* 38(5): 41–53.

Skeldon, Ronald (1997) *Migration and Development: A Global Perspective*, Essex: Longman.

Smith, Michael Peter (1994) ' "Can you imagine?" Transnational migration and the globalization of grassroots politics', *Social Text* 39 (Summer): 15–33.

Smith, Michael Peter (2001) *Transnational Urbanism: Locating Globalization*, Massachusetts: Blackwell.

Smith, Michael Peter and Luis Eduardo Guarnizo (eds) (1998) *Transnationalism from Below*, New Brunswick: Transaction Publishers.

Stolcke, Verena (1993) 'Europe: New boundaries, new rhetorics of exclusion', Sidney W. Mintz Lecture given at Department of Anthropology, Johns Hopkins University, November 15.

Sørensen, Ninna Nyberg (1995) 'Some comments on the anthropology of lower income urban enclaves: Dominican newcomers in the city', in Freidenberg, Judith (ed.) *The Anthropology of Lower Income Urban Enclaves. Annals of the New York Academy of Sciences*, 749: 211–17.

Sørensen, Ninna Nyberg (2000) 'Crossing the Spanish-Moroccan border with migrants, New Islamists, and Riff-Raff', *Etnologia Europaea* 30: 87–99.

Sørensen, Ninna Nyberg and Finn Stepputat (2000) *La Población Desplazada entre la Asistencia y el Desarrollo en los Andes Centrales del Perú*, CDR Working Papers 00.6, Copenhagen: CDR.

Tilly, Charles (1990) Transplanted networks, in Virginia Yans-McLaughlin (ed.) *Immigration Reconsidered: History, Sociology, and Politics*, New York: Oxford University Press, pp. 79–95.

Tuan, Yi-Fu (1974) Space and place: Humanistic perspective, *Progress in Geography* 6: 211–52.

van Hear, Nicholas (1998) *New Diasporas*, London: UCL Press.

Vertovec, Steven and Robin Cohen (eds) (1999) *Migrations, Diasporas and Transnationalism*, Cheltenham UK: Edward Elgar.

Wallman, Sandra (1979) 'Introduction', in Sandra Wallman (ed.) *Social Anthropology of Work*, ASA Monograph 19, London: Academic Press, pp. 1–24.

Waters, Mary C. (1994) 'Ethnic and racial identities of second-generation black immigrants in New York City', *International Migration Review* 28(4): 795–820.

Waters, Mary C. (1999) *Black Identities: West Indian Immigrant Dreams and American Realities*, New York: Russel Sage Foundation.

Weiner, Myron (1997) 'The global migration crisis', in Gungwu, Wang (ed.) *Global History and Migrations*, Boulder: Westview Press.

Weismantel, Mary and Stephen F. Eisenman (1998) 'Race in the Andes: Global movements and popular ontologies', *Bulletin of Latin American Research* 17(2): 121–42.

Wilson, Fiona (1999) 'Gendered histories: Garment production and migration in Mexico', *Environment and Planning*, A, 31: 327–43.

Yans-McLaughlin, Virginia (1990) 'Metaphors of self in history: Subjectivity, oral narrative, and immigration studies', in Virginia Yans-McLaughlin (ed.) *Immigration Reconsidered: History, Sociology, and Politics*, New York: Oxford University Press, pp. 254–90.

Part I
Mobile livelihoods
Regional and historical perspectives

1 Representing the local

Mobile livelihood practices in the Peruvian Central Sierra

Ninna Nyberg Sørensen

'I'll be in Huancayo until Friday', Guillermo explained, 'but from Friday I'll be in the village'. Referring to his rural community of origin, he continued by saying that this was how he lived, *acá y allá*, in several places: 'I usually go up once or twice a month, spending more time in the village during the sowing and harvest seasons, and more time in Huancayo the rest of the year'. Like Guillermo, many other 'rural peasants' and 'urban city dwellers' whom we included in our research on mobile livelihoods prior to, during and after the armed conflict in Andean Peru[1] would tell us where they intended to stay for the next few months or so. Sudden or unexpected occurrences would, nevertheless, often change their plans. Like other hyphened populations who challenge the boundaries between the 'centre' and the 'periphery', appearing one day as professionals or informal street vendors in the city, another day as dedicated *comuneros* (legitimately recognized members of the community) in the countryside, the women and men we met in Peru during 1999 and 2000 constantly transformed and re-created our notions of mobility and belonging through their everyday livelihood practices. Indeed, as I will argue in this chapter, constant movement between various rural and urban sites has been a central element in their livelihood practices.

Migration is not a new phenomenon in central Peru. Given that Peruvian social science has been influenced by the early work of John Murra and others on livelihood adaptations to the ecological diversity of the Andes from pre-Hispanic times, there has been greater sensitivity to translocal mobility in Peruvian ethnography (cf. Murra 1975; Favre 1977; various contributions in Lehmann 1982) – often studied under the heading of regional identities (Roberts 1974; Long and Roberts 1984) – than one finds elsewhere. Gavin Smith's discussion of livelihood and resistance in a Peruvian highland community prior to the armed conflict is another good example (Smith 1989). Smith explores confederations of households through which resources dispersed in space are fashioned into family livelihood strategies. Although belonging to a rural community has not always meant being divorced from a specific geographical locality, the institutionalization of migration has meant that the links established between villagers, not just within the rural area but also between the various work centres (both rural and urban), play a major part in how people achieve their identity. Moreover, the social relationships established between dispersed villagers reflect not only the production of a livelihood but also the political protection of its continued reproduction. Finally, and most importantly, as migration became an institutionalized way of life, it acted to select out some villagers for ex-residence while confining others to the village. Given that mobility has been the norm rather than the exception, there is a case for taking Smith's analysis further and exploring the extent to which rural and urban areas constitute a single space. If so, should movements within a single space be conceptualized as migration? And what happens to such spaces when social inequality and political discontent escalate into armed conflict, as it did in Peru in the early 1980s?

Given that mobility has been a central element in the livelihood strategies of both poor and better-off Andean people, research into the specificities of Andean livelihood practices is central to the analysis of contemporary processes of both rural–urban mobility and the socio-spatial consequences of the civil war that was waged between insurgent groups and the Peruvian military during the 1980s and early 1990s. Although often discussed separately, these two issues are linked. In this chapter I shall therefore explore the historical links between various patterns of displacement and spaces of livelihood practices, and the social institutions and networks that facilitate and sustain these practices.

The discussion is limited geographically to the Central Sierra, and more specifically the urban area of Huancayo (department of Junín) and the rural districts of Vilca and Acobambilla (both in the department of Huancavelica). My theoretical point of departure is that, within the context of everyday life, displacement (defined as coerced or involuntary movement as a result of, or in order to avoid, the effects of armed conflict and situations of generalized violence) may be indistinguishable from migration (defined as 'voluntary' migration in search of better living conditions). Not only are both 'forced' and 'voluntary' mobility characterized by a combination of compulsion and choice: both forms of movement seem to be motivated by a mixture of blocked opportunities, repression, discontent with current livelihood potentials, and aspirations for better futures. In terms of mobility patterns, both groups tend to follow the same 'routes', and in the so-called areas of destination, they often live alongside each other.[2]

At the same time, classification into the categories of 'internally displaced population' (IDP) and 'migrant' has powerful effects on both formal and informal social organization. Under certain political circumstances, therefore, being defined as respectively a migrant or an IDP may marginalize a group of people, while it, in other circumstances, may provide access to special entitlements or resources (Sørensen and Stepputat 2000; Stepputat and Sørensen 1999). For example, rural–urban migrants have traditionally been marginalized by city dwellers, and throughout the 1980s they were directly subject to state repression (due to their being linked with the Maoist guerrilla movement, *Sendero Luminoso*). Nonetheless, recognition of the IDP category and the opening up of state-sponsored return or re-population programmes in the mid-1990s (the so-called PAR programmes), including access to emergency aid and development funds, has given rise to new struggles for recognition. But movement is not only imposed from above, it is also induced from below, for example by extending social networks through which the reproduction of social ties, economic organization and politics become transformed.

In the following, I shall focus on a particular mobile livelihood strategy, one that seems to be common to both 'migrants' and 'internally displaced' persons in the central Peruvian highlands, namely that of forging or sustaining a multiple residence practice. One key objective is to highlight the complicated and often ambivalent relationship between rural points of origin, current urban settlement areas, *and* different settlement or return strategies. Drawing on the experience of individuals and families who at various times since the early 1950s have left their rural 'areas of origin' in the department of Huancavelica and who currently live their lives, or at least part of them, in the city of Huancayo, I shall reflect upon the variety of mobile livelihood practices they employ. The first section provides a broad overview of the Central Sierra region and the historical mobility patterns that Andean peasants practised prior to, during, and after the armed conflict. It also describes the different mobility patterns to be found among migrants and displaced persons in the city of Huancayo, social stratification, and the variety of social relations sustained between rural and urban communities. In the second section, I discuss the outbreak of the civil war and the ways in which the conflict affected mobility in the area. The third section discusses the multi-residence strategy found among migrants and displaced persons alike. To illustrate my point, I describe one particular case of organized return. In the concluding section, I make an attempt to situate these experiences in the broader context of migration.

Establishing mobile livelihoods

Peruvian territory is geographically complex and divided into three major regions: the western coastal plain (*la costa*), the eastern lowland jungle of the Amazon Basin (*la selva*), and the high and rugged Andes in the centre (*la sierra*). For comparative purposes in respect of the history of mobility, it may be useful to provide a few figures. Until the 1940s, approximately 65 per cent of Peru's population lived in the Andes. At the end of the twentieth century, less than 30 per cent of the total population, which is officially estimated at roughly 24 million, were rural, and the larger cities have grown tremendously (Markwick 1999). This development has generally been portrayed as a threat to stability in which negative images of rural migrants in the city prevail. Following the perspective adopted in this volume, however, mobile livelihoods should rather be understood as being embedded in Andean strategies to sustain a living, as well as in socio-cultural institutions, customs and ideologies.

In the Central Sierra, Huancayo functions as the capital of the Department of Junín. The city is located at an altitude of 3,260 metres in the flat Río Mantaro Valley, one of the most fertile areas of the Central Andes, which supports a large rural population. Being the major commercial centre in the region, Huancayo is of great importance as a market town for the surrounding rural area. For centuries it served as a *centro de descanzo entre caminos* (a resting place between trips; Manrique 1978), and as an unavoidable crossroads for travelling people, livestock and agricultural products. But it was not until the rapid expansion of commercial agriculture and livestock production in the late nineteenth century that it gained status as a regional centre. Since then, the population has steadily increased, most dramatically during the last ten to fifteen years, in which the city's population has tripled to close to one million, including the adjoining municipalities of El Tambo and Chilca.[3] Today, Huancayo is the third most important city in Peru in terms of transport, trade and production of electricity, and the fifth largest in terms of size.

Amongst Huancayo's newcomers, quite a few originate in the districts of Vilca and Acobambilla. Although these districts belong administratively to the province and department of Huancavelica, distance (in kilometres and accessibility), colonial history (unlike Huancavelica, the location of the infamous mercury mines of the colonial period, Huancayo was never a seat of the colonial administration), cultural belonging (to the Huancayan Wanca Nation as opposed to the Huancavelica Wari Culture),[4] and a widespread feeling among the *comuneros* of having been neglected by the Huancavelica local administration for decades, have all contributed to the creation of an actual feeling of belonging or at least relating to Huancayo.

Forms of mobility

Until around 1980, the only means of transportation in the districts of Vilca and Acobambilla was by foot and/or pack animal. From around 1930, a railroad was built connecting Huancayo and Huancavelica. The nearest station, Tellería, was located some seventeen kilometres north-east of Vilca, and considerably further from Acobambilla. Villagers had to walk or ride the mule path between Acobambilla and Vilca, and from there to Moya, from where they could get a ride to the train station. From the early 1980s, the district of Vilca became connected to Huancayo by road. A road over the high *puna* was established from Acobambilla to Puente Mellizo in the late 1990s, allowing villagers direct 'high-road' access to Huancayo without having to descend to the 'low-road' connection from Vilca – a fact of enormous importance, thanks to prevailing racial hierarchies. Communication between the districts or the various villages (*anexos* and *barrios*), especially those located higher up, is still by foot or horse. In the rainy season flooding and *huaicos* (landslides) may block travel by road for weeks.

A poorly developed infrastructure has not prevented villagers from high levels of mobility, especially between the different ecological zones in the district, which are linked to the pasturing of livestock on *estancias* (pasture land) in the high *puna* areas, the cultivation of different crops at different altitudes, and attending local and regional markets. Since the turn of the century, villagers have provided labour for the mining industry in Casapalca, Morococha, Huancavelica and La Oroya, and also for various infrastructural developments. From the 1930s, migration to the mining complexes increased, as did temporary migration to more distant places, such as Cañete (the sugarcane plantations and cotton fields on the south coast towards Ica and Pisco), the *Ceja de Selva* or jungle's eyebrow (for coffee, plantain and yucca production), and trade in la Selva Central. From the 1950s, migration to Chilca or Huancayo (education, petty trade, domestic service and agricultural labour), and to Lima (primarily to work in the garment industry and poultry farms) became a widespread livelihood strategy, especially among the younger, but still landless villagers.

From this brief sketch a picture emerges of extended spaces of livelihood, maintained through high levels of mobility between subsistence production in different ecological zones, between subsistence and wage work, and between wage work in different localities at different times of the year (in accordance with the agricultural calendar in the different climatic zones in Peru). Temporary migration to the coast, the jungle, the mines and elsewhere has provided the rural population with extra-agricultural incomes, which again have facilitated their maintenance of village life (Favre 1977) as well as their establishing themselves in the city of Huancayo (de la Cadena 1988). The fact that migration to Huancayo has been conditioned not by a demand for industrial labour, but rather by the possibility of employment in smaller workshops, the informal sector and the surrounding agricultural sector of carrot and potato production further leads de la Cadena to characterize Huancayo as a *ciudad de campesinos* (a city of peasants; ibid.: 46), that is, a complementary space in which agricultural livelihoods are supplemented with urban lives. Paerregaard has reached a similar conclusion and argues that it is rural–urban interdependence rather than separation that provides the key to understanding the complex, heterogeneous nature of Peruvian society (Paerregaard 1997: 2). Thus, contemporary rural communities in Peru are situated within regional, national, sometimes even transnational or global contexts (see Chapters 5 and 6) that effectively blur the conventional oppositions of rural–urban, traditional–modern, peasant–non-peasant dichotomies on which earlier studies of migration have built.[5]

Social stratification and mobility

Most Andean rural communities are characterized by social stratification into two social classes: *los gamonales* or the local landlords, who generally possess more land and livestock than others and act as the intermediaries between the community and the national institutions; and *los comuneros*, who are generally exploited by *los gamonales* and often have less or no power or possibility of direct contact with the political centre. This division corresponds to some extent to location in lower or higher zones, the lower zones being the wealthier and more powerful, and has clear origins in the old highland hacienda system (the formal granting of land to Spaniards or highly placed Criollos) and the concentration of 'Indians' into village settlements (Smith 1989).

It has clear reference to race too, not least to what de la Cadena has termed 'silent racism', a form of social exclusion based on education and intelligence. It is hegemonically inscribed in Peruvian geography, in which a socio-cultural division between *gente decente* (decent folks from the city) and *gente del pueblo* (Indian and *mestizo* Others) is played out. While 'silent racism' acknowledges the right of every Peruvian to belong to the nation, it simultaneously positions individuals on a differentiated scale according to their intellectual capacity. It contains a presupposition that educated people are legitimately destined for political leadership, a role Indians are seen as being unable to fulfil, due to their 'emotional dependence on the old order' (de la Cadena 1998). Thus races have their proper places. The higher the geographical altitude of origin, the closer one's 'natural' relationship with the soil and with agriculture, and the lower one's social standing and closeness to Indianness or inferior *chuto* identity. The lower the geographical altitude of origin, the closer the 'cultural' relationship to 'superior education', and the higher the social standing and closeness to a new generation of *mestizo* or *cholo* identity.[6] Rural–urban migration has in principle offered the 'Indian' the possibility of social *mestizaje* or gradual incorporation into the *cholo* identity through education. The problem is that most professionals who come from Vilca and Acobambilla (and rural communties in general) have had their hopes of social mobility through education disappointed, given the unevenness of academic training in Peru and the racial discrimination that places Serrano students from the interior provinces at an objective disadvantage (Manrique 1998: 199).

For most of the twentieth century, *los vilquinos* from Vilca proper (the district capital) have played the part of the landowning elite. As well as believing themselves to be whiter and descended more directly from the Spanish than the highlanders, they have exploited people from these higher communities, at times in a servile manner. Being relatively wealthier, they have also been the first to establish themselves in Huancayo.

A larger exodus from the district took place after the earthquake in 1947, which had devastating effects on agricultural outputs for years. But it was not until the mid-1950s that wealthier *vilquinos* began to buy land and build property in Huancayo. Establishing a house in Huancayo served two purposes: to be closer to employment outside the sowing and harvesting seasons (several *vilquinos* established ready-to-wear clothing sweatshops in Huancayo), and to *buscar cultura* (court culture), first by enrolling their children in the city's superior school system (*secundaria*), and from the early 1960s in university education;[7] and secondly by being exposed to city culture themselves. The following extract from an interview illustrates this period well:

> I was born in Vilca in 1935, my permanent home until the age of 17; later on I lived there occasionally. I am constantly in Vilca and in the annexes and communities. I have lived for a time in all the annexes of Vilca . . . I remember the year 1947 very well; I was an orphan by that time, and the harvest was a disaster. The low rate of agricultural return has contributed to the migration of the people . . . a central factor. For example, to Cañete – a large per centage of my compatriots have gone there . . . few to the jungle because of fear of *los males* (evil), of the diseases. To Huancayo, yes, but people from Huancavelica were not welcome here. A few to Lima, more to the mining centres . . . until today, people migrate in order to survive. There is a local phrase for this model: "A man who leaves his community is a wanderer (*andadero*)", one criticized by my compatriots because he leaves to find a livelihood (*buscando*

vida), always on the move, because he has no affection for his community. It is no longer like that. Today it is he who stays who is criticized. Today the adventurous leave, in order to survive and find culture, this is today... I left my community for two reasons: work and schooling. I worked as an assistant in a joiner's workshop during the daytime and went to school in the evening... during this time I lived in the house of my aunt... in Huancayo.

Comuneros from communities lying higher up also migrated for temporary wage work during this time, albeit on a much lower scale than people from the district centre. However, they did not have the economic means to buy property in Huancayo or elsewhere. To a certain extent they therefore relied on the traditional *compadrazgo* relations that had been established between *gamonales* and *comuneros* back home, a system in which city lodgings were often paid for by working the fields of the old *gamonal* back home. Wages earned from migration nevertheless made a powerful contribution to enhancing and diversifying their rural livelihoods and gradually disengaging themselves from the old social order of dependence on the *gamonal*-dominated communities lower down.[8]

The outbreak of civil war

It was in relatively isolated Andean environments like Vilca and Acobambilla that the guerrilla movement dramatically escalated terrorist activities in the 1980s (Gonzalez 1988; Degregori 1998). The Maoist insurgent group, Sendero Luminoso (the Shining Path), grew out of the worsening of relations between the USSR and the People's Republic of China in the 1960s, which in 1970 caused the Sendero leadership to leave the pro-Soviet communist party PCP and form its own Maoist-inspired one. Political violence, massacres, selective killings, the destruction of buildings and livestock and other enormities were committed not only by Sendero Luminoso (and with less intensity and different characteristics by the Tupac Amaro Revolutionary Movement, MRTA), but also by government troops in the Peruvian state´s not very successful attempts to subdue the insurgents. While government troops managed to dampen down terrorist activities in the mid-1980s, much of the area was again under Sendero Luminoso's control from the late 1980s until 1992, when Abimael Guzmán Reynoso, formerly Professor of Philosophy at the University of Huamanga and the founder and ideological leader of Sendero Luminoso, together with several top lieutenants of the movement, were captured and sentenced to life imprisonment (Oré Cardenas 1998; see also Wilson 2000, especially on Maoism in the Andes and the politization of schoolteachers).[9]

According to Sendero Luminoso's ideology, the *guerra popular*, the people's war, would proceed from the countryside toward the city, making the 'peasantry' the principal base of the revolution. Initial local support for Sendero was facilitated by the incomplete and largely unsuccessful land reform of the Velasco government, the fragmentation of the parties of the left over the issue of reform, and the unsatisfied economic and social needs of the rural population. In this way, Sendero Luminoso became a path for social mobility among Andean youth

(Degregori 1998: 130) by offering 'concrete alternatives in the face of structural problems of backwardness, abandonment, poverty and marginalization' (del Pino 1998: 161). The movement had particular appeal for young men and women who had hoped to escape rural poverty and racial marginalization through education (Wilson 1999, 2000). Sendero Luminoso emphasized revolutionary violence as the fundamental mechanism for obtaining political change, but the extreme brutality of their strategy quickly led to several points of rupture and clashes with the rural population, as did the response in kind by the armed forces. The first attempts at resistance developed along two lines, the first (and the only one being discussed here) being massive displacement to the cities, the second being the formation of *rondas campesinas* or civil defence patrols.[10]

Violence and displacement

Of the main zones of displacement, those from which people fled in the greatest numbers, mainly to the provincial capitals, were the departments of Huancavelica, Ayacucho and Apurimac. It is estimated that 27,000 Peruvians were killed or 'disappeared' during the civil war. Some 600,000 people were still displaced in late 1996.[11] In the Central Sierra, the displaced tended to move first to nearby larger communities, and then to the provincial capitals (Stavropoulou 1998: 469), not least to the Mantaro Valley and the city of Huancayo. Soon people from other departments added to the number of IDPs in Huancayo, in particular people from the surrounding highland peasant communities and the central and north-east jungle region.

Sendero's initial arrival in the rural communities of the districts of Vilca and Acobambilla in the early 1980s was 'peaceful': they came in small groups over the mountains, approached the *comuneros* as 'comrades', and introduced new ways of thinking to village herders and agriculturalists. A young male villager from one of the high-lying communities describes the meeting between villagers and Sendero agitators in the following way:

We began to hear of 'incidents' in Ayacucho in 1980, but in the village life proceeded as normal. Shortly thereafter, I believe it was in 1981 or 1982, these people arrived. They were designated to go to a primary or secondary school in some village, including the teachers who were already there. They began to talk to the people, to make them see how things were, softly, nothing but softly was the way they talked to you, and you became convinced. Because, in reality, what we saw was exactly what they told us, the truth, that the government did not act over poverty. We could hardly cultivate enough produce to eat, let alone buy clothes or pay for education, this was the plain situation. Hence, in this scenario, they told us how things were, they explained to us that the state, well, that the movement could take over (the state), as had happened with Mao Tse Tung . . . that we were all one big community, and with that understanding people began to draw nearer to them, well, began to have confidence in them.

In the firm belief that villagers were actually going to take over power, a few joined the movement and participated in the destruction of some of the smaller haciendas in the area and in attacks on rural police stations. With the arrival of the military, however, Sendero began to attack villagers as well. A woman from a high *puna* community remembers the following series of events:

> The social movement began to arrive in the community in 1981. At first they arrived armed only with political brochures. They obliged the local schoolteachers to read out the texts to the students. Later on they began to punish thieves and abusive villagers as well as the *hacenderos*. The *comuneros* were forced to participate in weekly meetings, during which we were taught that the movement was fighting for the poor, for villages abandoned by the state, against the bad authorities. They promised to build roads and establish water and electricity services, and many villagers thought they were right. However, overnight, and without any previous warning, they began to kill villagers who publicly opposed Sendero policies. Shortly afterwards, the military arrived and, like Sendero, abused and violated the population, forcing people to give them food and other goods. Even when people fulfilled the military's demands, they were accused of being *terrucos* (terrorists). After this, the villagers stopped sleeping in their houses and fled to hide in their fields during the night. We fled to Huancayo.

Escalating violence forced villagers to change their well-established mobile livelihood strategies for at least two different coping tactics: either to follow the demands of Sendero not to leave the villages at all (a measure to prevent villagers from informing the Peruvian military about Sendero's presence), or else to abandon their fields and livestock and flee to safer urban or not yet 'liberated' rural areas, thus displacing themselves on a more permanent basis. The latter tactic was also a response to the military presence in what the Peruvian government soon declared the *zona roja*, or red zone. Military bases were established in Vilca and Mantas (overlooking Acobambilla) in 1984. While the military closed down the base in Vilca in 1988, it has only recently abandoned the base in Mantas (1997).

In the mid-1980s district roads and bridges were blocked, the railway was occasionally bombed and travelling by road or rail became extremely dangerous. It became impossible to transfer livestock to the local and regional markets, and commercial travellers were prevented from entering or leaving the zone. One of Sendero's first moves was to close off rural markets and fairs. By doing so, they severely interfered with local mobile livelihood strategies, which were based on networks encompassing both the countryside and the cities.[12] Thus, the presence of both Sendero and the military mostly caused the discontinuation of well-established mobile livelihood practices. Or, to put it differently, political violence led to less mobility. But it also created distinct new forms of livelihood, namely more permanent settlement. The poorest, and the landless generally, had few options other than staying in the countryside. People who had rotated between the villages and various urban settings for decades had to stay in the cities for security reasons. Yet others had to leave all their belongings behind and flee under cover of darkness. To the extent that they managed to sell their possessions (land, livestock and houses), they did so at throwaway prices.

> My uncle had a *tiendacita* (a small grocery store) in the community. This was after the first attack on the SAIS Cahuide production unit.[13] Thus the police continuously came to look after the *hacienda*. One night they arrived silently. Apparently they had nothing to eat. When they didn't find anyone in the village they began to rob, they took everything from the store, even the entrance door. They went to look for the people who had fled the community. They killed several *comuneros*, found my uncle in one place and my brother-in-law somewhere else, and put them in a car. No one actually saw my uncle get into the car . . . but they killed him . . . his body was first brought to Chongos Alto and later to Huancayo, where he was put in the mortuary. After he was dead, my aunt couldn't stay in the community. She had a few animals, goats, cattle, horses, all these animals she had to turn over to a trader, a commercial buyer, a traitor, I tell you . . . because in those days the traders had very little money. [Before my uncle was killed] he brought the animals to Huancayo where he sold them for half their value, and my aunt was never given the total price agreed upon. But she had her little house in Huancayo, she already lived there, my uncle used to come down only once in a while. So she stayed in Huancayo. She had a daughter who later returned to live in the family house in the village. She is the only one there of the ten children my uncle raised. Another one lives in Satipo, the rest in Lima, and another one in Huancayo.

Different paths of displacement

Several villagers were forced to flee the community during the years of violence, in and around Vilca mostly in 1983–85, in Acobambilla after a military attack in 1983 (in which most houses in the district capital were destroyed), and after the 1989 massacre, in which seventy-eight people, who mainly worked for the local authorities, were killed. In many cases, however, flight was able to follow well-established routes of mobility. In addition, many had family and fellow villagers to 'move in with' and to facilitate their entry into the city of Huancayo. A few of them defined themselves or organized collectively as *desplazados* (internally displaced persons), but several affiliated themselves with the *Club de Vilca*, a migrant and hometown association established in the early 1970s, and the more informal group of *Residentes* (city-dwellers of rural origin) from Acobambilla.

Poorer *comuneros* from the higher zones of Vilca and neighbouring Acobambilla had also intensified their mobile livelihoods through trade (bartering animals and meat for sugar, salt, rice and other commercial foodstuffs) and temporary migration to the mining districts, the *Ceja de Selva* and the coastal area throughout the century. From the mid-1980s, however, when the escalation in political violence prevented these villagers from returning home to invest their migrant earnings in the local community, or forced livestock farmers to sell out, some highlanders also began to establish themselves more permanently in Huancayo. Unlike the *vilquinos*, and mainly because they did not own property in Huancayo, a majority defined themselves as *desplazados*. Among these a few organized collectively with other peasants from the higher zones of Huancavelica, Ayacucho and Apurimac. Many found their former livelihoods totally destroyed.

> When the violence escalated, my oldest son – he was attending school in Huancayo – said "let's all go to Huancayo", but what were we supposed to do here? The people (of Huancayo) are very jealous . . . but we went because the terrorists wanted to bring in my sons, and when they didn't want to join [Sendero], they were going to kill all my children, so they said, all of us in the house, they would kill us when the soldiers left for Mantas. Therefore we left and have never gone back. Ever since, we have had to find work in Huancayo, all of us, also my sons. I work here, yes, but there is no work to be found. Therefore, I have to sell my *manzanilla* (camomile tea) on the streets. I left everything I had, my fields, my animals, everything. My husband's sister was a bad person, she treated my animals very badly, gave the cows back-breaking work; all my animals are dead . . . and I am left with nothing, I can't even buy a plot for a little house.

The narrative quoted above points out two important aspects of the armed conflict. The first is the central role women played in deciding and organizing the family's dispersal. The second is that not all local conflicts were due to the war; inter-communal and inter-familial conflicts in many instances preceded the armed conflict, which nevertheless served as a neat 'cover' for simple theft and family feuds during the war. Among the many complaints of illicit land seizure I heard, the majority concerned close relatives who, in a few cases, had used Sendero's land re-distribution politics to 'settle' old disputes over inheritance.

Today, social stratification in terms of area of origin and time of arrival is echoed in the spatial division of *barrios* in Huancayo. *Vilquinos* live mainly in central Huancayo and in the more developed areas of Chilca. Lately, upwardly mobile *vilquinos* have moved into 'residential areas' in El Tambo. *Acobambillanos* and poorer *comuneros* from Vilca's annexes have settled in the semi-rural areas on the outskirts of Chilca. More collective settlements have taken place in El Tambo on ex-SAIS Cahuide land and in squatter settlements on ex-hacienda land (see Tamagno, this volume).

Ironically, the early exodus of richer and to some extent better educated families from Vilca, coupled with the blocking of mobility between village and city during the violent period in the 1980s, has led to both depopulation and impoverishment of the district centre, whereas rural annexes have experienced a growth in population. The opposite is currently the case in the district of Acobambilla, basically because the district capital is located at a higher altitude than many of its annexes. Even an old *gamonal* admits of the highlanders that:

> Vilca used to be a living community, good agriculturalists – yes, they had a regular economy, living fathers, were good agriculturalists and pastoralists.

It's no longer like that: Vilca is empty, no people left. In Huancalpi and beyond it is still like that. Soil of God, it's the only community still firmly engaged in agriculture and animal husbandry. And their students are all professionals; this rural community has surpassed the district capital. In Vilca, by comparison, there is only poverty.

During the years of violence in the zone, highlanders from Acobambilla and Vilca's annexes have maintained mobile livelihood practices between village and city to a greater extent than the *vilquinos*. The more dispersed community structure, coupled with the total destruction of infrastructure like roads and electricity, made military control over these communities more difficult. But the continuous mobility may also have to do with the highlanders' later entry into the wider educational system. It probably has most to do with the fact that the highlanders were forced to move to the city at a time when urban survival was becoming more difficult, and the maintenance of rural ties was therefore of paramount importance in making a livelihood. Thus difficult urban circumstances (high rates of unemployment, low levels of income among professionals, and harsh competition in the informal sector) have led *los vilquinos* and a few middle-strata city dwellers originating in Acobambilla to 'reverse' their livelihood strategies towards the rural communities, or at least to reconsider the economic potential of the countryside.

To illustrate these contradictions, I shall briefly present a case of collective return to Acobambilla in which the question of multiple residence is played out.

Of mobility and sedentary notions

In Peru, as elsewhere in the world, most of those who were displaced by the violence have moved within, rather than beyond, the borders of the state in which they hold at least nominal citizenship. Beyond the war's extremely destructive effects on life and livelihoods, economic resources and general political culture and institutions, the marginalized population have to some extent managed to refashion themselves as citizen subjects, to claim their rights, and especially to acquire a voice in the politics of post-war reconstruction (Stern 1998: 472–5). The following case, relating to return migration and dual residence, illustrates this point well.

The organized return

In 1991, a National Technical Commission for the Problem of Displaced Populations in Peru was formed by the Council of Ministers. The commission's mandate was to present an operational plan for the return of displaced persons to their communities of origin. As a follow-up to this process, and in response to a project in support of resettlement, Programme for the Assistance for the Repopulation of rural Peru (PAR) was created in 1993 (Stavropoulou 1998) and began work in 1994. In 1996, it was turned into a presidential programme for resettlement, and later the same year it became the 'Programme for support for the resettlement and development of the emergency zones'. PAR represents the first official recognition of the existence of displaced persons in Peru. Pressure from international and transnational organizations such as IOM, UNDP and UNHCR, local NGOs and particular donor governments was instrumental in this process.

PAR is basically directed towards those displaced by terrorist violence who wish to return to the communities they have previously left. However, both NGOs and organizations of displaced persons complain that the government and PAR have no institutional policy of consultation with civil society and its organizations. Partly as a result, return or resettlement projects carried out under the auspices of PAR have generally not been very successful. Many 'returnees' have migrated back to the urban areas of refuge, in response to both experiencing hostility from their communities of origin ('stayees' may perceive those who fled as deserters; general poverty levels have led to competition over scarce resources; young people who fled with their parents may have little interest in rural life and be perceived as 'problematic'; land conflicts may arise, and so on), and inadequate and ineffective funding for reconstruction. Still, the meagre funds connected to PAR programmes tend to be seen as the only available resource by impoverished city dwellers of rural origin.[14]

This was also the case for a group of people who had arrived in Huancayo from various communities in Acobambilla at various times, and who in the autumn of 1998 decided to organize a collective return to two rural communities located on the borders of Vilca district in Acobambilla. The group was quite a motley crowd, consisting of old and young, professionals and illiterates, employees and street vendors, home-owners and squatters. They were all poor, but I believe it is fair to say that their poverty ranged from 'impoverished' middle class to extremely poor. The professionals (mostly schoolteachers) had experienced rapid downward mobility, the street vendors or day labourers had not really had a chance to 'move up' in economic terms, and the single mothers and/or widows all had extremely precarious economic means. Their social backgrounds and current aspirations were signalled in styles of dress, the younger male professionals wearing jeans and leather jackets, the older peasants felt hats and woollen sweaters. Among the women, the schoolteachers and nurses could be distinguished by their polyester jeans and light perms, the peasant women by their traditional skirts, aprons and pigtails. The participants' urban living quarters were scattered around Greater Huancayo, the largest concentration being in Chilca, around 'El Parque de los Heroes', the traffic roundabout from where buses depart daily to the various rural communities, and in the neighbourhood of 'Coto Coto', the fairground for the purchase and sale of live animals (the function of places being indicative of continuous mobile livelihood practices).

The initiative to organize was taken by two male schoolteachers who had heard about state-assisted PAR returns elsewhere. They contacted the PAR committee in Huancavelica, where they were told what was needed to qualify for PAR assistance, namely that larger groups of individuals or families 'organize themselves' to submit a 'collective request for permanent return', that only persons who left after 1983 and before 1994 would be accepted, that all the individuals involved 'must sign up voluntarily', and that each of the participants should have 'a health test taken before they climb aboard the bus'. Back in Huancayo, the two schoolteachers began to form a group to meet these conditions.

When I first met the group in March 1999, 117 families (a total of 420 persons) had signed up for the collective return. Eventually, it became clear that several had done so without really knowing the conditions quoted above, and, as quite a few said, because they had been told by the organizers that it was 'either all of us or none of us', and that some had therefore felt under some pressure to sign up in order not to ruin the project for the rest. Thus, a considerable number of the participants were actually still in the process of considering whether they should return or not. I was also made aware that some fellow villagers had not been 'invited' or told about the return project. During one meeting, an older man and his wife showed up to complain to the PAR official that they had been deliberately excluded by not being invited to participate in the preliminary meetings. In their complaint, they referred to their former position in the community, their authority, and their rather large landed properties. They were told that it had been impossible for the leaders to contact all the villagers in Huancayo, but it was quite obvious that the entire group considered the old couple to be a nuisance they would rather avoid having to include in their return community. Since the tacit aim of returning was to obtain access to agricultural land and pasture, no one in the group was eager to include former *gamonales*.

Whether participants were actually seriously considering return or not, they had quite different visions of return than PAR. During the three official planning meetings in which I participated, most negotiations between the PAR official in charge of the return process and the group revolved around the question of *how permanently* they had to settle in the rural communities, how much *mobility* in and out of the community would be accepted, and the extent to which families could *divide* themselves between the city and the rural communities. The participants argued in favour of maintaining two homes, one in the city and one in the countryside. Time and time again, the PAR official explained that 'the government does not provide assistance to help people continue living in the city. Upon return participants are expected to become *comuneros activos*' ('active peasants' in the traditional agricultural community structure). Only people with special skills such as musicians and traders would be allowed to remove themselves from their communities for brief periods of time: women wanting to stay in Huancayo with school-age children, for example, would not be allowed to do so. In PAR's vision, entire families were expected to return and to stay together in the rural communities as a family.

Participants gave quite different reasons for their personal involvement in the group. However, a recurrent theme was the deteriorating living conditions in the city, especially after the Fuji-shock in 1990.[15] Wage work had become increasingly difficult to find, and earnings had gone down, as had the purchasing power of the lesser amounts of money being earned. *No hay plata* ('There's no money') and *En la ciudad todo es plata* ('You need money for everything in the city') were commonly agreed explanations for wanting to 'return'. Likewise, skilled jobs in the public sector had become less attractive, thanks particularly to increased competition among a steadily growing group of people and declining salaries. Thus, a majority came to see renewed access to farm land for the cultivation of food as a welcome contribution to the family economy. In addition, the fact that only a few of the participants possessed legal title to the lands they had left behind made it imperative to return and demonstrate to those remaining in the communities that these lands might have been temporarily abandoned but had certainly not been given up.

Nevertheless, only a few participants saw themselves as future permanent residents in their rural communities of origin. Rather, they wanted to go back at sowing and harvest time, or, as was stated time and time again, to *develop* and start *new projects* in the communities, activities that demanded continuous mobility. One of the leaders expressed it in the following way: 'We are not going back to be the same, *así como comunero* ('like traditional peasants'). We are not going back to compete for scarce resources. We are going back to re-create *vivencias* ('livelihoods')'. The participants had several concrete development plans, ranging from raising guinea pigs to pig-farming, from establishing new market places to micro-enterprises for repair work, to building a hotel in Huancayo for the many *comuneros* who need lodgings when they come to town (the latter idea was not presented to the PAR official).[16] As such, their ideas were all built on the traditional mobility patterns in the region. They therefore demanded that PAR allowed them some mobility after their return.

The PAR official tried to meet some of these demands by stating that no one was expected to go back to being herders and agriculturalists the way they were before. Rather, they would have 'fatter animals' and a 'larger yield of return' from the fields because of the 'technological inputs' secured by the second phase of the return programme, the development phase.[17] These 'development' promises did not really satisfy the most eloquent spokesmen of the group, who decided to organize opposition to the rigidity of PAR's conditions.

My interviews with some of the activists in the group showed that many had in fact signed up to the PAR programme in order to obtain access to what they saw as the only available resource. In reality, quite a few could not meet the objective poverty criteria (they owned property in the city and/or had left the rural community before 1983 or after 1992), but nevertheless felt that only renewed access to farmland and livestock could secure a future urban living. Thus, their vision of return was not permanent settlement in a rural community, but rather a livelihood based on multiple residence. For this vision to materialize, however, they were, in their own understanding of things, less dependent on assisted return than on the improvement and extension of the infrastructure, in particular the road system connecting villages with market towns and the improvement of existing irrigation systems or the creation of new ones. In sum, if the state provided public works (e.g. roads, irrigation, and electricity), they felt quite confident that they could manage the rest themselves as private entrepreneurs.[18]

Another small group of participants consisted of single mothers (widows and divorcees) or, in one case, of a married woman who had secretly signed up in order to escape a violent husband. The single mothers generally viewed city life with small children as a difficult exercise in survival. They lacked a network of female relatives who could care for their smaller children while they attended work. They also found themselves in extreme poverty, often unable to feed their children properly, and the prospect of obtaining access to farm land as well as the promised 'gifts' (tools and kitchen utensils) was found to be a better alternative than the continuous struggle for survival in Huancayo. At least initially, these women had little interest in continued mobility to the city. Interestingly, and in contrast to the (male) entrepreneurs, the battered wife saw state-assisted return as an opportunity to escape her husband in a 'safe' and 'protected' way. Being 'fixed in place' and protected by communal institutions was in her eyes the best alternative to domestic violence.

During one of the last planning meetings between the now smaller group and PAR in April 1999, a group of women once again raised the question of education. They strongly opposed the PAR requirement that they should remove their children from the city school system 'when everybody knows how inferior village schools are'. Again the PAR official gave in a little by assuring the group that children enrolled in secondary schools could stay in Huancayo. He claimed, however, that mothers were supposed to take their smaller children with them, thus ensuring 'the return of whole families'. In addition, he attempted to convince the mothers with the weighty argument that rural schools would only improve if there were sufficient parents present in the countryside to assert local claims for better educational facilities. His last words of reassurance were that others would soon join them in their demand for better schooling, since this return was the first in a whole series. His words made the women giggle among themselves: '*Ay si*, returns back to Huancayo, ha, ha, ha'. To them, as to most of the other participants in the group, the bounded territorial spaces envisioned by PAR were too fixed in place to resonate with their personal experiences of sustaining a livelihood through spatially dispersed networks.

Less than half of the families who originally signed up for the PAR-assisted return actually 'jumped on the bus'. Among those who did, very few were present in their new village houses when I visited the district in April 2000, primarily because of the heavy rain in spring 2000, which had washed away some of the newly built family houses and communal buildings. Other houses were still under construction, their yawning window casements looking as ghostly as the gaping wounds between the few returnees and those who remained in the villages (of whom the conduct of a few during the violence could clearly be attributed to either side). More than two-thirds of the returnees had re-migrated back to the city, primarily because of the heavy spring rain, but also because they had not been given access to communal land. Several of them, nevertheless, noted with pleasure that their new 'PAR houses' allowed them to stay in their 'own' houses instead of in the houses of difficult family members or old *gamonales*, reflecting both a continuous wish to cultivate relationships with the village and potential changes in the social structure. 'Down' in Huancayo, others were arranging a new collective return. They will not necessarily have to travel the long and wearisome gravel road up over the *puna* to negotiate the return with village authorities. The president of the community structure lives part of his life in Huancayo, as does the current mayor, who has established a temporary local government office in Huancayo while a new one is being constructed in the village.

Conclusion

In this chapter, I have examined livelihood patterns in the Peruvian Central Sierra and demonstrated that these are not confined to local communities, but rather involve a range of spatially extended social and economic activities. By taking a longer historical perspective, I have been able to show that contemporary rural–urban migration is not happening at a hitherto unprecedented scale furthered by the violent conflict. Throughout the twentieth century, mobility was a central element in the livelihood strategies of the poor as well as the better off. To a large extent, this has been a selective process in which the landowning and slightly better educated families have had better opportunities than the poorer *comuneros* of Indian origin to establish themselves in urban centres. In this respect my analysis indicates that high levels of spatial mobility have not led to the resolution of the deep economic and political problems that beset them, nor to the undermining of the deep structures of social and racial inequality in Peruvian society. Where people came from in the rural areas (district centres or rural annexes higher up), and the power relations between places like Vilca and Acobambilla, seem to have been of crucial importance to both the livelihoods people have been able to sustain and the social mobility strategies open to them.

The violence destroyed the possibility of circulation, which had the spatial effect of immobilizing the population in either the city or the countryside. This temporal fixity impoverished rural residents and city dwellers alike, and led to the rapid downward mobility of the small educated and professional class. As urban poverty grew throughout the 1990s and violent incidents declined, urban dwellers began to look to the countryside to sustain a living. Many re-established mobile livelihood practices on their own, while others organized collective returns towards the end of the 1990s.

In the reverse process of re-establishing rural livelihoods, however, it is not inevitable that the old socio-racial order will prevail. The violence has apparently altered the scope for negotiation, and it seems, for example, that the more 'settled' the former *gamonales* from the rural districts have become in Huancayo, the more 'displaced' they are in their home communities. The negotiations between PAR and the organized group of 'returnees' further indicate that people's efforts to recover lost ways of life are staged at a 'mobile point of time' in which it is no longer totally clear who will 'represent the local' and be in charge of political power in the countryside.

The analysis has also considered the somewhat problematic distinction between, on the one hand 'voluntary' and 'forced' displacement, and on the other hand rural and urban livelihoods. As my discussion has hopefully shown, the categories of migrant and IDP tend to lose meaning and analytical applicability when complex processes of violence and displacement generated by civil war combine with already established patterns of mobility. These patterns, I have suggested, involve the construction of social relationships across space, as well as the forging and sustaining of multi-residence practices that include both the city and the countryside and, at certain times, other migration destinations for temporary work. Given the spatially extended character of social relationships and networks among villagers, most persons who were displaced by the violent conflict were familiar with life in other places prior to their flight. However, this does not mean that social networks were not damaged by the violence. Indeed, most people, including city residents who left their rural communities prior to the conflict, have been impoverished and traumatized in both material and social terms.

We may therefore conclude that, while the armed conflict in Peru led to the discontinuation of well-established mobile livelihood practices, it has not led to the breakdown of the idea and consequent resort to spatially dispersed networks or of attempts to construct new ones based on multi-residence in the post-conflict period. Nevertheless, these strategies are totally ignored by the ways in which the state envisages return, resettlement and future development. In order to qualify for state-sponsored return programmes, people need to stay put in one, and only one, place. Policies that restrict migration are costly, and they generally hurt the poor more than the better off. Given the central importance of mobile livelihoods in the Peruvian Central Sierra, policies that aim at poverty reduction should therefore accept, if not encourage, the various forms of mobility that contributed to people's livelihoods throughout the twentieth century. Such policies could include the support of multiple residence strategies, thus facilitating the development of the very resources inherent in mobility. In Peru, as in most other places of the world, it nevertheless remains to be seen whether policies based on this kind of thinking have any prospects.

The analysis has pointed out the importance of including the social, economic and political contexts within which mobile livelihoods are practised. These contexts are not just locally defined, since mobility is not only about the movement of people, but also of ideas. Transnational ideas about human rights, the rights of internally displaced people and development have played a crucial role in Peru. Although few of the people discussed in this study have ever left Peru, they have had access to such ideas and discourses, not least through local and international NGOs.

Michael Kearney has argued that the relationship between a state and its citizens is normally conceived and enacted as an internal affair. But in cases such as Peru, when state authority comes to be identified by international human rights agencies or UNHCR as abusive, the relationship between the state and the citizen becomes transnationalized (Kearney 1996: 184). Seen in this perspective, one could argue that the current negotiations between 'migrants' or 'displaced people' and the state are taking place at a time when the state has been forced to recognize the existence of the internally displaced within its own borders, but also when formerly marginalized indigenous communities, displaced peasants and urban migrants are not only claiming to have rights, but also daring to assert them.

Acknowledgements

Many people helped move my arguments along the way. First and foremost are the Andean people who related their experiences to me, the local associations and NGOs who facilitated important parts of my fieldwork, and the Peruvian anthropologist, schoolteacher and community organizer Andres Sappallanay, who, besides assisting me in the study, joined me on walking tours in the migrant districts of Huancayo and on a visit to the community of Huancalpi, his home village. Special thanks go to the indefatigable activists of *Jateriy Ayllu*. I would also like to acknowledge my colleagues Finn Stepputat and Henrik Rønsbo, without whom this work would never have materialized. The final version of this chapter grew out of a paper I presented at the workshop on 'Migration and Transnational Theory Re-examined' held in April 1999 in the Dominican Republic, and revised for a workshop entitled 'Migration Processes: the Temporal Perspective Re-examined' held in connection with the American Anthropological Association's Annual Meeting in November 1999 in Chicago. I am grateful for the valuable comments made by participants in these two workshops, especially those made by Vered Amid in her capacity as discussant. Finally, I must thank Fiona Wilson for initially talking a Caribbeanist into going to Peru, inspiring my thoughts by countless pleasant discussions, and continuing to be a dear friend and travel companion.

Notes

1 The empirical data collection on which this paper is based was undertaken jointly with Henrik Rønsbo (in 1999) and Finn Stepputat (1999–2000). The enormous inspiration stemming from this collaboration cannot be emphasized too strongly. However, Finn and Henrik should not be held responsible for any assertion made in this chapter.

2 For an elaboration of this argument in relation to international migration and refugee movements, see Crisp 1999, and van Hear 1998.

3 The last national census was taken in 1993 and reports a much lower number of inhabitants, namely 342,843. This number probably excludes Huancayo's adjoining urban environments. Taking these environments (Chilca, El Tambo), the high percentage of non-registered persons and the frequent travelling between urban and rural areas into account, the estimate of one million inhabitants becomes quite probable.

4 This cultural difference was related to me by several *comuneros*. According to historical sources, the Wari stronghold was centred on what is today Huancavelica, the Wankas on Huancayo (Wankayo). The Wari Empire was the first to occupy the Quebrada de Vilca (*c*. 800). The Waris were overthrown by the Incas around 1460. The Spanish conquest of the Inca Empire (*c*. 1532) was aided by the Wankas (Fagan 1991). At a later point, the Wankas allied themselves with the Incas in a failed uprising against the Spanish (Stern 1982).

5 I do not have the space to develop the debate over the terms 'peasant' and 'peasantry' here, but some remarks are in order. Both terms have been criticized (1) for not taking into account the multiple extra-agricultural economic activities in which sectors of the rural population engage and the degree to which peasant-migrants penetrate into distant and diverse socio-economic spheres; and (2) for ignoring the existence of ethnic identities that are not reducible to class analysis. In his reconceptualization of the peasantry, Michael Kearney has come a long way in developing a post-peasant theory based on a dismantling of binary oppositions and an integration of ethnic politics into the analysis. He argues that ethnicity brings with it a wider spatial focus than the usual concentration

on villages, local towns, neighbourhoods, regions and so forth (Kearney 1996). The Peruvian historian Nelson Manrique nevertheless persists in seeing usefulness in these terms. He argues that, instead of doing away with them, social scientists should rather consider to what extent family labour is organized around the agricultural calendar and subordinates other needs to the seasonal demands of agriculture (Manrique 1998). In the Peruvian context, race and ethnicity have generally been culturally constructed as being closely related to geography. In order to avoid the cultural essentialisms and notions of homogeneity inherent in both class and ethnicity concepts, I have chosen to use the term 'rural community' here.

6 *Chuto* is a condescending or pejorative term used by lowlanders to label indigenous people from the high puna zone. According to del Pino (1998), it denotes 'igno-rant', 'brutish' and 'savage', and is grounded in the (mis-)conception that monolingual Quechua speakers from the puna are weakly articulated with the market and the city. In the district capital of Vilca, this racist term is widely used by *vilquinos* when they refer to or even address villagers from higher communities in and beyond the district. *Cholo* used to be a negatively loaded term used to denote Andean migrants aspiring to assim-ilate to *criollo* culture. During Alberto Fujimori's reign and the subsequent political campaigns of presidential candidate Alejandro Tolodo, cholo has come to symbolize the true Peruvian identity.

7 The Universidad Nacional del Centro was founded in Huancayo in the early 1960s. The university concentrated a significant contingent of students of precarious means from the region and close ties with the region's rural *comuneros* were established (Manrique 1998: 199).

8 For a more extended discussion of the relationship between migration and the political independence of the *comunidades*, see Favre 1977.

9 Neither Sendero Luminoso nor the MRTA has managed to destabilize the country at the levels experienced in 1992. Sendero Luminoso has nevertheless continued to carry out armed actions (selective killings, bomb attempts, raids, etc.) in several departments of Peru. From 1995 to 1997, 1456 violent actions occurred, causing 851 deaths (Hampton 1998). The MRTA re-emerged in December 1996, when fourteen guerrillas took some 600 hostages in the Japanese ambassador's residence in Lima. Due to CNN and other global television networks' intense coverage of this event, people throughout the world witnessed the killing of all fourteen guerrillas (and one hostage) when Peruvian special commandos stormed the residence in April 1997.

10 *Rondas campesinas* were formed by the peasants in 1987–89, on the pattern of traditional self-defence groups set up to fight cattle-rustling. The military also created new self-defence committees. In 1993, the military was given full authority over both the *rondas* and the committees.

11 Estimates vary. The UN Commission of Human Rights estimated the number of IDPs in Peru as ranging from 600,000 to 1,000,000 in 1996, the Global IDP Survey around 250,000 in 1998 (Hampton 1998). The estimate given above is based on government and NGO sources.

12 According to Degregori, this move was basically due to Sendero's failed (or a lacking) analysis of the Peruvian rural condition. He writes: 'Such (the peasants') spatially dis-persed networks clashed with Shining Path's strategy of taking over bounded territorial spaces and converting them into support bases that tended toward isolation' (Degregori 1998: 151).

13 *La Sociedad Agricola de Interés Social* (SAIS) Cahuide, was born with the agrarian reform of Velasco Alvarado in 1970 with the principal objective of distributing hacienda-land to poor and landless peasants. It grew to one of the largest operations in Huancayo, but was totally destroyed by the civil war.

14 Some other Peruvian government agencies are mandated to cover emergency and devel-opment needs. For example, FONCODES, the National Fund for Compensation and

Social Development, is charged with administering the state social investment in favour of the poorest sectors of the country, and PRONAA, the National Food Assistance Programme, with providing emergency food assistance to the poorest sectors of the population (Stavropoulou 1998).

15 In August, 1990, Peruvian President Alberto Fujimori agreed to the terms of a neo-liberal stabilization and structural adjustment programme. The programme involved reducing public expenditure in health, education, housing and social services, and increasing the price of foodstuffs and the unemployment rate overnight.

16 Interestingly, a few villagers in the rural community of origin had planned ahead of the city returnees. When I re-visited Acobambilla in March 2000, the shell of a six-room hotel had already been built on the village square. The village authorities had planned to use some PAR-donated *calaminas* (tin plates) for roofing. This plan was abandoned after a PAR inspection during which the village authorities were coerced into redistributing the *calaminas* to 'the poor and needy'. In their discussion with the PAR official over the issue, villagers pointed to the reasonableness of constructing a hotel for ex-residents who occasionally visit the community. 'Why construct family houses for people who are not permanent residents anyway'?

17 PAR assistance is generally divided into two phases. The first phase is called *apoyo de emergencia* or relief aid, consisting of building materials (corrugated iron, hardboard, and so on), kitchen utensils, agricultural tools and some first-aid equipment. This phase is followed by *apoyo de desarollo*, a development phase, in which people are given seed grain and some small livestock.

18 This is apparently in sharp contradiction to other IDP groups. The UN Commission on Human Rights reports that many IDPs criticize 'the lack of consultation with organizations of the displaced and the emphasis on large infrastructure projects rather than family and community rehabilitation programmes . . .' (UN Commission on Human Rights, 1 April 1996: 101,102).

References

Crisp, Jeff (1999) *Policy Challenges of the New Diasporas: Migrant Networks and their Impact on Asylum Flows and Regimes*, Geneva: UNHCR, Working Paper no. 7.

de la Cadena, Marisol (1988) *Comuneros en Huancayo: Migración campesina a ciudades Serranas*, Huancayo: Instituto de Estudios Peruvianos, Documento de Trabajo No. 26.

de la Cadena, Marisol (1998) 'From race to class: Insurgent intellectuals *de provincia* in Peru, 1910–1970', in Steve Stern (ed.) *Shining and Other Paths: War and Society in Peru*, 1980–1995, Durham and London: Duke University Press.

del Pino H., Ponciano (1998) 'Family, culture and "Revolution": Everyday life with Sendero Luminoso', in Steve Stern (ed.) *Shining and Other Paths: War and Society in Peru*, 1980–1995, Durham and London: Duke University Press.

Degregori, Carlos Iván (1998) 'Harvesting storms: Peasant *Rondas* and the defeat of Sendero Luminoso in Ayacucho', in Steve Stern (ed.) *Shining and Other Paths: War and Society in Peru*, 1980–1995, Durham and London: Duke University Press.

Fagan, Brian (1991) *Kingdoms of Gold, Kingdoms of Jade: The Americas before Columbus*, London: Thames and Hudson.

Favre, Henri, (1977) 'The dynamics of Indian peasant society and migration to coastal plantations in Central Peru', in Duncan, Kenneth and Ian Rutledge (eds) *Land and Labour in Latin America: Essays on the Development of Agrarian Capitalism in the Nineteenth and Twentieth Centuries*, Cambridge: Cambridge University Press.

Gonzalez, Raúl (1988) 'Sendero: los problemas del campo, la ciudad . . . y ademas el MRTA', *Que Hacer*, Lima, No. 50: 46–63.

Hampton, J. (ed.) (1998) *Internally Displaced People: A Global Survey*, London: Earthscan Publications.

Kearney, Michael (1996) *Reconceptualizing the Peasantry: Anthropology in Global Perspective*, Boulder: Westview Press.

Lehmann, David (ed.) (1982) *Ecology and Economy in the Andes*, Cambridge: Cambridge University Press.

Long, Norman, and Bryan Roberts (1984) *Miners, Peasants, and Entrepreneurs: Regional Development in the Central Highlands of Peru*, Cambridge: Cambridge University Press.

Manrique, Nelson (1978) *El desarollo del mercado interior en la Sierra Central 1830–1910*, Series Andes Centrales, No. 6, La Molina.

Manrique, Nelson (1998) 'The War for the Central Sierra', in Steve Stern (ed.) *Shining and Other Paths: War and Society in Peru, 1980–1995*, Durham and London: Duke University Press.

Markwick, Sandy (1999) 'Peru, History and Economy', in *South America, Central America and the Caribbean 2000*, Europa Publications Limited, 8th edn.

Murra, John (1975) Formaciones Económicas y Políticas del Mundo Andono. Lima: Edición IEP.

Oré Cardenas, Edilberto (1998) *Ayahuanco: bajo la sombre de Sendero. Un testimonio de parte sobre la violencia*, Lima: Instituto de Defensa Legal.

Paerregaard, Karsten (1997) *Linking Separate Worlds: Urban Migrants and Rural Lives in Peru*, Oxford: Berg.

Roberts, Bryan R. (1974) 'The interrelationships of city and Provinces in Peru and Guatemala', *Latin American Urban Research* 4: 207–35.

Smith, Gavin (1989) *Livelihood and Resistance: Peasants and the Politics of Land in Peru*, Berkeley: University of California Press.

Stavropoulou, Maria (1998) 'Will Peru´s Displaced Return?', in Roberta Cohen and Francis M. Deng (eds) *The Forsaken People: Case Studies of the Internally Displaced*, Washington D.C.: Brookings Institution Press.

Stepputat, Finn and Ninna Nyberg Sørensen (1999) 'Negotiating Movement', in Ninna Nyberg Sørensen (ed.) *Narrating Mobility, Boundaries, and Belonging*, Copenhagen: CDR Working Papers 99.7: 85–109.

Stern, Steve J. (1982) *Peru's Indian Peoples and the Challenge of Spanish Conquest*. Madison: The University of Wisconsin Press.

Stern, Steve J. (ed.) (1998) *Shining and Other Paths: War and Society in Peru, 1980–1995*, Durham and London: Duke University Press.

Sørensen, Ninna Nyberg and Finn Stepputat (2000) *La Población Desplazada entre la Asistencia y el Desarrollo en los Andes Centrales del Perú*, Copenhagen: CDR Working Paper no. 6.

United Nations (UN) Commission on Human Rights, April (1996) *Internally Displaced Persons*, Report of the Representative of the Secretary-General, Mr Francis M. Deng, submitted pursuant to Commission on Human Rights Resolution 1995/57.

van Hear, Nicholas (1998) *New Diasporas: The Mass Exodus, Dispersal and Regrouping of Migrant Communities*, London: UCL Press.

Wilson, Fiona (2000) 'Representing the State? School and Teacher in Post-Sendero Peru', *Bulletin of Latin American Research* 19(1): 1–116.

Wilson, Fiona (1999) 'Recuperation in the Peruvian Andes', *EADI Journal*, pp. 231–45.

2 Mobile minds and socio-economic barriers

Livelihoods and African-American identifications among youth in Nairobi

Bodil Folke Frederiksen

The title of this chapter refers to the way in which the barriers to spatial mobility experienced by young people in a Nairobi slum may generate forms of mobility and identifications, which are not necessarily confined to the slum area, ethnic group or nation. More specifically, I would like to discuss the significance of mobility and diasporas in the light of young people's dreams and experiences and in relation to their local construction of livelihoods and transnational opportunities for cultural identifications. I argue that for young people in an African city such as Nairobi, being African and being urban carry greater significance than belonging to a nation, in this case Kenya, and or to an ethnic group. This can only partly be explained by local histories of migration. Another significant factor is the transnational cultural products that are used and produced by the young people themselves.

Images and narratives made familiar by the electronic media feed into the dreams young people in particular have of a wider spatial and social mobility. There may be a lack of fit, however, between travel and migration routes, that is, the mobility of bodies, and the routes of popular culture – the mobility of meaning. Only rarely do narratives emerging from these two draw upon and conjure up the same culturescapes. For young people flows of meaning and images from a global popular culture may be more appealing than those rooted in actual movements of people on a more limited regional and national scale, although the latter may have the immediacy and authenticity of family experience. A mental mobility, which is related in complex ways to the realised mobility of persons, contributes to the development of skills and the invention of livelihoods. Such forms of mobility are of special importance for the quite well-educated but largely unemployed young women and men who are found in the poor areas of East African cities.

Which narratives and identifications, then, give pleasure and make (economic) sense for deprived but alert young people in an African city? Which places are imagined, and what are the reasons for certain patterns and preferences?

In his overview of theoretical work on 'diaspora', James Clifford discusses collectivities other than the nation which may produce sentiments of identification, and suggests that 'world historic political/cultural forces such as "Africa" . . . may produce diasporic identification for blacks in Britain and the Americas' (Clifford 1994). The global importance of reggae and the Rastafarian movement is an obvious instance of a genre which captures the experience and history of mobility in a particularly poignant manner. In his examination of the diffusion of Rastafarian allegiance and reggae music in West Africa, Savishinsky argues that 'the spread of Rastafarian music and fashions in West Africa appears to represent but one more chapter in the ongoing assimilation by urban-based African youth of the culture of the Diaspora.' He goes on to point out that the diaspora culture itself obviously 'represents a reworking of elements derived from indigenous African sources' (Savishinski 1994: 30).

The following discussion makes a similar but more general argument about black popular culture. It suggests that a West Indian and African-American diasporic consciousness, building on the loss and utopia of African roots, is in turn reimported to Africa and transformed in dialogue with local culture. This re-emerges as a black popular culture and fuels pan-African identifications and to some extent political ideals among young people in the urban centres of East Africa. Impulses from Rastafarianism mix with other important strands of pan-Africanism and with a multitude of expressions of black popular culture. Together they contribute to constituting a global Africanness, which is attractive for urban youth in Africa and influences their thinking about livelihood, mobility and their place in the world.

The data presented here on the livelihood practices, mobility and cultural identifications of young men and women in Pumwani, a poor Nairobi neighbourhood, are based on my own research into youth culture. The research focus has been popular cultural production, activities, discourses and reception – the localisation of global, transnational or translocal cultural flows – in relation to young people's livelihood activities and the changing family structure in urban East Africa.[1]

Setting and people

The residential neighbourhood of Pumwani has a population of around 18,000, who share an area of less than half a square kilometre. Pumwani is located close to the important Nairobi markets of Burma (fashion, salons, food), Kariokor (handicrafts, utensils), and the large Gikomba market, which encompasses the most dynamic congregation of informal (*jua kali*) production activities in Kenya. It is a rundown but lively, busy, culturally diverse neighbourhood, neglected by the powers that be except for a few long-standing Islamic and Christian organisations, and politicians when elections are close.

Pumwani, which literally means 'place of rest', was established by the city council of colonial and racially segregated Nairobi in the 1920s, as a neighbourhood for the African population of the newly established capital of Kenya.[2] The core inhabitants were Muslims, who had come up-country from the Indian Ocean coast at the beginning of the century. They called themselves Swahili, worked as safari guides, soldiers and hunters, and settled in villages on the eastern outskirts of tiny, white, colonial Nairobi. In about 1920 their urban villages were demolished and the inhabitants, who now included women from the coast and from rural areas near and far, were moved to Pumwani, where land and some infrastructure were provided. During the coming decades, more groups of women settled in the neighbourhood, some seeking to escape rural poverty and the lack of opportunities, others fleeing polygynous families dominated by fathers or husbands. They all wanted to settle in the city, and very few women came with their husband or parents (Burja 1975: 217). Many worked as prostitutes and also provided associated services like brewing of beer and tea, and cooking. Several female migrants managed to earn enough money to build their own houses and subsequently ran a profitable business renting out rooms. Unlike the male labour force, who usually returned to their rural areas to invest in houses and land there, most of the women did not return, but stayed in Nairobi with the families they had established there – children and possibly a husband or boyfriend – until they died.[3]

In the view of the colonisers, women did not belong in towns. They were more interested in migrant labour consisting of men who would stay in the city while working and then return to the rural areas, where their wives and children would ideally reside. The cost of labour could then be reckoned in terms of the upkeep of a single man rather than a family, and housing provided in town could be in the form of barracks for single men or bachelor quarters, as they were euphemistically known. As we have just seen, the reality was that women were highly motivated and suited to creating independent lives and earning livelihoods in urban areas. So although Pumwani, like other African urban areas, was primarily intended for men, history played a trick on colonialism, and women ended up being the core of the population.

Communities in Kenya have a long history of mobility and migration, not least between the city and rural areas. All ethnic groups in Kenya have migrated to Nairobi and are represented in Pumwani. Luo from western Kenya came to the neighbourhood in the 1940s to work on the railway, and Maasai and Kamba, who were recruited into the colonial army and police, had their living quarters there. Kikuyu traded from their nearby agricultural land, many being employed by the colonialists as house servants, but they lived in the slums. Their mobility was restricted, especially in the 1940s and 1950s, when the British colonial authorities attempted to keep Africans out of the city and practised segregation based on passes.

The history of families in densely populated Pumwani also includes large-scale overseas movements of people from India and the Middle East, and the migration of a very small number of people to Great Britain, the rest of Europe and the United States. However, from the perspective of the contemporary inhabitants of this urban slum, the experience of migration and mobility has been dominated by destitute refugees from neighbouring countries coming into the city and relatives fleeing rural conflict and poverty more than by large-scale and long-distance migration. Hundreds of thousands of internally displaced persons and refugees live in camps, towns and cities all over Kenya, where the majority of the population already live in a situation of poverty and political and economic instability.[4]

Large groups of refugees and immigrants from neighbouring countries live in Pumwani. Refugees from civil wars in Ethiopia, Uganda and more recently Rwanda, Burundi, Somalia, the Sudan and Congo/Zaire have settled in the neighbourhood. Most lead highly insecure lives there as illegal aliens, are prone to harassment by the authorities and dependent on the good will of their neighbours. Families displaced by ethnic clashes over rights to land between President Moi's tribe, the Kalenjin, and Kenya's largest tribe, the Kikuyu, have migrated to the neighbourhood since 1994. Thus rural–urban migration is still considerable, and around seventy percent of Nairobi's growing population live in slums.

Today, the built environment of the neighbourhood is crowded. The predominant form of housing is the square Swahili-type of mud houses with inner courtyards. They were introduced by the coastal population and were once spacious and separated by strips of grass. Rooms have repeatedly been subdivided and added, and the houses are now separated not by grass, but by narrow mud lanes criss-crossed by open sewers and overflowing with garbage. The provincial administration is still present in the shape of chiefs and headmen. As in colonial days, nobody can add to a house or start a business without greasing their palms.[5]

Modern Nairobi is still a largely segregated city, with Whites, Asians and Africans each living in their own neighbourhoods. To a large extent this segregation expresses economic rather than racial differences. However, although it is an African area, Pumwani has always been frequented by Nairobians of all colours. In the late afternoon the roads and lanes between the houses begin to fill up. The numerous restaurants, hotels and video cinemas are run mainly by people of Swahili origin and other long-standing African urbanites. Muslim life styles are influential, beyond what is warranted by the twenty percent of the population who follow Islam, and are seen by locals as indicating a commitment to urban living. The neighbourhood is close to the industrial area, so throngs of weary workers pass by on their way home to estates far and near, some staying for a snack or drink in one of the bars. Young men disappear into video cinemas, wooden shacks where the latest Indian or American action films are shown; later pornographic films are featured; cars with single males go round in search of prostitutes; groups of young Somalis, Asians and a few Whites search for *miraa*, a plant drug which produces a mild euphoria when chewed. A few middle-class African families have come to enjoy the good Swahili cooking for which the neighbourhood is known. The whole area is humming with business activity. Young men sell second-hand clothes, dye, wash and iron clothes, run barber salons and do *jua kali* (informal sector) metal work. Women sell fresh milk, vegetables and cooked food, and some sell their own bodies and companionship. They also brew beer and illegal liquor, always ready to pack up their businesses and bolt for it when the police or chiefs come into sight.

Young women and men: Livelihood and style

Young people of the neighbourhood think of themselves as urbanites. The majority have lived in the city for more than half their lives. Some spent their early childhood in the countryside, but very few intend to move back there, although most people value their connections with rural relatives. City life is associated with freedom, but also with temptations and dangers: 'Young men are exposed to Western ways and many different things like drugs. When you go to the country, you find that the youth are not exposed that much and you find that they are more morally upright than the people of the city'.[6] Many single mothers who live and work in town prefer their children to grow up in the rural area in the care of the grandparents. On the other hand, in the view of another young man, a highly valued exposure to the world starts early in the city:

> I like to be a young person in the city. Because you learn many things that you cannot learn in the rural area . . . . It is better to be brought up in the city because social facilities and education are better. A youth in the city can feed on solid food while still crawling. Those people on the other side, they are more bushy. They don't know the latest thing, maybe clothes. It is important to keep up with the world, the latest music; you have to be in touch with it.
>
> (ibid.)

Most young people have had eight years of schooling or more and speak English, Swahili and their mother tongue. They all make use of Sheng, described by one of them as 'Swahili with spice', an ever changing topsy-turvy language made up of most of the languages current in multi-lingual Nairobi, and understood mainly by young people.

Young women and men are experts in the world of fashion, style and popular culture. Although few have travelled outside Kenya, they are familiar with most parts of the world through their education and from mass media. Everyday conversations are interspersed with references to African-American film, music and sports stars. Young people will refer to Eddie Murphy, Fresh Prince (Will Smith), Michael Jordan, Janet Jackson, Toni Braxton, Whitney Houston and the Marley family much as they do to friends and acquaintances in the neighbourhood. According to one young woman:

> You have to wear like Fresh Prince; if you don't catch Jordan you are '*mshau*' (bushy). You must look like Toni Braxton. You must force yourself to look like that. That is the stealing part of it. You must steal to get the blocks (platform shoes). The American youth are more independent. We try to copy, but we can't.[7]

In a very direct way these icons serve as points of identification and models, as illustrated by the following extract from a group discussion among young men on the role of media:

> I think I can get ideas because – something like Fresh Prince – you know I am such a kind of a person, I like high life, so maybe from it I can learn how I can interact with the people, joke, maybe – such kinds of things. American kind of life. Mostly the teens get fashion, the new things, from a famous person like Fresh Prince. A ring like this one, and the broken suits. As you can see from my head I follow the Jordan hairstyle.[8]

Young men especially are walking advertisements for the goods and activities they are turning into profit. Those selling *mitumba* (second-hand clothes) will be dressed up in the sharpest African-American fashions, mainly of the hip-hop variety, or in dress styles copied from Zairian *sapeurs*, locally called *bolingo*. The young barbers running *Soul Brothers* themselves exhibit the sucession of hairstyles made fashionable by African-Americans. One small group of young men have appeared on national television, and teach dancing and performance to hopeful groups of entertainers and acrobats, a few setting themselves up as teachers of Lingala, the language of Zairian *soukous* music. Pumwani is a centre of entertainment, and the Kenya Broadcasting Company (KBC) send talent scouts to the neighbourhood when they want to recruit actors and musicians for their radio and TV shows.

In one interview, the leader of a struggling local dance group, Group Africa, told how he would copy and develop further the dancing and music styles seen on television. In this case the music is from South Africa:

> We use the music which has hitted in the Chart. We just go and buy it and train the music ... Now we are practising the South African music .... The name of the guys I don't know but I think they are soldiers from the South African government .... In the group there are seven ... People like that music very much, the way they dance, ... they dance funny. That song, we have it, we had a problem with the music, because here in Kenya it is hard to get. It is one LP that we hear; it is in KBC (Kenya Broadcasting Corporation). Getting tapes is hard. We decided to record the music and now we are into dancing .... On TV they take only half part .... But we ourselves, we want to do the dancing full, from the beginning to the end. Most of the style we create ourselves. We search for the funniest style that we can put there. The soldier styles we have seen in movies, and we combine them.

The local version of the South African show is directed at a particular audience, families with children, who visit the open-air restaurant where Group Africa has a temporary engagement:

> Our idea is to do different things than the soldiers do. Opposite. So if a soldier is supposed to do "at ease" we do "alert", if it is supposed to be March time going forwards we do it going back. We do things opposite with the music so that people be happy – laughing and laughing. Makes the manager happy [and he] requests you to come there so that he can get more people who buy drinks. When the people are many, things go easily.[9]

For most young unmarried people everyday life is a continuum between leisure and work, with no sharp boundaries separating one set of activities from another. In contrast to the young black men in Amsterdam described by Sansone, with whom they share cultural preferences and who are experts on 'leisure', young people in Pumwani exploit their knowledge of popular culture diligently in work activities. Many wish to earn a living from what Sansone calls 'ghetto outlets', such as 'fashion, professional sport and crime' and some do so; but ideas derived from an expert knowledge of popular culture influence the form and content of a broader range of business and service activities (Sansone 1995: 128, 137).

Work and family relations

The idea and practice of 'business' is imbued with a particular significance and radiance in the neighbourhood. Business is known as the *shamba* (field) of the city. In terms of status, business people rank higher than those involved in the production of goods, regardless of whether they are *vibarua*, casual workers who walk daily to the nearby industrial area to offer themselves at a factory's gates for a day's employment, or involved in *jua kali* (informal sector) production. Locally, the idea of business includes provision of services, and many of those in search of legal or illegal livelihood activities will describe themselves as business people. White-collar workers, or working-class people as they are also called, are a less flexible category. They have a similar high status to business people, and are mostly employed in the formal sector.

Almost half of the young men in the sample described themselves as business-men, and also listed business as their preferred activity. Those who had finished school after eight years or less had modest ambitions.[10] Their ambition was to sell shoes, second-hand clothes, baskets, food, herbal medicine, and products from the informal sector such as stoves, or provide services like haircutting, ironing of clothes or driving a taxi. Their more educated age mates, those who had finished Form Four, that is, twelve years of school, usually listed their most desired occupation as owning or managing a business or a large store. Several men in both groups dreamt of professional careers such as becoming a judge, a banker, a pilot, or even a provincial commissioner. As it is, many slide in and out of illegal activities – theft, the sale of stolen goods and muggings locally or in the town centre. A few are organised in gangs. Most are self-employed and flexible, always on the lookout for new opportunities.

Competition is tough within the limited range of work activities pursued, but all the same more than a third of the young men surveyed limited themselves to pursuing their activities in the close neighbourhood. Another third worked both in Pumwani and outside, and the rest worked only outside the community. Young men are prone to be picked up by the police and asked for identification papers when they move into the central business district of Nairobi, a practice reminiscent of colonial days and one of the barriers to mobility. Fathers of the young men surveyed in Pumwani had a higher frequency of being involved in a varied set of livelihood activities than their sons. An important activity, though one out of the reach of young men living in Pumwani, was farming. In many cases the sons of fathers who were reported to be in the professions (journalists, doctors and civil servants) said that they were unemployed, despite their background and education.

Half the women in the sample had lived in Pumwani for more than ten years. One in four described themselves as engaged in business. A similar number considered themselves unemployed or looking for a job. The business activities they pursued were typically very small in scale, such as selling vegetables, helping their mothers with the production and sale of cooked food or home-brewed beer or liquor, hairdressing, and sewing or washing clothes. They were less mobile than their male age mates, in both their work and leisure activities. The few women who were in formal employment were nurses, receptionists or doing secretarial work.

Young women were also asked about their mothers' work experience. Around a third of mothers were said to work in sale and services, and a third were farmers. Very few were reported to be unemployed, in marked contrast to their daughters.

Many lived in informal marriages. In a survey which asked for comparisons between formal and informal marriages, one respondent described the latter as a 'business'. Women living in informal marriages agreed that men were expected to look after them economically. In situations in which the possibilities for young women to obtain work are extremely limited, entering into informal unions and having children as an investment in the future may be a reasonable economic strategy. Around one-third of informal marriages are formalised at some point by parents' blessings, a bride price is paid, and they are usually solemnised in a Church or mosque.[11]

National or transnational imaginings

Transnational imaginings are local, being influenced by the history of mobility in a particular setting. The idea of a strong African-American culture is one of the answers for young people longing for identifications that make sense of the world. The memories and present realities of mobility in East Africa, on the other hand, are bleak. The master narratives of bodily mobility are the outcome of struggles over land and other sources of livelihood: slavery, the wanderings of nomads, trade, colonialism, alienation of fertile land by the British, forced labour migration to estates and plantations, villagisation in the case of Tanzania, rural-urban migration, internal displacement following ethnic clashes, and flight across borders, away from civil wars or repressive political regimes.

Young people dream of migrating, not to neighbouring countries, but to regions of the world outside Africa. An imagined United States, visualised as being inhabited by African-Americans, is the desired space. A young unemployed man, one of seven brothers and sisters, sums up local desires: 'Me, I see myself somewhere in the United States. Somewhere like Michigan State. But it is just a big dream. And also there are some small steps which I need to seriously embark on, like uplifting my family's financial position, and also for myself I need to go to college, get a good paying job, and then I fly off.' He also thinks that 'it is easier to get to heaven than to get a visa to the US.'[12]

If the United States contributes to young people's daydreams, neighbouring countries often give rise to nightmares. In the following quote, a young man from the neighbourhood makes a sketch of the kind of instability which is most immediately relevant and problematic to him and his associates:

> Worshipping God is something great . . . . It was shocking that our neighbour-ing countries like Uganda, Tanzania, Somalia, Rwanda, Burundi – they've got clashes and many people have lost their families, many people have died, so, and that's what we Kenyan people, we pray for our country not to be with clashes. And that's why politics here is not strong, 'cause we are afraid that when it is strong there will be clashes like in neighbouring countries, 'cause what we see shock us. You see parents dead, a small child there alone crying for his parents; other things you see – bodies floating in the rivers . . . . Politics, I can't support it to be in our country.[13]

Among the younger generation, the idea and experience of the nation state, with its compromised politics, do not evoke values and dreams as appealing as does an imaginary 'Africa'. Those who are in their twenties now have no memory of the euphoria of national independence more than thirty years ago, memories that their parents still have and that their grandparents share. That moment of united national purpose has long since been shattered by the realities of unequal development and rivalry between different groups of the population, organised around politicised ethnic identities. Most importantly, young men and women have not found the jobs which the government led them to believe would be available once they had finished their education, and many have lost faith in the state.

In terms of popular culture, the Kenyan nation does not provide activities or genres which are exciting and popular with young people, with a few exceptions. Swahili-language situation comedies, depicting the ups and downs of ordinary Kenyans in urban settings, which are shown on national television, are popular. A few local music and dance groups who dress up in mock ethnic gear, such as Rare Watts, who perform in full Maasai regalia, have a large following. If the nation as such is at all associated with cultural activities which reach out to the mass of the people, they are of a state-led kind: parades, *barazas*, mass meetings, flag ceremonies, uniforms and the 'invented traditions' of tribal dancing and rituals (Haugerud 1995). Together they constitute a non-participatory culture from above, whose predictability and rigid form have little appeal for young people. Cultural forms associated with religion have more appeal, but gospel performance, Christian and Muslim crusades and festivals, which masses of young people take part in, are associated with ideas larger than those of the nation. Most importantly, however, national forms of popular culture are confronted with a resourceful global popular culture industry.

The nation and pan-Africanism

As Sansone notes, writing about the Surinamese diaspora in Holland, 'the leisure industry, music industry and mass media . . . play a key role in what is commonly considered black or white.' The industry makes 'trendy a certain way of being young, gifted and black' (Sansone 1995: 116, 136). For the last decade or two, popular culture has contributed significantly to making 'African-America' the most powerful culture-scape for young people living in African cities – a particularly receptive public. Television series and popular music with associated videos present young Americans and West Indians who share looks and styles with youth in Africa inhabiting a utopian space of black youthfulness and afflu-ence. Not surprisingly, the question which was most commonly asked of me when I discussed American stars and shows with young women and men in Pumwani was, 'Are they real?' When a group of young men in their twenties were asked whether they identified primarily with their ethnic group, the nation or 'Africa', they all said that first and foremost they felt themselves to be Africans.[14] 'I am first an African, then I become Kenyan after. I don't think of myself at the tribal level. When I meet others we think of ourselves as Africans and Kenyans. In that way we can go forward.' The political revival of the idea of 'Africa' among young people in an urban setting has to do with the combination of a pan-African political ideal and 'African' presence in music, narratives and images. The cultural interaction between Africa as a region and the African diaspora, coming together as an idea of 'Africa', is a key cultural resource. The preference for African-American, West Indian and African stars, shows, sportsmen and -women, fashion and music can be seen as pan-Africanism in a contemporary guise. Or to put it differently, the present popularity of what are seen as the stars and genres of African-origin pop-ular culture is supported by the memory and imagining of pan-African ideals and space.[15]

On the adoption of the new South African Constitution in 1996, President-designate Thabo Mbeki famously said, 'I am an African', taking in the whole continent, instead of just the new nation of South Africa. In present-day South Africa the majority party, the African National Congress, increasingly stresses an all-African perspective on culture and development, a perspective which earlier characterised its rival movement, the Pan African Congress. There is a whole cul-ture industry and management philosophy which advocates a return to African values under the heading of the 'African Renaissance'. The core values are con-tained in *ubuntu*, an African humanism that supposedly values community and collectivity higher than individual achievement. The South African youth maga-zine *Tribute* is one expression among many of this new trend. These ideals are also influential among youth in Kenya, for whom the new South Africa is a model. Young people in Pumwani thought of South Africa as being midway between the First and Third Worlds, successful and advanced in terms of politics, human development and popular culture.

The 1990s African Renaissance has a long and distinguished history. It can be seen as the latest flowering of a pan-Africanism which goes back at least to the beginning of the twentieth century. The Jamaican Marcus Garvey demanded 'Back to Africa', and the American reformer William DuBois fought for black national-ism in the United States, based on African values (Allen 1970: 83). In Africa itself, the 1930s intellectual and politician Leopold Senghor eulogised African philoso-phy and aesthetics in poetry and prose. Aimé Césaire, from the French-speaking

West Indies, imagined and practised a pan-African cultural 'Negritude', while in the same vein Léon-Gontran Damas wrote of the 'glory of being black'. Franz Fanon, Walter Rodney and George Padmore, all West Indians, chose Africa as their life's work, and wrote strong and influential political treatises on the economic, political and mental consequences of slavery and colonisation. Their influence, often coupled with the language, imagery and ideals of Rastafarianism, was central to African independence and revolutionary movements from the 1930 onwards. When the youth-based National Provisional Ruling Council took power in the 1992 coup in Sierra Leone, reggae was played all day long on the radio, murals depicting 'Rasta Man', Marcus Garvey and a weeping Mother Africa appeared in Freetown, and urban youth supporting the 'revolution' greeted each other with the Rasta slogans 'One Love' and 'Respect' (Opala 1994).

Jamaican Rastafarians built on Garvey's ideas, which stressed racial pride and dreamt of a symbolic return to Ethiopia/Africa from slavery among whites in Babylon. The notion was that colonisation by Babylon carved up the original Ethiopia, which before colonisation included all of Africa. 'Ethiopia' was an idea of 'blackness' or 'Africanity' more than a concrete physical space connected with the nation of Ethiopia (Cohen 1997: 38). The dream spread, in the form not only of the Rastafarian movement in the wake of West Indian migration to Western Europe and the United States, but also of footloose reggae, one of the most influential genres of global popular culture.

The famous sixth pan-African Conference, held in Manchester in 1945, was a watershed: American and West Indian intellectuals, including George Padmore and C. L .R. James, planned the conference with young Africans of the stature of Jomo Kenyatta and Kwame Nkrumah, and laid the political and intellectual foundations for African independence (Legum 1962; Abdul-Raheem 1996). Important elements in their visions came from the fight against slavery and for liberty undertaken by blacks in the Americas and West Indies.

When Kenya's future President, Jomo Kenyatta, lived and travelled in Europe in the 1930s and 1940s, he was both a nationalist and a pan-Africanist. When he returned to Kenya the nationalist politician in him took over. His own movement for independence and the mobilisation of the peasant-based Mau Mau liberation movement did not look beyond the horizons of the nation. The anti-colonial struggle in Kenya has often been accused of being even narrower, a fight primarily for the rights of the country's largest tribe, the Kikuyu, rather than for a Kenya of united tribes, the nation to come. The Mau Mau freedom fighters became a negative emblem in the West, and their star was never high after independence even in Kenya.

Although at the time Kenyatta dissociated himself from the movement, his pragmatic and conciliatory nationalism was always tainted with tribalism. The same has been the case with the regime of his successor, Daniel Arap Moi. However, pan-Africanism has not been discredited, but has survived as a distant political and cultural ideal, and for some as a desired direction for development. The Organisation of African Unity lives on, despite some staggering problems, and is widely respected. The political survival of pan-Africanism has coincided with its constant multifaceted presence in music, narratives and images.

On music: Region and diaspora

The role of music is an example of the predominance of popular culture of African origin. Genres and stars of African and African diaspora origin dominate popular music in many parts of the world. The prevalence of such music in East Africa in general, and in a Nairobi slum neighbourhood in particular, is no surprise. It is a question of relevance, quality and availability. Surprising or not, the pride taken in black music is of some importance for the identity and dreams of young people.[16]

As we have seen, local music entrepreneurs worked on bringing South African music to Kenya and reworked a particular genre to suit their own purposes. The predominant regional genre, however, is *soukous* music, which originates from neighbouring Zaire, now Congo, and is performed in Lingala or Swahili. *Soukous*, like most other musical genres, is transnational. It started with the introduction of the Hawaiian guitar by Belgian musicians into the Congo in the 1940s, and later incorporated Cuban rumba and other West Indian influences from genres like the *merengue* and *matiniqué* (Seck and Clerfeuille 1993: 42–3).

However, *soukous* music is indigenous to Kenya. Ideas travel more easily than people, and *soukous* is performed live in clubs and bars by a few young performers from the former Zaire and by a host of would-be Zairians. The latter are young Kenyans, who exploit the Zairian musical know-how and high status, have picked up Lingala, the *lingua franca* of parts of Congo/Zaire, and sometimes pretend to be immigrants. Here, one of them, the leader of Group Africa, tells about his favourite music:

> I like Bilenge Musica. They are Zairian musicians, but now they are here in Kenya, and they are national Kenyans. They dance Lingala music, and they are same like us because they are four. We copy from them and modify it. Outfit we make it for ourselves.... The music that I like is that Lingala music, African music, *soukous*, Zairian. I like even funk music, slow jam, I was dancing funk.... As a Lingala dancer, even if you are old you can dance, even if you have beards, like funk... I like mostly Lingala music and then slow jam. Those are easy musics – and blues.

On the other hand he is critical of reggae, not of its political message, but of its association with drugs and crime – issues and problems all too familiar to slum dwellers:

> Reggae music I don't like it very much.... Those people who like reggae they take *bhang* and those other things. Most of the reggae musicians like Bob Marley, he used to take *bhang* before he went to the floor. Even Peter Tosh. In many reggae clubs here in Kenya you see some crimes happen, you get some people stabbed because they take *bhang* on the floor.... Even if you come with your own girlfriend, maybe it is your first time, it will end with you being stabbed or they will go away with your girlfriend. I don't like that

reggae music because of the behaviour of those people. The music has got a nice message but . . .[17]

His is, however, a minority position. Reggae is present everywhere in Pumwani: 'Here we like Jamaica'. The United States, Zaire and Jamaica, in that order, were thought of as the countries most famous for music. In a survey of music stars, in which a sample of a hundred young men and women named their favourite musicians, one in four of those named was a reggae musician. Bob Marley came top, followed by Burning Spear (William Rodney), Gregory Isaacs and the South African reggae artist Lucky Dube. Other popular African reggae artists are Alpha Blondy, Ras Kimono and Majek Fashek, all from West Africa. The names of the reggae group Black Uhuru and the singer Burning Spear remind Kenyans of independence (*uhuru*) and the national contribution to the realisation of the aims of pan-Africanism. 'Burning Spear' was a nickname of the future president of Kenya, Jomo Kenyatta, when he was the hero of the Kenyan nationalist movement. It is fitting that a skilful mural painting of the reggae star who shares the name and radical politics of the young Kenyatta adorns a wall in Pumwani, which saw the early rise of Kenyan nationalism.

Modern versions of funky rhythm and blues, locally named 'slow jam' and performed by young African-American stars like Brandy, Boyz II Men and Toni Braxton, are particularly popular with young women, as is gospel music, which is enjoying a revival connected to the rise of charismatic forms of Christianity. Rap music is the most important runner-up in terms of popularity. The late Tupac Shakur is a cult figure, and his photo adorns the living quarters of numerous teenagers. There may be a class dimension to allegiance to different styles. Young men from Pumwani jokingly called the followers of the hip-hop culture from the better-off estate across the street *wa-babylonies* or *wa-softies*. They are seen as rich kids who can afford the expensive outfit that is required. Reggae and rap muster an almost equal number of male and female fans, and in general audiences are eclectic, shifting loyalties frequently, and there are no strong dividing lines between followers of the different genres. A young local musician described his age mates in the neighbourhood in this way: 'They dress like Tupac and dance like Marley'.

Conclusion

The aim of this article has been twofold: to argue that an identification by young urban Africans with a global black popular culture makes sense for them in their context of urban poverty, and to characterise their livelihood strategies and activities in the light of their cultural identifications. I have argued that poverty and political oppression and neglect contribute to immobilising them, even though they are living in a neighbourhood characterised by past and present mobility. In this situation access to popular culture is of great importance, and black American and Caribbean culture as well as regional African culture provide models, pleasure and entrepreneurial ideas. I have given examples of the way young men and women model themselves on global black stars and styles, and traced the reasons why pan-African ideals are more attractive than those of the nation state.

In a certain sense young men and women in Pumwani lead more restricted lives than did their parents in terms of social and spatial mobility. Most of their parents had access to a rural home, and quite a number of them were farmers, an option which is not open to young people, nor desired by them. The rural–urban dichotomy is still a fact of life, important for young people's identification as urbanites, but not particularly useful in terms of opening up livelihood opportunities. For many young people, the slum is a prison and poverty is the jailer. Some do manage to leave, however, in most cases helped by education and a supportive and comparatively well-connected family network. Others make a decent living by exploiting the opportunities connected with communication, entertainment and new forms of services.[18]

Young people make enough money to eat, to dress in the latest African-American or Zairian fashions, to add a room or two to their parents' mud house when they enter into relationships or marry, and to send their children to school. They also have easy access to electronically transmitted mass popular culture and may pluck business ideas from shows and styles. But the majority do not make enough money to move to other areas of Nairobi or Kenya, let alone dreamt-of places like the Britain or the United States.

From the perspective of poor people in Kenya (the majority of the population), mobility is associated with poverty, instability and often the use of force, rather than something people willingly engage in. The kind of movement that poor people, like everybody else, wish to undertake – visiting relatives, studying and doing business abroad – is surrounded by impassable barriers. The vast and suggestive cultural space of an Africa–America continuum, underscoring the connections between home and the most dynamic economic and cultural region in the world, is proving productive for young people's life and work.

Writing on Caribbean identities, Stuart Hall suggests that 'the African diasporas of the New World have been in one way or another incapable of finding a place in modern history without the symbolic return to Africa' (Hall 1995: 9). In an opposite move, groups of economically disadvantaged young people in African cities are making use of the culture and imagined space of an African diaspora to find their place in Africa and their home in the world.

Notes

1 Eight months of fieldwork between 1996 and 1999 was funded by the Danish Council for Development Research as part of a research programme entitled 'Livelihood, Identity and Organisation in Situations of Instability'. During my research I benefited from being a Research Associate at the Institute of Development Studies at Nairobi University. I thank them for their support, and also my research assistants in Nairobi, Isabel Munandi, David Mita Aluku, George Mouria and Julius Mwaniki. I also thank the editors of this volume for much needed and helpful comments on earlier versions of the paper.
2 For the history of Pumwani, see Hake 1977, McVicar 1968 and White 1990.

3 Some groups, like the Haya women from Tanganyika, came to earn an income in order to support their families in periods of drought and agricultural crisis, stayed for a while and returned home with their earnings (White 1990).

4 At the moment East and central Africa are among the most unstable regions in Africa in terms of small-scale wars, some across borders, ethnic conflicts and ensuing mass movements of people. 'Of the 7 countries from which over 94 per cent of Sub-Saharan Africa's 3.9 mill. refugees originate, only one (Angola) is not in East Africa; of the 10 countries that receive over 92 per cent of the refugees only two (Zaire and South Africa) are not in East Africa' (World Bank 1990: Vol. 1. 15). In the late 1990s, however, the West African region began catching up (See Zlotnik 1999).

5 Chiefs and headmen are Government-appointed civil servants.

6 From a group discussion on attitudes to youth, Nairobi, April 1997.

7 From a group interview of young women on the role of mass media, Nairobi, October 1998.

8 Nairobi, April 1997.

9 From a life history interview, Nairobi, October 1998. I have not been able to identify the music described, but it seems likely that it is Isicathamiya, the singing and dancing genre invented by black miners living in hostels, made famous by Ladysmith Black Mambazo, and turned into 'World Music' by the American musician Paul Simon. On Isicathamiya, see Erlmann 1996.

10 Based on surveys of samples of 100 young men and 100 young men and women, and follow-up group interviews.

11 For a more detailed discussion of a changing family structure in Pumwani, see Frederiksen 2000.

12 From a group interview of young men, Nairobi, December 1999.

13 From a life history interview, Nairobi, October 1998.

14 From a group interview, Nairobi, December 1999.

15 From the point of view of radical politics, the sting and critique associated with earlier pan-Africanism is not present in this contemporary version. William Ackah describes the present diffusion of black culture as the globalization of a conservative culturalist pan-African-Americanism (Ackah 1999: 94 ff.).

16 For an example of what is seen as black music in Uganda, see Ssewakiryanga 1999.

17 From a life history interview, Nairobi, October 1998.

18 The percentage of people working seems to have been higher in earlier generations, in terms of both employment and self-employment. However, the information on parents' work provided by their sons and daughters may not be accurate.

References

Abdul-Raheem, Tajudeen. (1996) *Pan Africanism*, London: Pluto Press.

Ackah, William B. (1999) *Pan-Africanism, Exploring the Contradictions: Politics, Identity and Development in Africa and the African Diaspora*, Ashgate: Aldershot.

Allen, Robert L. (1970) *A Guide to Black Power in America*, London: Victor Gollancz.

Burja, Janet. (1975) 'Women entrepreneurs of early Nairobi', *Canadian Journal of African Studies* 9(2): 213–34.

Clifford, James. (1994) 'Diaspora', *Cultural Anthropology* 9(3): 302–38.

Cohen, Robin. (1997) *Global diasporas*, London: UCL Press.

Erlmann, Veit. (1996) *Nightsong. Performance, Power and Practice in South Africa*, Chicago and London: The University of Chicago University Press.

Frederiksen, Bodil Folke. (2000) 'Popular culture, gender relations and the democratization of everyday life in Kenya', *Journal of Southern African Studies* 26(2): 209–22.

Hall, Stuart. (1995) 'Negotiating Caribbean Identities'. *New Left Review* 209: 3–15.

Hake, Andrew. (1977) African Metropolis. Nairobi's Self-Help City, Sussex: Sussex, University Press.

Haugerud, Angelique. (1995) *The Culture of Politics in Modern Kenya*, Cambridge: Cambridge University Press.

Legum, Colin. (1962) *Pan-Africanism: A Short Political Guide*, Westport: Greenwood Press.

McVicar, Kenneth. (1968) *Twilight of an African Slum: Pumwani and the Evolution of African Settlement in Nairobi*, Los Angeles: University of California Press.

Opala, Joseph A. (1994) ' "Ecstatic Rrevolution". Street Art Celebrating Sierra Leone's 1992 Revolution', *African Affairs* 93(371): 195–219.

Sansone, Livio. (1995) 'The making of a black youth culture: Lower-class young men of Surinamese origin in Amsterdam', in Amit-Talai and Helena Wulff (eds) *Youth Cultures: A Cross-cultural Perspective*, London & New York: Routle 114–43.

Savishinsky, Neil J. (1994) 'Rastafari in the promised land: The spread of a Jamaican socio-religious movement among the Youth of Africa', *African Studies Review* 37(3): 19–50.

Seck, Nago, and Clerfeuille, Sylvie. (1993) *Les Musiciens du Beat Africain*, Paris: Bordas SA.

Ssewakiryanga, Richard. (1999) 'What has become of our teens? Popular music and the youth in Uganda', in Guhathakurta (ed.) (1999) *Culture and the Disciplines: Papers from the Cultural Studies Workshops*, Enreca Occasional Paper Series 5, Calcutta: Centre for Studies in Social Sciences 108–20.

White, Luise. (1990) *The Comforts of Home: Prostitution in Colonial Nairob*, Chicago: The University of Chicago Press.

World Bank Discussion Paper (1990) International Migration and Development in Sub-Saharan Africa, Vols 1 and 2.

Zlotnik, Hania. (1999) 'Trends of international migration since 1965: What existing data reveal', *International Migration* 37(1): 21–61.

3 Mobility, rootedness, and the Caribbean higgler

Production, consumption and transnational livelihoods

Carla Freeman

Migration, travel, and transnational production have defined the Caribbean region since its inception as a terrain of colonial conquest more than 300 years ago. Indeed, one could argue that they have been integral to the region's development strategies. From the forced movements of slaves and indentured labour to voluntary moves of adventurers and fortune seekers and continuous circulation of people within and outside the region, flux has as much defined Caribbean livelihood as stasis. This paper addresses the relationship between movement and rootedness, transnationalism and locality, by turning its attention to a legendary Caribbean figure, the 'higgler'. A 'higgler' in the Caribbean context is defined as a market intermediary, a buyer and seller of produce and goods who typically purchased these in small quantities from rural growers and sold them in the town marketplace. Traditionally, she travelled back and forth between country and town, buying and selling agricultural produce for manufactured and imported goods, and, in turn, making these commodities available in rural areas. The country higgler has been a powerful figure in Afro-Caribbean history, most often depicted as a woman who embodies local economic ingenuity and female independence.

I map here some of the ways in which this figure, in her contemporary form, pushes us to think more flexibly about livelihoods and their changing meanings within and across space and time. The women I will describe here straddle a number of economic pursuits, identities, and ways of living that challenge fundamental dichotomies that remain persistent in our models of development and analyses of contemporary life in general: production/consumption; formal/informal economies; work/leisure; and within the Caribbean region specifically, the gendered paradigm of 'respectability'/'reputation'. My argument can be summarized as follows: if migration and development studies have both tended to privilege the realm of labour and production, and production has historically been situated in opposition to consumption, there is also a deeply gendered dimension to this dualism in which men produce and women consume/shop. What we miss in such a polarized formulation are the ways in which together modes of consumption and modes of production, and labour across formal and informal sectors, may have ironic and potentially transformative effects for configurations of status and class groups as well as ideologies of gender and race.

By linking a discussion of economic development through particular modes of production to the realm of consumption, I will suggest that we interrogate some of the ways in which transnational theories of late have painted a rather faceless, historyless, and ironically fractured portrait of contemporary life in which movement and flux take the following forms: people move across the globe (e.g. as either cosmopolitan elites, as pleasure-seeking tourists, or as destitute migrant labourers seeking economic gains); media and goods move (largely from rich to poor countries) and generate new meanings and value by those who consume them in their 'local' homes and communities; footloose factories move to low wage parts of the developing world, incorporating and spitting out Third World (female) labour at the whims of corporate demand; and capital circulates through the hidden electronic manoeuvres of multinational firms. As a Third World female producer/consumer, the higgler represents an intriguing dimension of transnationalism that has yet been little studied – one in which participants within the informal sector are themselves transnational actors and not merely globalization's effects. These women are not only incorporated into the international division of labour through processes of global demands for cheap labour. They are also crafting new dimensions of economic and cultural exchange through modes of travel that tap into but are not reducible to the patterns of late twentieth-century transnational capitalism that have by now been so well documented. Positioned at the intersections of production, consumption, and formal and informal sectors, transnational higglers provide a unique opportunity to bring together discussions of the international division of labour with those of the culture of consumption. My aim here is to bridge this discussion and to focus on its particular implications for analyses of migration and for conceptualizing mobile livelihoods more broadly.

Caribbean higglers as global/regional/local subjects

The historical importance of the Caribbean higgler has been multifaceted. From the days of slavery, the early higgler was integral to establishing the internal marketing systems that have come to define much of the Caribbean region (Mintz 1955; Katzin 1959; LeFranc 1989). Her role under slavery was profound, both symbolically and practically. By transporting and making available a wide array of produce, herbs, and root crops, grown by slaves on provision grounds during their 'free' time, and providing the dietary staples for slave and planter alike, she both subsidized and gained some autonomy from the plantation system (Beckles 1989; Bush 1990). In so doing, the higgler helped to establish a patterned diet that has characterized West Indian life across class and racial boundaries by travelling between peasant producers in the countryside and emergent urban centres. In contrast to the plantation mistress, whose lifeways and movements were circumscribed by the limits set by expectations of 'respectable' domestic duty and propriety, the higgler operated in the public space of markets and roads in her island home as well as on sojourns to neighbouring islands. Over nearly two centuries, she has come to embody a figure of womanhood in which travel and business acumen are defining characteristics. Indeed, as a cultural icon the higgler is marked more by physical movement than by stasis, more by vivacity and toughness than by a demure Victorian demeanour.

Historically, the higgler's trade has not been restricted to produce and consumables; central to her trade have also been news, information and gossip (Katzin 1959). Her style of banter and prowess over modes of negotiation are well known and admired traits of West Indian womanhood. Indeed, this figure has been one of the most highly commodified images of West Indianness generally. The colourful country higgler, wearing head tie and printed skirt, proudly balancing her bountiful tray of fruit atop her head or nestled beneath her generous bosom, has become a synecdoche for Caribbean womanhood, and even nationhood. Her image is produced for tourist as well as local consumption on post cards, key chains, tea towels, as well as on the canvases of local artists. She signifies a femininity that is at once that of a mother and a worker, a provider and a consumer, she is both the definition of 'locality' and of movement. As such, her particular enactment of femininity – that of independence, strength, and fortitude – has formed a powerful counterpoint to that of a more middle-class European model denoted in the region's well known concept of 'respectability'.[1]

One can still find today Caribbean market women who resemble closely these descriptions. While few travel on donkey cart, foot, or banana boat as they once would have done, they still can be found in the region's rural areas and marketplaces buying and selling many of the same sorts of produce and goods of days gone by. Additionally, a new form of higglering has expanded in the region, in which women[2] travel on commercial airlines buying clothing and other consumer goods rather than mangoes or provision crops, and re-selling these in an active (and illegal) informal market at home. Otherwise called 'suitcase traders' or 'informal commercial importers' (ICIs), these Caribbean higglers are a well-known and much discussed but little studied group (French 1989; Quinones 1997; Ulysse 1999; Witter 1988). The suitcase trade (named for the large bags carried abroad empty and returned full upon higglers' return home) is an international phenomenon witnessed in many of today's major metropolitan areas as well as Third World cities within Africa, Latin America and the Caribbean. These 'informal commercial importers' represent a growing dimension of an expanding informal sector in Barbados and the region at large. Today, the transnational higgler travels not only beyond the rural/urban loop of her agricultural counterpart, but to metropolitan cities in which many find relatives and friends who have migrated abroad and, quite significantly, to places within the region that were defined outside of the traditional inter-regional boundaries that were established centuries ago by colonialism.

For transnational higglers, many of whom are simultaneously employed by foreign corporations, and others who devote the majority of their labour to the buying and selling of consumer goods on the informal market, their motivations and experiences can, in one sense, be usefully interpreted through the lens of migration studies as their livelihoods and relationships straddle 'home' and 'host' societies. As regular sojourners, whose labour requires that they travel between sites within and across the Caribbean region, they follow in the footsteps of nearly three centuries of Caribbean higglers and other labour migrants, and raise questions about temporality as well as locality in what might be argued to be a model of Caribbean livelihood defined by movement as opposed to stasis and settlement. As producers and consumers of goods and services, their labour as higglers is situated within the informal economy, itself embedded in the transnational circulation of imported goods. For many, higglering is integrally tied to wage-earning jobs in the formal economy's transnational export sector. Higglering, then, can be understood as bound up within circuits of labour that are both transnational and local (one might say multi-local or multi-sited). However, higglering can also be considered a form of tourism among the lower and middle classes who turn travel into profit. It is at once an expression of production and consumption, work and leisure. Counterposed to migration, higglering entails both frequent movement as well as rootedness. While its goals are certainly economic, higglering is also embedded deeply in an array of cultural ideologies and practices which define 'livelihood' in broad and multiple determined ways. Here, I attempt to contribute to efforts to re-conceptualize transnational livelihoods and migration by foregrounding three themes: the relationship between formal and informal economic sectors and their embeddedness in the expansion of the global economy; relationships between production and consumption and their implications for local identities, and finally the ways in which gender (femininity in particular) is central to each of these processes.

The Barbadian woman whose grandfather went to London to work as a conductor on public transport, and whose mother lived away for 20 years as a nanny in New York, leaving her to be raised by her granny back home, now finds herself travelling to the culturally distant but geographically closer territories of San Juan and Caracas, across the linguistic/colonial divides of the region's past.[3] All her life, she can recall letters and phone calls, packages and trips linking her family in Barbados with kin in Canada, England, the US, and Trinidad – all points along the Anglophone colonial continuum. By contrast, her view toward her Latin American and Hispanic Caribbean neighbours conjures up only cultural remoteness verging on disdain. Colonial history has forged patterns in which long past independence, the cultural ties within the ex-British territories, are largely mapped to England, Canada, and more recently the US. Now, however, phrase book in hand, she finds herself negotiating the streets and shops of San Juan, with the same savvy expertise of the country higgler aboard a local mini-bus, or donkey cart in days gone by.[4]

Contemporary transnational higglers are both hailed for their ingenuity and bemoaned for the illegality of their trade by their local governments and state development planners.[5] Their trade contributes in significant ways not only to providing income to the formally unemployed or under-employed, but also to sup-plementing the low wages of many situated within the transnational industries in Free Trade Zones across the region. It is a group of this final category of contem-porary higglers to whom I turn in this paper – those women employed within one of the region's newest and fastest growing industries, off-shore informatics, who find themselves propelled into the additional pursuit of weekend higglering. Their lives as such have become intimately bound up with a multitude of dimensions of globalization. Even more so than the traditional higgler dealing in produce and travelling across national and regional spaces, the informatics worker/higgler is multiply embedded in global processes. In my fieldwork among informatics workers in Barbados in the 1990s, I quickly discovered that, demanding as these jobs were in terms of sheer discipline and rigour of the labour process as well as expectations for over-time, most of the women operators simultaneously engaged in one or more forms of informal income generating activity 'on the side', including baking and decorating cakes for special occasions, hair styling in their kitchen 'salons', and buying and selling clothing and accessories to networks of kin, friends and workmates. This last form of informal work, what I am calling here transnational higglering, is tied in intriguing ways to women's formal jobs in informatics. To distinguish them from other groups of contemporary higglers, I refer to this group of women employed within or formerly linked to the offshore sector as 'high tech higglers'. This is not a label which these women would likely use to define themselves. Indeed, one aspect of these sojourns that distinguishes them from those of other higglers (past or present) is the fact that they are not necessarily seen as 'work' at all. While economic advancement is undeniably part of their goals (at the very least, paying for the trip itself, and ideally profits that can be used for such home-based expenses as children's school uniforms, home improvements/building, the purchase of a car, etc.), these trips are seen by the high-tech higglers in direct contrast to, and as a welcome reprieve from, their formal jobs. What is notable to the observer, however, is the degree to which this combined set of activities (their formal jobs in informatics and their informal marketing pursuits) places this group of higglers in an intriguing new category of economic actors. Though in both capacities – as global export producers and as travelling market intermediaries – their historical roots are deep (dating back to the earliest days of colonial sugar exports and rural-urban higglering), they demonstrate some of the convergences across structural spheres (culture/economy; formal/informal sectors of the economy, mobility/rootedness) that have been only narrowly portrayed in the recent globalization literature. Further, each of these realms and their dynamic intersections demonstrate the integral place of gender in the dialectics of local/global arenas.

It came as a bit of a surprise to me, when interviewing nearly 100 Barbadian women about their jobs in informatics and their simultaneous informal economic pursuits (many of which also take a transnational form), that not a single one expressed any interest in migrating abroad. These are women whose families are often scattered between Toronto, Trinidad, London and New York, whose dreams of the future are infused by references to 'globalization', and whose labour and leisure involve many transnational dimensions. Their jobs as information processors link them electronically to sites scattered across the US, and they recite with pride the litany of American cities and states they have committed to memory by processing airline tickets and insurance claims from across North America. Their lunchtime conversations are peppered with references to the latest Hollywood films and evening soaps. Their holidays are as likely to find them picnicking in a park nearby and listening to calypso and dub music, as boarding planes for Miami, enjoying American nightclubs and shopping malls, hamburgers and fries. Why then, when there is such a clear and unambiguous sense of their rightful place 'at home' in Barbados, for so many others across the region, migration continues to be believed to represent a desirable set of possibilities? How might we interpret what seems to be a simultaneous embrace of transnational movement and culture formulated across transnational space, and a clear rootedness in local place and Barbadian identity? What emerges from this research is a sense that this particular form of higglering presents a counter option to migration for these young women, an opportunity to pursue economic ends and cultural/tourist goals, but remain firmly embedded in kin and extended social networks at home. Like many migrants, when possible, higglers regularly tap into kin networks abroad when they plan their marketing trips. One might see them as intermediaries between immigrant family members and those who have remain settled in Barbados, much as traditional higglers linked town and country in days gone by. They bring back and forth gifts and food, money and news, and in turn rely upon networks of support and contacts in both places. Indeed, the presence of kin and social networks in American and Canadian cities has reinforced the desirability of these sites as higglering destinations. On the other hand, the difficulty of accessing tourist visas to the US and Canada and the availability of inexpensive airfares to other regional destinations have introduced new venues for the higglers to explore.

Straddling transnational formal/informal sectors

In the Caribbean region, much of the past decade's research on the relationship between globalization and economic development has emphasized two related phenomena: the neo-liberal emphasis on the expansion of exports, the proliferation of the informal sector in these societies, and the central participation of women within both of these arenas (Massiah 1986; Safa 1991, 1995; Momsen 1993). The expansion of the informal sector has often been described as a by-product of these export-oriented industries, and patterns of labour migration are often linked to the specific configurations of these two economic realms.[6] Recently, there has been some speculation as to the linkages not only between these two sectors institutionally (Harvey 1989; Portes and Walton 1981; Portes *et al.* 1989), but also at the level of the individual, where increasing numbers of people are simultaneously engaged in formal export industrial labour and additional informal economic activities (St. Cyr 1990; Quinones 1997). Today's suitcase traders invite a new sort of investigation of the relationship between the region's emphasis on export industrialization, its expanding informal sector, and the gendered nature of these processes, both individually and in their complex intersections.

Though the focus of my earlier research was the formal employment of Barbadian women in the new service industry of informatics, I found that these jobs could not be seen in isolation of numerous dimensions of the informal sector in which the informatics workers engaged as active consumers as well as producers. The majority of the high tech informatics workers who were the subjects of my study also participated in at least one other form of informal income generating activity (e.g. buying and selling clothing and accessories, hair styling in their kitchen 'salons', or baking and decorating cakes for special occasions.) *All* were active consumers within the informal economy of prepared foods, imported goods, and a wide array of services (e.g. babysitting and dressmaking). Not only was informal labour and consumption part of these workers' everyday lives, but I found as well that employment in these zones also fosters directly their capacity to engage in the specific practice of transnational higglering (Freeman 2000).

For example, the employees of Barbados' largest foreign-owned informatics facility are rewarded for high levels of productivity with travel vouchers on American Airlines. These coupons enabled many of the women in this company to travel abroad for the first time in their lives. Their destinations were influenced in part by networks of kin and friends living overseas, as well as by the limits of their coupons (e.g. two redeemable for a trip to San Juan, Americans' Caribbean hub, three for New York, and four for London). Further, in a more indirect way, a number of other factors have propelled employees' participation in the suitcase trade. I argue that the company dress codes and emphasis on 'professionalism' foster both discipline among the workers and a determined effort to distinguish themselves from other factory workers. In order to do so, women go to great lengths to make, commission, and purchase new clothes and goods that mark their non-factory status. The suitcase trade represents one of the major sources of this attire. In this case, the demand for new styles and new consumer products is integrally tied to the particular formation of a 'pink collar' worker within the informatics sector, a process which I argue is configured by a complex set of factors including foreign and local gender ideologies, modes of discipline, and aesthetics.[7]

The fact that these Barbadian women juggle formal and informal sector work[8] is not in itself remarkable in the history of Barbados, or the region at large (Comitas 1964/1973; Carnegie 1986, 1987; Senior 1991).[9] However, the particular linkages, both structurally and symbolically, between the formal export sector and the emergent trade in consumer goods fostered by these transnational higglers remains unexplored as a dimension of globalization and local development. They also raise questions about the 'exceptionalism' of migration/movement as opposed to the presumed 'normative' goals of settlement that migration theories have long asserted. As Charles Carnegie pointed out more than a decade ago, the 'speculator' or higgler who spends regular portions of the year outside her native island would seldom have been classified as a migrant by social scientists. However, he argues, their patterns of movement are very similar. 'We do know that they have been leaving for some considerable time; that many end up having lived in several host societies; and that they return to the West Indies in large numbers. It would seem that from the emic point of view these are not distinct conditions; *'speculating' and 'migrating' are not, for West Indians, qualitatively very different'* (Carnegie 1987: 41 italics added). We can extend Carnegie's insight here by exploring how multiplicity and 'flexibility' in all of their creative, resistant, and disciplined forms, represent both a long cultural tradition in the Caribbean,[10] as well as a newly configured and intensified demand of contemporary globalization (including dimensions, for example, of David Harvey's time-space compression (Harvey 1989) and Judith Stacey's 'flexible families' (Stacey 1990)). As Trouillot has argued, for Caribbean peoples there are 'obvious reasons why the urban and rural poor, women heads of households, migrants and other people seeeking out a living under social and economic strain would want to be sceptical and bank on multiple adaptive strategies. Yet . . . what strikes most ethnographers is something more than risk management. First, the systematicity with which people maintain multiplicity is prevalent enough for observers to phrase it *not in terms of movement between roles or types but in terms of types or roles that include movement.* Second, Caribbean peoples seem to have fewer problems than most in recognizing the fuzziness and overlap of categories, and multiplicity is not confined to the economic realm or to the poor' (Trouillot 1992: 33, italics added). The high tech higglers I highlight here exemplify precisely Trouillot's points. For them, these travels are not about economic strategy alone, but about 'survival' in the most basic sense.

Aihwa Ong has argued recently (Ong 1998) that '. . . while mobility and flexibility have long been part of the repertoire of human behaviour, under transnationality the new links between flexibility and the logics of displacement on the one hand, and capital accumulation on the other, have given new valence to such strategies of manoeuvring and positioning. *Flexibility, migration, and relocations, instead of being coerced or resisted, have become practices to strive for rather than stability'* (Ong 1998: 19 italics added). Again, perhaps for the higgler, and Caribbean people more generally, as Carnegie and Trouillot have suggested (Carnegie 1986; Trouillot 1992), flexibility has defined dominant modes of livelihood from the region's very beginnings. The higgler, then, in past and present renditions, prompts us to re-think the relationships between a past defined by stasis and global capitalism's 'new' pressures toward movement and flux. The higgler demands a historical basis from which we might assess these contemporary transformations, and she invites us to examine formal/informal economies as not only mutually dependent, but as simultaneously anchored within transnational movements. As neither migrant in the pure sense, nor exclusively 'settled', her labour demonstrates these linkages in space and time and in ways that make plain the interconnectedness of production and consumption not only spread across a global assembly line of Third World producers and first world consumers (Mies 1986), but in the life experience of 'Third World' women, who themselves enact both roles simultaneously.[11]

Higglering and the gendered enactment of production/consumption

Although a small number of historians have engaged the significance of consumption in the process of assimilation/distinction between immigrant groups and their host societies, migration scholarship (like most other forms) has privileged production over consumption as the fundamental anchor upon which immigrant identity and experience is based (Auslander 1996; Heinze 1990; Peiss 1986).[12] Contemporary sociological and anthropological scholarship on migration frequently notes striking symbols of 'modernity' or 'Americanization' as they are displayed by people situated across the broad continuum of transmigration. The new Eastern European immigrant in turn of the century New York, whose first step toward assimilation, Peiss says (Peiss 1986: 63) was 'changing one's clothes' and in particular, buying a hat to go to work; the rural Salvadoran in Nike sneakers, and sporting a cell phone rather than a machete on his hip (Mahler 1999); the girl of 16 from Pustuniche who replaces her traditional Mayan dress (huipil) with spandex (Greene 1994) and dozens of other such sketches exemplify the evocative power of consumption in the context of transnational movement and changing modes of livelihood. Remittances have been shown to transform lifestyles and boundaries of class for family members and communities left behind. It is ironic, however, in light of the recent interest and focus upon consumption within studies of globalization,[13] that the flows of goods and their meaningfulness along economic as well as cultural lines are rarely of central concern in our theorizing 'transmigration'. Here again, there has been an analytical division of labour – the study of people in movement has largely centred on their *productive* roles, and the study of things in movement has largely focused upon changing patterns of consumption. To put it crudely, those people who move/migrate are defined primarily as workers, and those who stay put as consumers within the transnational continuum. The two processes, it seems, have remained relatively separate as categories for transnational analysis. Where consumption is at issue in analyses of transnational identities, it is largely seen as a mark of 'tradition' yielding to 'modernity', and sometimes a bemoaned sign of the seductive illusions of American prosperity.[14] In light of the recent call by several scholars (Grasmuck and Pessar 1991; Hondagneau-Sotelo 1994; Mahler 1999) that gender be engaged not merely as a variable, but as inextricable from the very concept and practice of migration, it is particularly vital that consumption and its meanings be more rigorously engaged.

In this regard, the higgler is a particularly intriguing figure since her labour is bound up entirely in changing practices of consumption for herself, her family, her community of customers, and potentially, for the nation at large. Perhaps, more than the average consumer, she epitomizes the argument that consumption is itself a form of economic activity equal in importance to that of production. Just as was clear in my earlier work on the centrality of clothing and appearances among informatics workers in forging new gender and class identities among 'pink collar' 'professionals', the higgler is involved in a two-fold process of utilizing material goods to negotiate new gendered practices, meanings, and identities. As such, the contemporary high-tech higgler represents a striking convergence between two competing models of West Indian feminine gender ideologies: that of 'respectable' femininity (generally thought to be expressed through the conventions of marriage, church-going, and conservative mores) and that of strong black womanhood (best personified in the figure of the buxom and savvy market higgler, whose travel and style of business brought her into greater contact with poorer or less 'refined' elements of society). The contemporary higgler who is also a wage earner in a transnational firm in a sense collapses this dichotomy by articulating at once a figure of respectable working woman – in her 'professional' clerical worker garb – and by engaging in an old practice of trade that also requires business acumen, sharp wits, and guile more usually believed to be part of the masculine realm of 'reputation'. Because the contemporary higgler's primary goal is the provision of consumer goods to markets 'back home', she faces the task on her sojourns to translate tastes and desires between 'home' and 'host' cultures, as well as to manage her own relationships and movements on foreign territory, to a large extent, through modes of consumption. Barbadian high-tech higglers are adopting not only new modes of consumption (new goods) but also new modes of femininity that both conform to and transgress, for example, middle-class 'respectable' ideals, and in so doing, may be engaged in a process in which traditional class distinctions are being blurred. Just as modes of bodily display and adornment, stature, and movement among the 'pink collar' informatics workers have begun to more closely resemble that of office and 'professional' women workers than that of traditional agricultural and factory operators, we witness through their transnational higglering new configurations of femininity that depart from stereotypic mappings of working class women's gender performance.[15]

Bourdieu in *Distinction* (1984), and Simmel in *Fashion* ([1904] 1957) explore such tensions between self-invention and constraints to mobility through consumption, and make clear that modes of consumption are never merely a set of processes which reveal or express existing differences across groups, but are equally utilized as mechanisms to establish these boundaries and distinctions. Indeed, recently, several scholars have argued that 'life style' is quickly replacing 'class' as the defining characteristic for mapping social groups in the late twentieth century (Featherstone 1990: 83; Shields 1992; Miller 1998: 14), while others are intent to assert that the mere consumption of middle-class goods and styles does not in and of itself confer middle-class membership to the consumer-imitator. The questions raised by Caribbean higglers are not simply the meanings of goods and travel in these West Indian women's experience, but also the relationships between these and particular modes of femininity as they relate to class, race and nation. Through the increased centrality of cultural capital (e.g. embodied in activities such as travel, learning languages, and presenting oneself in a certain manner of femininity), there are ways in which these higglers are simultaneously enhancing their economic positions as well as their status. The process is a dialectical one, much like the relationship between their formal and informal sector labour, and the modes of production and consumption that have come to define what they do and who they are. And since, for the transnational higgler, consumption is both an *individual personal* practice carried out as she travels and as an entrepreneur back home, as well as a *social practice* that has a bearing on the circulation of goods, and potentially their gendered enactments more broadly, these processes are particularly potent. For herself and her family, the transnational higgler may primarily be involved in the pursuit of income and her own self-fashioning, but at the same time she is deeply engaged as an arbiter of styles and taste for the customers she supplies with goods.

Interestingly, though these movements of trade are increasingly common among diverse groups of Caribbean women and across the region, they appear to be manifesting themselves in distinct ways. Where Jamaican women ten years ago may have made Haiti and Miami their regular destinations for trade, and Barbadians travelled regularly to Miami and Caracas, today the latter are travelling to St Lucia and San Juan.[16] The modes of operation, scale and items of trade also vary across class and national lines, for example, airline flight attendants have long been known to engage in a high form of higgler trade in clothes, fashion accessories, perfume and cosmetics, and other duty free items tied to their employment travel and access to foreign exchange; lower class higglers, by contrast, trade in less expensive clothing, shoes, small appliances and house wares. In Martinique, men rather than women are the predominant transnational traders.[17] Further, there appear to be specialty market 'niches' for different groups of higglers. In Barbados, men who participate in transnational trade specialize in electronics and hardware more than clothing and household adornments. The form and significance of these modes of trade are themselves dynamic, shifting with national, regional and global economic fluctuations as well as in relation to changing tastes and desires. How these movements help us think differently about production and consumption, locality and transnationalism, and the complexities of mobile livelihoods, may be read in part through Danielle's story.

From informatics to entrepreneur, hard work and 'dressing hard'

Danielle was employed in one of the largest data processing firms in Barbados when I first met her in 1989. She was open then about her simultaneous pride in and boredom with her job as a 'materials controller'. Her day was spent on slippery feet, handing out pages of text to sedentary keyers whose job it was to enter them electronically for foreign publishers. While she complained about the boredom and frustration of being squeezed between keyers' demands and supervisors' mandates, she enjoyed the regular pay check – 'It helps me budget better, and plan for things.' Even in the early days of our meeting, she let on that her real ambition was to open her own business and 'be my own boss'. During those months, she was perfecting her sewing, and making skirt suits for herself and her fellow workmates on commission. Learning how to cut her own patterns by hand, she could soon turn out a simple suit in a matter of an hour or two. Soon, Danielle was supplementing her formal wage in informatics with fairly regular income earned informally by needleworking.

The relationship between her sewing pursuits and her formal job revolves closely around expectations for professionalism that I explore elsewhere (Freeman 1995, 2000). For the purposes of this paper, suffice it to say that a particular professional style became integral both to defining the work and workers within the informatics sector, and to fuelling several informal sector economic practices among growing numbers of these working women. In addition to seamstressing, engagement in transnational higglering expeditions over bank holiday weekends had become a widespread practice among many of Danielle's workmates, and she and several friends arranged a trip together first to San Juan over an Easter Holiday weekend. As is typically the case, Danielle arranged a package ticket with a local travel agency, including ground transportation to a reasonable motel (costing roughly USD 55/night for a double room). On these trips, she generally travels with her close friend and previous workmate, Marcelle, who has worked her way up in the informatics industry to a managerial position in a new firm. Their trips are planned so as to accommodate Marcelle's work schedule, and she arranges a day or two away from her formal job in order to extend the week-end over four days. Their husbands and other relations take care of their children (two apiece), and these trips are spoken about with the simultaneous dimensions of profit-seeking work and pleasure-seeking escapade. They board a plane out of Grantly Adams International Airport, each woman having checked two large empty suitcases. Danielle carries with her ticket a 'wish list' of orders to fill for herself, her family, and her customers. On their last trip to St. Lucia, for example, they are met by the husband of Danielle's cousin, who has been liv-ing and working in Castries for many years. Their four-day trip includes a busy combination of shopping in reasonable retail stores for jeans, children's clothes, and casual leather shoes, an excursion to see dramatic waterfalls and the famous Pitons, and evenings out in popular nightclubs. In the shops, Danielle straddles the roles of consumer and eventual broker, and balances the requests on her list against prices, availability, and new styles she ventures her customers will like. In her display of snapshots from this trip (following the familiar convention of posed portraits in front of both St. Lucian national sites as well as inside shops), one would be hard-pressed to decipher this higglering journey as anything but a long weekend tourist excursion away from Barbados. The particular mean-ings of these ventures, however, are significant precisely in their multiplicity – as opportunities for generating income, but equally, for seeing new sites, enjoying themselves, feeling fashionable and adept at finding 'good deals', and in construct-ing forms of feminity that defy some traditional boundaries that are both gendered and formulated along the lines of class. Danielle and her friend Marcelle are both married women, mothers, and 'professional' working women – one in a high prestige industry in a position with responsibility, the other as a business owner and entrepreneur. They go to church with some regularity, and could generally be described as part of the lower middle classes. Their higglering pursuits, when seen amidst their wider relationships and responsibilities, powerfully exemplify the false dichotomy of the persistent gendered paradigm of respectability and reputation. They are neither the 'uptown ladies' nor the 'downtown women' of Ulysse's Jamaican paradigm (Ulysse 1999). They move easily between 'proper', 'respectable' etiquette of middle-class family life and work, facilitated by the new modes of consumption they now enjoy, and the 'reputation'-like practices of foreign travel, night-clubbing, and bold bodily display formerly construed as masculine practices (Wilson 1969). The purchase of sensible-looking skirt suits and conventional leather dress shoes for work, as well as the lycra and gold lame evening wear are all integral to these practices of femininity. Like their prede-cessor's trading in agricultural goods, who have long been a strong presence in Caribbean marketplaces, they proudly occupy an increasing array of public spaces (airports, planes, shopping malls, etc.). They also demonstrate the simultaneous valuation of tourist experience and economic pursuit that echo comments made by

Joan French (French 1989) about the motivations of lower-class Jamaican higglers. French asks,

> What are the things then that the higglers in this context find nice about higglering? The first thing from what I have been able to gather, is that it is nice to spend your own money and get nice things; very nice. The nice things that they buy are usually things that are meant to either reduce labour – the blender or things like that – or increase the level of leisure, or pleasure of their surroundings of their lives . . .. The other thing that is nice about higglering is that it is nice to travel . . . .. It is a way to get out of the home . . . these women just loved to get out and about there and liked the whole excitement and adventure of the trips. Making money was important, but really if they didn't make any this trip, too bad. Next trip you would try and make up for it, because it was nice to be out there.
>
> (French 1989: 33–35)

Discussion and conclusions

Transnational theory of the past decade has found useful and even seductive notions of flexibility and deterritorialization to challenge previous models of social and economic life that presumed for migrants and other travellers an eventual if not given state of sedentariness and assimilation. Indeed, this new language and theorizing under the rubric of 'transnationalism' has had some liberating conceptual dimensions, which have, in turn, given rise to debates about the historical underpinnings and expressions of these transformative movements. There have been useful arguments against the 'newness' and novelty of these circuits, and some recent challenges to the sense that fluidity necessarily implies freedom and liberation.

Hondagneau-Sotelo and Avila (1997), for instance, take issue with the very claim that foreign-born Latinos demonstrate the patterns of indeterminance of settlement, transnational political organization, and circuits of belonging that some proponents of transnational theory have claimed, arguing that these communities are, indeed, more settled in the US than such accounts would seem to imply. They also (like Ong 1998 and Smith and Guarnizo 1998) object to the celebratory tone with which these processes have been described, above and beyond the costs and struggles, and exertions of state power within which they are experienced. Finally, along with others who have begun to challenge the genderless grand theories of transnationalism (e.g. Stivins 1998; Freeman 2000), they advocate a model of transnationalism which is defined not in spatial or physical terms of movement, but 'as the circuits of affection, caring, and financial support that transcend national borders' (Hondagneau-Sotelo and Avila 1997: 550).

Taking a somewhat different approach in re-thinking gender transnationally, Mahler has argued that flexible expressions of gender across transnational spaces may be less stable and transformative than one might first assume, and that they may operate differently for men and women (Mahler 1999). She describes patterns in which female migrants from El Salvador living in Long Island are seen to adopt radically new modes of dress and appearance – replacing modest dresses with tight fitting pants, bold makeup and nail polish, and revealing necklines – only to have to eliminate them as return-migrants. She argues that migration for them has not proved ultimately liberating along gender lines, but has rather reinforced traditional expectations of modest femininity. In contrast, new transnational expressions of masculinity are more supported, and even embraced upon return. For male transmigrants, the bold flaunting of new clothes and accessories and of even more striking importance, new pick-up trucks, work to re-assert and enhance masculinity primarily, Mahler argues, for the purposes of demarcating generational and class lines. In short, metamorphosis occurs for women inside the US but does not travel back home. For men, 'pariahs in the US, they transmute into paragons in their home towns' (Mahler 1999: 30). Among the Barbadian higglers, by contrast, the fluidity of their movements between Barbados and their marketing destinations and their simultaneous rootedness in Barbados imply less of the radical disjuncture experienced by the Salvadoran migrants Mahler describes. Higglering trips may invite opportunities of experimentation and boldness of style that are less available at home, however, these journeys are short and less charged with dramatic reversals in gendered protocols and behaviour. They act more to punctuate or embellish Barbadian women's gendered practices at home than to radically oppose them. While both Danielle and Marcelle's husbands *worried* about the sexual infidelities that might accompany such travels, and the women enjoyed teasing and joking about such activity, in fact none had occurred.

While the activities of the Caribbean higgler, straddling production and consumption through the medium of travel, might transgress gender expectations in many parts of the world, and even other parts of the region itself, for Barbadian women, these patterns of movement have roots that stretch much before the contemporary era of globalization. The consumption practices in which the higgler engages are directed towards the feminine body (clothing/fashion, make-up, hair products, accessories), children's needs (clothing, toys) as well as the domestic space (curtains, sheets, small kitchen appliances, and clothes) – all reinforcing her roles (and her female customers' roles) as mother and homemaker. These can be read as both challenging and reinforcing conventional gendered roles – on one hand women experiment with new modes of feminine self-fashioning through dress, accessories, and activities such as night-clubbing, and on the other, they reinforce their central responsibility within the domestic arena. As such, they demonstrate, again, how expressions of 'reputation' and 'respectability' converge in the travels and practices of transnational higglers. Where consumption is generally thought of as a 'localized' set of practices, for the higgler it involves both local and transnational pursuits. Further, the marketing pursuit of the higgler, not merely for herself and family but for the goal of generating income, places her consumption squarely in the mode of production. For the informatics worker cum higgler, production and consumption of goods and services are mutually reinforcing, indeed *melded* activities, and both have become highly transnationalized. Femininity, in its various guises is an integral dimension of them all.

As 'Third World' women, whose livelihood intimately connects the realms of production and consumption across transnational space and within their 'local' island home, today's higglers are enacting new modes of globalization patterned on centuries-old modes of movement within the Caribbean region. For these women, migration is only one among many 'solutions' to livelihood, and only one expression of possible forms of movement in the world. In short, rootedness and movement are not, for the higgler, two different options, but two dimensions of the same life and complex of identities. Returning to the question posed at the outset, then, as to why these women have little interest in migration, it appears that their engagement as higglers represents a powerfully persuasive alternative. In short, they are able to experience both economic gains and the sense of adventure of travel as well as connectedness with networks of kin and friends abroad without actually uprooting themselves from the fabric of their lives in Barbados. Their motivations share some similarities with those of migrants, however, the temporariness of their sojourns and range of destinations both act to solidify their sense of 'home' in Barbados. As such, higglering and migration represent different points along a continuum of transnational livelihood. The case I introduce here is not meant to assert that these transnational Barbadian higglers are new de-nationalized global subjects, but rather that they are multiply territorialized, and that their very identity as 'Bajans' or Barbadian is enhanced by this multiplicity. They are local subjects living across and within a transnational terrain both in Barbados (as informatics workers, as well as in numerous other forms of consumption and contact with global goods and culture), and on their sojourns abroad (as consumers and marketers of goods, and as 'tourists' engaged in the consumption of other languages, people and cultures). They are rooted in Barbados, and their Barbadian-ness is increasingly defined and sharpened through new modes of production, consumption, and travel in ways that link Barbados with numerous other sites across the global terrain.[18] Their notions of themselves as women, as members of the working and middle classes, as Barbadian, West Indian/Caribbean and Black, are, not surprisingly, increasingly defined in relation to others they encounter, and selves they are more consciously reflecting upon through their travel. Higglering, then, is a form of labour and consumption, of travel as well as stasis, transnationalism and rootedness. It becomes a realm in which identities (national, regional, class, racial, gender and sexual) are articulated and re-defined through a complex of social, economic and cultural relationships that rely upon modes of livelihood that are at once grounded in transnational movement and ever-changing meanings of locality and home.

Acknowledgements

I wish to express my thanks to Karen Fog Olwig and Ninna Nyberg Sørensen who organized the stimulating workshop that gave rise to this paper, and whose comments have sharpened my own thinking about transnationalism, the specificity of the Caribbean region, and of the case of Caribbean higglers, in particular. Thank you as well to Alejandro Portes, Maria Patricia Fernandez-Kelly, and Marta Tienda, whose conference of Migration and Development at Princeton University provided a marvellous forum in which to present the paper and debate 'transnationalism' among a geographically and disciplinarily diverse audience. Viranjini Munasinghe also read a draft of the paper, and her excellent questions and comments continue to challenge and motivate me. Unfortunately, there have been numerous fine suggestions made by the many people who read or heard this paper that I have not been able to incorporate. I wish to acknowledge, finally, the University Research Committee of Emory University, who have provided me with the funding to pursue these questions in the coming year through on-going fieldwork with Caribbean higglers.

Notes

1 First proposed by Peter Wilson (1969), the duality of respectability/reputation has held wide currency in scholarship of the region. His formulation proposed that two cultural models have framed Caribbean societies: one modelled on European norms of respectability in which propriety and decorum are emphasized through practices of marriage, monogamy, and the tenets of Christianity. Women are described as the main bearers and arbiters of respectability, residing largely in the interior realms of home and church. Reputation, on the other hand, refers to those cultural practices and beliefs which foster 'comunitas' or a levelling of social hierarchy. Forms of verbal jousting, and display, in which small groups gather in exterior, public spaces, are depicted as derived from African tradition, and are said to be practised more by men. Numerous critiques of this formulation have been articulated (Barrow 1986; Besson 1993; Freeman 2000; Miller 1994; Yelvington 1995), challenging various dimensions of the starkness of this proposed duality. Nonetheless, virtually every ethnography from the region takes up this paradigm in one form or another. As such, its heuristic value has been great, and it is in this spirit that I engage it here to counterpose Wilson's version of feminine 'respectability' with another equally strong version of powerful, black womanhood embodied in the figure of the higgler. What Wilson's model fails to convey are the competing and co-existing models of femininity that encompass not only those attributes and qualities of 'respectability' but also elements that he would have located under the masculine heading of 'reputation.' In light of the centrality of the marketplace in Caribbean societies, it is notable, as Yanique Hume (personal communication) has noted, that this institution figures nowhere in the 'reputation'/'respectability' paradigm. As a public gathering place outdoors, but one in which women are primary participants, it contradicts many of the defining parameters of gendered practices within Wilson's original formulation. See Freeman (2000) for an expanded discussion of competing ideologies of femininity in the context of the transnational informatics industry in Barbados.

2 Although women are known to predominate in this form of higglering, like its agriculturally based antecedent, men represent an active minority in the trade. Some women have reported that men are more likely to import electronics than housewares, and to tie their trips to other forms of migrant labour, such as temporary agricultural work in North America (interview 1 May 1999). To date, there is no systematic research that has engaged this question of gender within higglering/ICI practices.

3 I base this scenario on the case of one of the informatics worker/higglers I interviewed, however, the general experience of kin of several generations following patterns of migration to Britain, Canada, and the US, as well as to other parts of the (largely Anglophone) Caribbean region is a common one in Barbados and across the region. Certainly, there have been significant migrations from Barbados and other parts of the Anglophone Caribbean to non-English speaking parts of the region, including Cuba and

the Panama Canal. However, in the popular imagination of the women in my research, the Hispanic territories have been figured as far more alien than even the more physically distant but culturally (language/colonial history) similar islands (e.g. Jamaica).

4 One could argue that the range of new destinations and the bases upon which they rest set apart the higgler's travel experience from that of recent Barbadian migrants. Where migrant destinations for Barbadians have been predominantly to England, Canada, and the United States, the tendency for higglers to cross former colonial/linguistic boundaries, prompted by the availability of cheap airfares, has been much greater.

5 During the early period of my fieldwork, in 1991, a desperate plea was made by the then Minister of Trade, asking 'Patriotic Barbadians' to boycott illegal suitcase traders. His call was made in support of local clothing manufacturers and storeowners who claimed that their businesses were being severely curtailed by the overseas trade by ICIs. More recently, in an interview with a local boutique owner, this complaint was echoed with despair. This shopkeeper has had to shift her market exclusively to tourists, selling Barbados tee shirts and related beachwear, facing the simple fact that 'Bajans could get their clothes and shoes cheaper from the traders.'

6 Today, the informal sector has largely shifted from being considered a drain on the formal wage earning sector of the economy or as 'resistant' to capitalist production, to one of integral co-existence, and a realm of 'self-help' income generation in the face of high unemployment and limited wage earning alternatives (Collins 1990). Portes and Walton's (1981) discussion of the relationships between formal and informal sectors and their simultaneous relationship to patterns of labour migration sets the stage for my point here that these are not only integral links structurally, but increasingly are all part of individuals' experience as well.

7 Kathy Peiss (1986) offers a striking parallel in the relationship between informal entrepreneurial activity, definitions of femininity and the practices of adornment, in her discussion of African American women's history.

8 For women workers in Caribbean export processing zones, many of whom are the mothers of small children, the practice of combining formal and informal work also raises central questions about divisions of labour within households. Indeed, Afro-Caribbean women have long been known for their high rates of labour force participation (47 per cent in Barbados), and household headship (roughly 30 per cent). Many studies of kinship, households, and women's work in the Afro-Caribbean have, likewise, focused on the particular mechanisms through which women have 'cut and contrived' to piece together a livelihood, often by combining formal and informal economic activities (Beckles 1989; Barrow 1988; Bolles 1983, 1996; Senior 1991). Some have attributed women's high participation in household decision-making and their high rates of labour force participation to traditions established in part by women's control over the internal marketing system as higglers after emancipation (Momsen 1993: 183). However, at the same time that women's participation in the export zones and the informal sector is expanding, so too is there a contraction of the traditional kin networks of support that women have relied upon in their efforts to 'make do' (Barrow 1998; Freeman 2000). It is as yet unclear how transnational higglers negotiate the multiple responsibilities of travel, work, childcare, and other domestic obligations, and what the relationships are between this form of informal labour and higglers' household forms and economies.

9 Carnegie (1987) extends Comitas' earlier concept of 'occupational multiplicity' in the Caribbean by arguing that 'strategic flexibility' is a more general cultural model with which West Indians approach most aspects of life. This is rooted in a history of movement, and expressed in numerous ways across the life course (e.g. migration, kinship, occupation, etc.).

10 Indeed, along the lines of Carnegie's argument, one could potentially read many dimensions of West Indian life, including family formations, multiple strategies of labour and habitude, etc., as bound up in such a cultural model of flexibility and multiplicity.

11 See Freeman (2000) for a fuller critique of Mies's mapping of Third World women/producers: first world women/consumers.
12 Leora Auslander's (1996) history of eighteenth and nineteenth century France engages the question of the role of consumption in the formation of national cultures in ways that were integral to allowing immigrants, for example to *become French*. For Heinze (1990), consumption was a vital means of adaptation to American culture among Eastern European Jews in the nineteenth and early twentieth century.
13 This literature is growing rapidly and is varied in methodology, theoretical framework, disciplinary approach, message and form. The crude extremes can be characterized by, on one hand, arguments which glorify the democratic and creative possibilities introduced by global goods, to those bemoaning the immoral transmission of consumerism to poor underdeveloped parts of the world.
14 Popular as well as scholarly treatments of migration to America are full of such examples. The wonderment in El Norte over having indoor plumbing (no matter the filth) is juxtaposed with the arduousness and servility of domestic labour for middle-class employers; lipstick and new clothes are depicted as simultaneously a mark of pleasure through 'Americanization' and presumably, false consciousness, in the face of real material destitution.
15 On this theme, Simmel [1904](1957) notes, 'Just as soon as the lower strata begin to appropriate their style – and thereby overstep the demarcation line which the upper strata have drawn and destroy the uniformity of their coherence symbolized in this fashion – so the upper strata turn away from this fashion and adopt a new one, which in its turn differentiates them from the broad masses. And thus the game goes merrily on. Naturally, the lower strata look and strive towards the upper, and they encounter the least resistance in those fields which are subject to the whims of fashion, because it is here that mere imitation is most readily accessible . . . the more closely one stratum has approached the other, the more frantic becomes the hunt for imitation from below and the flight towards novelty above.'
16 The reasons for these shifts in destination are as likely to relate to air carrier pricing and the ease of getting visas, as the availability of networks of family and friends in particular transnational locales.
17 Katherine Browne (personal communication 1999).
18 Transnational higglers also raise central questions about the development of methodological approaches to studying the cultural and economic complexities of globalization that are of particular relevance for those engaged in Caribbean studies. The crossing of linguistic/colonial cultural divides between historically balkanized Anglophone, Francophone and Hispanophone territories demands that our own scholarship move in these directions. By conducting 'multi-sited' or 'travelling' ethnographic fieldwork that engages both *travel and home, movement and stasis* as formative domains in which people enact and imagine themselves, sometimes at one and the same time, sometimes over a life span, we might better interpret 'flexibility' and not be inclined to privilege physical movement over other forms of connection, or the contemporary moment over history.

References

Auslander, Leora (1996) *Taste and Power: Furnishing Modern France*, Berkeley: University of California Press.
Barrow, Christine (1986) 'Male images of women in Barbados', *Social and Economic Studies*, 35 (3): 51–64.
Barrow Christine (1988) 'Anthropology, the family, and women in the Caribbean', in Patricia Mohammed and Catherine Shepherd (eds) *Gender in Caribbean Development*,

Monda, Jamaica: Women and Development Studies Project, University of the West Indies.

Barrow, Christine (1998) *Caribbean Portraits: Essays on Gender Ideologies and Identities*, Kinston, Jamaica: Ian Randle Publishers.

Beckles, Hilary McD. (1989) *Natural Rebels: A Social History of Enslaved Black Women in Barbados*, London: Zed Books, Ltd.

Besson, J. (1993) 'Reputation and respectability reconsidered: A new perspective on Afro-Caribbean peasant women', in J. Momsen (ed.) *Women and Change in the Caribbean*, Bloomington: U Indiana Press.

Bolles, Lynn (1983) 'Kitchens hit by priorities: Employed working-class Jamaican women confront the IMF', in June Nash and Maria Patricia Fernandez-Kelly (eds) *Women, Men and the International Division of Labour*, Albany, NY: SUNY Press.

Bolles, Lynn (1996) *Sister Jamaica: A Study of Women, Work and Household in Kingston*, Lanham, Maryland: University Press of America.

Bourdieu, Pierre (1984) *Distinction: A Social Critique of the Judgement of Taste*, Cambridge, Mass: Harvard University Press.

Bush, Barbara (1990) *Slave Women in Caribbean Society, 1650–1838*, Bloomington: Indiana University Press.

Carnegie, Charles V. (1986) 'Inter-island trading in the eastern Caribbean and the informal sector concept', *Medio Ambiente Caribeno* 2: 123–50.

Carnegie, Charles V. (1987) 'A social psychology of Caribbean migrations: Strategic flexibility in the West Indies', in Barry B. Levine (ed.), *The Caribbean Exodus* pp. 32–43, NY: Praeger.

Collins, Jane (1990) 'Unwaged labour in comparative perspective: Recent theories and unanswered questions', in J. Collins and M. Gimenez (eds) *Work Without Wages: Domestic Labour and Self-Employment within Capitalism*, Albany: State University of New York Press.

Comitas, Lambros (1964/1973) 'Occupational multiplicity in rural Jamaica' in L. Comitas and D. Lowenthal (eds) *Work and Family Life: West Indian Perspectives*, NY: Anchor Books.

Featherstone, Mike (1990) 'Global culture: An introduction' in M. Featherstone (ed.) in *Global Culture: Nationalism, Globalization and Modernity*, London: Sage Publications Ltd.

Freeman, Carla (1995) 'From higglering to high-tech and home again: Barbadian women workers in a transnational arena', *Folk* 6: 5–26.

Freeman, Carla (2000) *High Tech and High Heels in the Global Economy: Women, Work and Pink Collar Identities in the Caribbean*, Durham: Duke University Press.

French, Joan (1989) 'It nice', in Michael Witter (ed.) *Higglering/Sidewalk Vending/Informal Commercial Trading in the Jamaican Economy, Proceedings of a Symposium, Department of Economics*, Occasional Paper Series 4, University of the West Indies, Mona, Jamaica.

Grasmuck, Sherri and Patricia Pessar (1991) *Between Two Islands: Dominican International Migration*, Berkeley: University of California Press.

Greene, Allison (1994) 'The cultural politics of dress in pustuniche', paper presented at the Annual Meetings of the American Anthropological Association, Atlanta, GA.

Harvey, David (1989) *The Condition of Postmodernity*, London and New York: Blackwell.

Heinze, Andrew (1990) *Adapting to Abundance: Jewish Immigrants, Mass Consumption and the Search for American Identity*, New York: Columbia University Press.

Hondagneau-Sotelo, Pierrette (1994) *Gendered Transitions: Mexican Experiences of Immigration*, Berkeley: University of California Press.

Hondagneau-Sotelo, Pierette and Ernestine Avila (1997) ' "I'm here but I'm there" – The meanings of Latina transnational motherhood' *Gender and Society* 11(5): 548–71.

Katzin, Margaret Fisher (1959) 'The Jamaican country higgler' *Social and Economic Studies* 8(4): 421–40.

LeFranc, Elsie (1989) 'Petty trading and labour mobility: Higglers in the Kingston metropolitan area', in Hart, K. (ed.) *Women and the Sexual Division of Labour in the Caribbean*, Jamaica: The Consortium Graduate School of Social Sciences.

Mahler, Sarah (1999) 'Transnationalizing research on migration and gender: Notes and queries from a case study of Salvadorans' (Unpublished Paper).

Massiah, Joycelin (1986) 'Work in the lives of Caribbean women', *Social and Economic Studies* 35(2): 177–240.

Mies, Maria (1986) *Patriarchy and Accumulation on a World Scale: Women in the International Division of Labour*, London: Zed Books.

Miller, Daniel (1994) *Modernity An Ethnographic Approach: Dualism and Mass Consumption in Trinidad*, Oxford: Berg Publishers.

Miller, Daniel (1998) *A Theory of Shopping*, Ithaca: Cornell University Press.

Mintz, Sidney (1955) 'The Jamaican internal marketing pattern: Some notes and hypotheses', *Social and Economic Studies* 4(1): 95–103.

Momsen, Janet (ed.) (1993) *Women and Change in the Caribbean*, Bloomington: Indiana University Press.

Ong, Aihwa (1998) *Flexible Citizenship: The Cultural Logics of Transnationality*, Durham: Duke University Press.

Peiss, Kathy (1986) *Cheap Amusements: Working Women and Leisure in Turn of the Century New York*, Philadelphia: Temple University Press.

Portes, Alejandro, Manuel Castells and Lauren A. Benton (eds) (1989) *The Informal Economy: Studies in Advanced and Less Developed Countries*, Baltimore: The Johns Hopkins University Press.

Portes, Alejandro and John Walton (1981) *Labour, Class, and the International System*, New York: Academic Press.

Quinones, Maria I. (1997) 'Looking smart: consumption, cultural history, and identity among Barbadian "Suitcase Traders" ', *Research in Economic Anthropology* 18: 167–82.

Safa, Helen I. (1991) 'Women and industrialization in the Caribbean', in Sharon Stichter and Jane Parapet (eds) *Women, Employment and the Family in the International Division of Labour*, Philadelphia: Temple University Press.

Safa, Helen I. (1995) The Myth of the Male Breadwinner: Women and Industrialization in the Caribbean. Boulder: Westview Press.

Senior, Olive (1991) *Working Miracles: Women's Lives in the English Speaking Caribbean*, Bloomington: Indiana University Press.

Shields, Rob (1992) *Lifestyle Shopping: The Subject of Consumption*, London: Routledge.

Simmel, Georg ([1904] 1957) 'Fashion', *American Journal of Sociology* 62(6): 541–88.

Smith, Michael Peter and Luis Eduardo Guarnizo (eds) (1998) *Transnationalism From Below*, New Brunswick: Transaction.

St. Cyr, Joaquin (1990) 'Participation of women in Caribbean development: Inter-island trading and export processing zones', Report prepared for the Economic Commission for Latin America and the Caribbean (ECLAC) Caribbean Development and Co-Operation Committee.

Stacey, Judith (1990) *Brave New Families: Stories of Domestic Upheaval in Late-Twentieth Century America*, New York: Basic Books.

Stivins, Maila (1998) 'Theorizing gender, power and modernity,' in Krishna Sen and Maila Stivins (eds) *Gender and Power in Affluent Asia*, London & New York: Routledge.

Trouillot, Michel Rolph (1992) 'The Caribbean region: An open frontier in anthropological theory' *Annual Review of Anthropology* 21: 19–42.

Ulysse, Gina (1999) 'Uptown ladies and downtown women: Informal commercial importing and the social/symbolic politics of identities in Jamaica', Ph.D. Dissertation, Department of Anthropology, University of Michigan.

Wilson, Peter J. (1969) 'Reputation and Respectability: A Suggestion for Caribbean Ethnology' *Man*, 4(1): 70–84.

Witter, Michael (ed.) (1988) *Higglering/Sidewalk Vending/Informal Commercial Trading in the Jamaican Economy*, Department of Economics Occasional Paper Series 4, University of the West Indies, Mona, Jamaica.

Yelvington, Kevin (1995) *Producing Power: Ethnicity, Gender and Class in a Caribbean Workplace*, Philadelphia: Temple University Press.

Part II
Livelihoods extended

4 A 'respectable' livelihood

Mobility and identity in a Caribbean family

Karen Fog Olwig

You had to leave for economic reasons and to develop yourself. After O- and A-levels your studies are limited here. That is it. . . . Dominica is a small place, it is surrounded by sea, and where else can you go? If you want to expand and develop you must go out.

This is the reply that Janet, a woman in her early 60s, gave me when I asked her why she had left Dominica when she was a young woman. It is apparent that, to Janet, the question of why she had moved away was almost irrelevant – it was a foregone conclusion that she would have to leave the small Caribbean island when she had reached a certain age if she wanted to go further in life. This was not a matter of dire economic necessity. With her A-levels she was well educated by local standards and had had relatively well-paid jobs, first at a secondary school, then at a bank. She was also a key person in her family because she maintained a home for her younger siblings in Roseau, the capital of Dominica, so that they might go to secondary school there. Janet wanted more out of life, however, so she left. She spent several years in Jamaica studying for her BA and one year in England pursuing post-graduate education before finally going to Canada to work in special education and have a family. After many years in Canada she returned to Dominica, where she worked in her area of specialization for several years before retiring.

The migration movements of people of middle-class background like Janet in the pursuit of the sort of life and career or livelihood that they find rewarding have not been subject to a great deal of study within the field of migration research. This area of investigation has tended to view international migration primarily as a low-class phenomenon involving the movement of largely unskilled labour to different parts of the world with expanding labour markets. The notion of migration as something that involves mainly the lower classes has been obvious in studies of Caribbean migration. Research on the development of the migration tradition in the Caribbean has thus emphasized the role of migration as a means whereby emancipated slaves, who later became landless labourers, could escape from the social and economic confines of the plantation regime (Frucht 1966; Thomas-Hope 1978; Richardson 1983; Olwig 1985). Studies of contemporary migration have focused on the relatively uneducated people with few economic resources who migrate for better opportunities abroad, often with a view to returning with enough money to live comfortably in their own home (Philpott 1973; Gmelch 1992; Olwig 1993, 1997a).

Yet, it is quite apparent that the middle classes have played an important role in Caribbean migration. They have often constituted an important model of upward mobility for people of the lower classes. Some of the goals sought by Caribbean migrants, in both their migration destination and their society of origin, therefore reflect middle-class aspirations. This model is largely a model of a 'respectable livelihood' grounded in trade, business and especially the professions, and granting a secure social and economic position in the middle layers of Caribbean society. Furthermore, the middle class itself has often held a precarious position in local Caribbean societies, and its members have engaged in migration, partly as a means of securing the livelihood that provides the basis of their position in society, and partly as a way out when this livelihood was seriously threatened (Lowes 1995; Thomas-Hope 1995, 1998). A study of middle-class migration therefore offers important insights into the cultural construction of a livelihood model that has been a central aspect of Caribbean migration.

In this chapter, I shall examine a model of livelihood as practised and conceived by specific social actors in a family network with roots in a Caribbean middle-class family. I shall investigate how this family's livelihood model was formed in the childhood experiences of the oldest generation in the family, led to extensive migration movements by family members, and became an ideal that gave this global family a particular identity. In doing so, I shall draw on Gudeman's definition of the concept of livelihood as a cultural model that is 'comprised of the beliefs and practices which constitute a people's world' (Gudeman 1986: 28). This model contrasts with the Western models of livelihood that have been dominant for the past two centuries and draw on 'logical and mathematical schemes' (ibid.: vii). However, it accords with an older, now obsolete notion of livelihood, where the term has a broader meaning and refers to 'course of life, life time, kind or manner of life' (The Oxford English Dictionary). This latter meaning is in many ways closer to more contemporary notions of livelihood as entailing specific career trajectories or ways of life that have important social and cultural, as well as economic, implications.

The ethnographic context is that of a family network that has its roots in the Caribbean island of Dominica. However, the geographical origins of the family are secondary to its socio-cultural background in the values of respectability that first emerged in the middle layers of colonial British West Indian society. These values revolve around educational achievement and moral standards centered on family life and holy matrimony. As family members appropriated these values, they developed their own understanding of a proper livelihood for themselves and their relatives, with regard to career trajectory and manner of life. In the process, they created an extended but well-defined field of social relations and cultural values that has provided them with an important framework for life. This field of relations and values, as practised and negotiated by members of this family network, constituted my research site. I investigated it through interviews carried out with fifty family members[1] who live today in Great Britain, Canada, USA, Barbados and Dominica.

Families have typically been investigated through participant observation of the everyday social and economic relations that are played out in family life. This might be combined with interviews on genealogies, marriage patterns, etc. When studying a non-local family network that is both a set of social and economic relations and an important source of identity for people who live in a variety of life situations, other sorts of research methods must be developed. I have found that life stories can offer both a very concrete research tool and the sort of data that generate insights into social fields of importance in situations of mobility. A life story entails accounting for an individual's movements through life – geographical as well as social, economic or cultural – in such a way that it portrays a sense of coherence that reflects the narrator's sense of self. Life stories, in other words, are constructed on a fine line between movement and change, continuity and identification. They are constructions because they need to be built out of the welter of occurrences and relationships that characterize most lives. They are also cultural constructions, because these constructions need to conform to certain established conventions concerning what sort of life is credible and socially acceptable. Life stories are, of course, also personal, because they reflect individuals' particular cultural understandings of themselves and the lives they have lived. By eliciting life stories from people, we may therefore obtain data on the life courses that people have lived, including the moves which these life courses may have entailed. We also gain insights into the socio-cultural order that the narrators establish in their life stories and their own particular understanding of themselves in this order.[2] Life-story interviews therefore offer a useful tool of investigation when doing research in extended field sites that exist by virtue of their being given purpose and meaning by those who identify with them by choice.

The development of a global family network

The family network that is the focus of my study consists of the descendants of a schoolteacher and his wife, who lived in a small village in Dominica during the 1930s, 1940s and early 1950s. This couple had eleven children, all of whom left not just the village, but Dominica itself, in the course of the 1950s and 1960s and moved to various parts of the Caribbean, North America and Europe. When I interviewed these siblings and their descendants during the 1990s, they were living in cities as diverse as Ipswich (England), Toronto (Ontario), Rochester (New York State), Bridgetown (Barbados), and Roseau (Dominica). This movement had occurred in the course of two generations and had turned the family into an extended field of social relations. Movements figured most prominently in the life stories of the eleven siblings, who comprised the oldest generation of relatives and had been born in Dominica. Their movements can be summarized as in Table 4.1.

Table 4.1 Movements between the locations of the first generation of siblings, listed according to the relative age of the siblings in the family

Ann, b. 1929:	Great Britain – Canada – Dominica
Chris, b. 1930:	Great Britain – Dominica – Barbados – Dominica
Mark, b. 1933:	Great Britain – Dominica – Great Britain – Dominica
Ben, b. 1934:	Jamaica – Dominica – Jamaica – Dominica – Great Britain – Dominica
Janet, b. 1935:	Jamaica – Dominica – Great Britain – Dominica – Canada – Dominica
Nelly, b. 1937:	Canada
Mary, b. 1938:	Jamaica – Canada – USA
Robert, b. 1940:	USA – Dominica
Alan, b. 1941:	USA
Rick, b. 1943:	USA – Antigua – USA
Vera, b. 1944:	Trinidad – Canada – Dominica – Canada

It is possible to view the movements of the siblings out of Dominica as part of the larger pattern of post-World War II Caribbean migration. In this migration, destinations were mainly chosen through the accessibility of specific locations and the social and economic opportunities offered there at the time the person concerned wished to travel. During the early 1950s, Ann, Chris and Mark went to England, which had an open-door policy and offered free education. During the 1950s and 1960s, Ben, Janet and Mary went to Jamaica for further education at the newly established University of the West Indies. During the late 1950s, Nelly moved to Canada on a domestic scheme which paid travel expenses and offered permanent residence after a short period of employment in domestic work.[3] During the late 1950s and early 1960s, Robert, Alan and Rick went to the United States, Rick to join a Roman Catholic order that ran a secondary school in Dominica, Robert and Alan to attend a university operated by the same religious order. Finally, during the 1960s, Vera, who is handicapped, moved to Trinidad for special education.

This brief account of the siblings' movements makes it clear that migration does not merely involve movement in physical space between different geographical locations that can be located on the map: it also entails movements in relation to social and economic spheres, corresponding to various institutional structures that may cross-cut separate locations. When examined from the point of view of these structures, the siblings' movements display an entirely different sort of migratory pattern based on the socio-economic spheres traversed by them:

1 Colonial (trans-Atlantic) or post-colonial (Caribbean regional) institutions
   • University-level courses offered in Great Britain for employees in the colonial administration, educational or health system
   • Schools of nursing, Great Britain
   • The University of the West Indies
   • Institutions of special education for the handicapped, the Caribbean
2 Religious (educational) communities
   • Religious Catholic Order
   • Catholic university

3   Labour market, imperial and transnational
    - Labour recruitment from the colonies (Great Britain)
    - Domestic scheme (Canada)
4   Family networks
    - Family reunification (Canada, USA)

While all the siblings' movements entailed travelling long distances and extended stays abroad, the spheres within which they moved were quite different, and it is questionable whether all these moves would be classified as migration *per se*. Scholars would probably regard moves that were sparked by labour needs, such as Ann's move to Great Britain and Nelly's to Canada, as classic examples of Third World migration to Western countries. Most researchers would also see typical instances of migration in Ann's, Janet's and Mary's moves to Canada, where they joined their sister, who sponsored their immigration into the country. It is less certain, however, whether they would view a movement abroad for the purpose of study or employment within the auspices of a large colonial or post-colonial organization, or within an international religious community, as a type of migration, even when it involves the crossing of a political border and extended stays abroad that may, eventually, become permanent.

A standard dictionary definition of migration, which presents the 'established' usage of terms in common language, will illustrate the problem. According to the *Merriam-Webster Collegiate Dictionary*, migration simply means 'to move from one country, place, or locality to another'. The concept does not specify what sort of movement is involved in migration, or whether a certain period of time must be involved for a movement to count as migration. We receive little help when we look up the crucial verb 'move', because it refers very broadly to any kind of movement a person can engage in. Meaning no. 1C offers some help, however, because it specifies that 'to move' means 'to change one's residence or location.' But this, of course, then raises the question of what we mean by residence or location, and again we run into a complexity of meaning that has to do with distinctions between temporary and permanent places of dwelling. Such distinctions can be made by immigration officials applying various laws that determine the length of stay and the type of social and economic activity allowed in a new place. Such legal definitions are, of course, highly relevant, because they determine, to a great extent, the rights of the movers in the migration destination. They only point to one aspect of a long, complex process that involves a variety of social, economic, political and cultural factors. Furthermore, such technical considerations may have little to do with how a particular move is perceived by the movers, and they certainly say little about the changes in meaning that the moves may attain through time for those who move. As an anthropologist, I have opted to make the social relations and cultural values staked out by the family members in the course of their life trajectories the core of an analytical framework that focuses on the ethnography of movement rather than the impact of migration on given fixed societies.

Life trajectories

From the point of view of the family members, it appears to have been of little significance whether or not a specific move could be classified as migration as such. They seem to have taken advantage of whatever possibilities they saw to pursue opportunities that would further the trajectory of their chosen livelihood. Sometimes these opportunites took them abroad, sometimes not. Their moves, in other words, were not caused by the action upon them of external push-pull factors causing a migratory pattern of movement. Rather, the siblings acted on their own, guided by their knowledge of the various opportunities open to them. Further-more, family members did not mention whether their move was of a temporary or permanent nature and probably did not know this at the time they moved. The only siblings to use the term 'migration' when describing their moving away from Dominica were Nelly, who went to Canada under an organized migration scheme, and Ann, who travelled to England in the mid-1950s at the peak of West Indian migration to Great Britain.[4] When relating their movements abroad, most siblings did not elaborate on their change of residence or the potential change in national allegiance implicated by this move. Rather, they talked about their particular stage in life when moving and the various opportunities that the move afforded them. They emphasized their wish to establish their own lives and prove themselves, and described the various moves involved in the process of pursuing this goal. In their life stories, their movements therefore did not begin when they left Dominica, nor did leaving Dominica necessarily constitute the most important or final move in their lives. By the time they had left Dominica, all the siblings had already moved away from their childhood home in the small rural village where they grew up to Roseau, where they attended secondary school.

In relating their life stories, many elaborated more on their experiences in mov-ing away from the childhood village to the capital than on their movement from Dominica to a foreign destination. Janet, for example, described her move to Roseau as involving a drastic change in life:

> I left home at eleven to go to Roseau. Going over things later in life, reflecting on it, I realize that it must have been traumatic leaving the free life in the village, where my dad used to take us to the beach, and where he would go with us on walks in the hills – rambles he called them – to go to town to live with my auntie . . . there. She was a very structured and organized person, and I was a little careless in my way of living . . . . She loved me, but I didn't recognize it at the time. . . . I felt she didn't love me, because she always told me what to do. She cared for us in Roseau, made sure that we stayed on the right track, and did well in school.

> We had to go back . . . for holidays. I dreaded the trip: there were no roads . . . from the village to the nearest port, and we had to walk the nine miles [to the port], where we had to take a boat to Roseau. I got sick travelling by boat, which was stopping at different places, just the diesel smell. Sometimes we

had to carry our suitcase on our head, walking the nine miles. Sometimes we could take a truck part of the way, and I would get sick on the winding roads.

The move to Jamaica, however, was just mentioned in two brief sentences: 'In 1958 Chris, who was my adviser, told me that they offered special scholarships for people to study in Jamaica. So I applied, got accepted, and went to study there.'

Similarly, Janet said very little about her year of study in England and the change in environment that this involved. It may seem curious that she said so little about her experiences in Jamaica and England, which would seem to be quite different from Dominica. I suggest that this reflects the fact that, from her life-story perspective, the initial, relatively short move out of the childhood home in a small, isolated village to pursue secondary education in the colonial capital may have been a bigger step in her life than the seemingly much greater move to the university in Jamaica. By the time she had passed her O-levels and A-levels, as she noted in the part of the interview quoted in the introduction, it was almost a foregone conclusion that, to move on in life, she needed to move off the island.

Janet's life story suggests that, when examined in relation to life trajectories, locations are defined and perceived in terms of their significance as demarcators in the movements through life that individuals undertake. One would therefore expect most people's life trajectories to unfold in relation to several different locations. The nature of the locations and the scale of physical movement involved between them can vary widely. In the case of this family, movement out of the parental home while still a child to attend secondary school in Roseau was a first step. Movement abroad as a young person for further education and better opportunities was, in general, a second step. This movement was not necessarily final, however, but contingent on various factors, such as social and economic opportunities in other possible destinations, and the personal relationships of the movers to persons in different areas. Ann, who moved to England during the 1950s, thus decided to join her sister in Canada during the 1960s, as did Janet, Mary and Vera, who had travelled mostly in the Caribbean for education. Within two years, Mary had married a Dominican who lived in the United States and moved there. Her husband had come to the US through the sponsorship of a distant relative of Mary's. Chris, Ben, Mark and Robert returned to Dominica to work in their professions once they had received their education abroad. Chris, however, later moved to Barbados to work for a large Caribbean regional organization, whereas Mark moved back to England to take up employment in his field. Rick, who had moved to the United States, spent several years in Antigua, where he worked for an institution run by his religious order before settling in the United States. Finally, during the past ten years, Ann, Chris, Mark and Janet moved to Dominica with the intention of (semi-) retiring there. Even though the siblings generally described their movements as integral to their personal development and life trajectories in general, the movement had not been an individual concern but had taken place within a larger framework of family relations.

Family and livelihood

The family constituted an important reference point in the narrators' accounts of their life trajectories and the movements these involved. Indeed, it may be argued that the narrators presented their life stories within a framework of family relations and the ideals that these relations embodied. A fundamental dimension of this framework was the particular livelihood that the family had come to identify as being proper for family members. This culturally constructed livelihood had educational achievement and moral worth as its basis. Economic gain and social status were not, in and of themselves, important goals: rather, the learning and mastering of a profession, as well as devotion to a morally upright life, were the key underpinnings of the kind of livelihood that was central to this family's identity.

In a Caribbean context, this ideal can be seen to be part of the value complex of respectability which Wilson and others (Wilson 1969, 1973; Abrahams 1983; Brereton 1993; Olwig 1993, 1995) have shown is associated with the middle class that emerged in the Caribbean in the post-emancipation era. In most of the British Caribbean, religious and educational instruction by Protestant missionaries provided an important basis for the development of this middle class. This was because, as S. Gordon notes (1963), education was one of the very few means whereby the local population could attain higher status in the highly hierarchical societies of the post-emancipation era (see also D. Gordon 1987). The self-image of the Caribbean middle class has therefore been one of a group distinguished primarily by a notion of a way of life grounded in socially responsible and civilized behaviour, not by its economic achievements (Alexander 1973). A 'respectable livelihood', in other words, is one that, by virtue of its grounding in European-oriented intellectual, moral and economic values, was granted a relatively high status in colonial society, and by extension in the society of independent nation states that emerged in the latter part of the twentieth century. An emphasis on 'respectable livelihoods' can be found in other British colonies throughout the world. It resulted in local populations associating social mobility with education and employment in the civil service (see, e.g. Parkin 1979; Ranger 1983).

In Dominica, where Catholicism has predominated,[5] there has historically been less emphasis on religious and educational instruction, and a weaker relationship between the Francophile Catholic Church and the British colonial administration. In the post-emancipation period, something of a cleavage developed between the British-dominated colonial capital of Roseau and the rather isolated local villages of independent peasants living under the moral guidance of the Catholic priest and the local schoolteacher. A local middle class which could assume a central position in the establishment of the island society and later the independent nation state, therefore came much later in Dominica (Gordon 1963: 33; Honychurch *c*. 1983: 8; Baker 1994: 117, 122, 125, 139). Nevertheless, as in the rest of the Caribbean, the local population has come to regard education as a means 'of improving their status and of obtaining white collar jobs in business or government service' (Fleming 1964: 7).

Because of the late development of an educated middle class in Dominica generally, the family I have studied represents the early establishment of such a class in
the island. It therefore attained particular importance in the emergence of the modern Dominican nation state. The family members' understanding of their livelihood
and its relationship to their background in Dominica, as well as their later life trajectories, were grounded in the foundational story of the family. Although they
identify the family as Dominican and associate it with the isolated village where
the siblings had their childhood, they do not see the family as having been rooted
there from time immemorial. On the contrary, movement to and within Dominica
constituted an important element in the foundation of the family. Some of the
older members of the family possess a family tree that shows its founder arriving
from France in the eighteenth century. This tree, however, stops in the nineteenth
century, and it is somewhat uncertain how it should be linked with the present
family, except that the Frenchman settled in Dominica and had descendants who,
somewhere along the line, mixed with the local population of African and Carib
origin. The oldest generation in the family traced its local origins to a small village
in the southern part of the island, where it had owned an estate and made a living
on cultivating the land and raising animals. Most of the helpers were paid in kind,
often with a piece of land, and consequently the land dwindled. The family was
comfortably off economically speaking, but it was not well educated, and apparently it possessed only one book, which contained all the names and dates of birth
of the children. It had no Bible, because the Catholic Church did not encourage
this. The oldest son in the family opted to move out of this environment to become
a schoolteacher, and when he had finished his seventh standard examination in the
local school, he was sent to a school in another area to train as a student teacher.
When he passed this exam he was transferred to several other schools, until he
became head teacher in a small village in the northern part of Dominica. There
he settled down, married a local woman (also of mixed descent), and sired eleven
children.[6]

The father's movements, as related by his children and youngest surviving sister,
provide an important key to the special status that the family attained in Dominica.
The arrival of the French ancestor signals the introduction of this particular family,
and its special family name, to Dominica. On the other hand, the long intervening
history, on which there is little information, indicates the family being settled on
its own land and mixing with the local population. The father's move away from
his parents' estate to be trained as a schoolteacher initiated a break away from the
rather isolated rural community and entry into the more educated upper strata of
colonial society. The father was described as a very ambitious and enterprising
man. Beside heading the local school, he had his own farming enterprise, where
he made use of his children to cultivate the land and carry produce to market.
He also helped organize community projects, including the building of public
baths and toilets in the village. He had grand plans for the construction of a
swimming pool for local children so that they could learn to swim, the surrounding
sea being too rocky and rough. The father had also been the first person in the
village to acquire a radio, and the older children remembered how the entire village

would congregate by their house to listen to radio broadcasts from the outside world.

The father's move away from the parents' land and a dependence on agriculture into an occupation as a school teacher was an important step which gave prestige to the family. Chris explained:

> My father became a teacher because teaching was available employment. He went to primary school, and then he went into teaching without formal education, he only received local training and took local exams, they had grades of exams they could take. He did not go overseas to college. Teaching was something to do, it gave status in the community.
> ['Teaching was better than farming?']
> Yes.
> ['Why?']
> Because of the income possibility. It was a regular income, though a small one, and it was associated with intellectual aspects – farming had no educational aspect – and this made you more important than a farmer in these days. And he worked for the government and had status as a government employee.

It is significant, however, that the father's social and geographical mobility ceased when he was appointed the head teacher of a small village school, because this signified in effect that his career would go no further. Several of his children recognized this connection between geographical and social mobility, and some thought that their father developed an alcohol problem because he felt that he had become isolated and stuck in the village, where he had little intellectual company. Others, however, thought that he had been barred from further promotion because of his drinking.

Though the siblings rarely spoke of class and described themselves as part of the local community, they realized that they had enjoyed respect in this community because of their father's special position. By virtue of this situation, they themselves were also expected to set a good example. Their father had thus raised them to be good students and hard workers, to speak proper English (never the local French patois, associated with uneducated people of the lower classes, though most of them learned it anyway), and to lead a morally upright life. The father's alcoholism had tarnished the image of the family somewhat, but by the time it had become a serious problem the family name had already been established, in part due to the older siblings' educational achievements.

It was quite clear that the father had ambitions for his children to obtain higher education, and he carefully tutored them so that they would not just become accepted at secondary school in Roseau, but also obtain scholarships. All, except for the oldest and youngest child, attended secondary school in Roseau, several of them on scholarships. In Roseau the siblings were no longer 'the headmaster's children' but became 'just country people,' as Janet described them. Mary recalled that, whereas her family had been somewhat better off financially in the village, it was quite apparent that children in the town dressed better and more expensively than she and her siblings could afford, though she added that her family was better educated and did better at school. A solid education was clearly more important than material possessions.

The father regarded education as the best road toward a secure middle-class livelihood. This was impressed on Mark when he did poorly at school:

> When I first came to Roseau I played too much football, cricket. So I failed my first term in high school. When my father got the report card, he just pointed to the mountain where we had gone to cultivate the provisions and said, "For the rest of your life, you will climb that mountain!" The next term I got a second grade.

A central aspect to this middle-class livelihood was obtaining a government job.[7] When Chris finished secondary school, therefore, his father arranged for him to get a position in the colonial administration:

> I started work outside the government, but my father was not happy about that. . . . It was not my choice to go into the government, [but] my father spoke to the chief secretary for the government who was a local person – over him there was an administrator who was English – and asked him for a job for me.
> ['Why did your father prefer for you to work for the goverment?']
> He didn't like me in a small firm, the goverment gave status in the community, and it was a secure job.

For Chris this was the beginning of a distinguished career that brought him to the very top in public service, not just in Dominica, but also in the Caribbean. When a younger brother received an island scholarship to study at the University of Jamaica, this established a strong tradition of personal achievement, well beyond the kind of livelihood expectations of the local middle-class society, in the family. This family tradition involved travel abroad for further education or training, ideally followed by a return to Dominica to serve the country.

The close association between movement, education and a successful life was a central leitmotiv in the life stories of all the siblings in the first generation, whether or not they had succeeded in living up to it themselves. Those siblings who did succeed in migrating to pursue a professional career of their own choice embodied the family ideal that the rest of the family strove to emulate. In their life stories, however, they tended not to elaborate on their successes, but presented their impressive professional careers as the most natural thing in the world. This is exemplified in the quotes from the life story related by Janet, who obtained scholarships to study in Jamaica and Great Britain. This in turn means that the burden of explanation and justification lay on those who had not had the same sort of careers, or who had had to struggle considerably more to achieve anything.

One of the few who did not obtain higher education was Nelly, who had travelled to Canada on a domestic scheme:

> I went to a Convent High school, taught by nuns. I went there until grade 12. When I finished there were no jobs, and I wanted adventures, to see another country. So I migrated to Canada.
>
> They had a special scheme to Canada to go as helpers in a home. You had to work in a home for one year, and then you could become a citizen. I came with quite a few girls, and we settled with families.
>
> . . .
>
> They were dentists. And they knew that I came from a good family – they knew my background – they treated me well, and we were close. And my brother came for a visit; he was attending a conference. I told them that I came from a large family, and my father wrote. I kept close to them, and they were our dentists, we were good friends, and I visited the daughter. I was on the phone with her for one hour yesterday, because she needed some help.

In this account of leaving Dominica, she emphasizes the importance of new experiences and makes it clear that, although she travelled as a domestic servant, she quickly became part of the family she worked for, because they recognized her good qualities. By pointing to the value of human relations, she created a life story which represented something of an alternative to the more career-oriented life trajectories represented by most of her siblings. This type of life story fitted her particular background in the family as someone who had experienced difficulties at school and just barely made it through secondary school, as she explained in response to my follow-up questions on her initial account of her life story:

> I always felt like I was not smart. My sister behind me was ahead of me. At high school they put us in the same class. She had a scholarship and books. I had to use her books, and this put me behind. She had to finish first.

Nelly's emphasis on the importance of moral rather than intellectual virtues was not just compensation for her failure to live up to a dominant family tradition of intellectual achievement, but pointed to another important aspect of the family's livelihood ideals that the siblings associated primarily with the mother. Whereas the siblings described their father as an intellectual and as a strict disciplinarian who had high ambitions for his children and the local community, they characterized their mother as a loving, caring and religious person with high moral standards. Her values were reflected in the emphasis that the first generation of siblings placed in their life stories on moral values, devotion to religion and the extension of help to needy relatives. All the siblings described themselves as members of the Catholic Church, and most described themselves as staunch church-goers; all regarded holy matrimony as the only foundation of a proper family; and all saw the family as a context of life where unconditional love and support were natural.

These virtues had not just been morally right, but also essential to the livelihood of family members. Nelly's life story reflected this. Thus, it was apparent that she had helped her sisters move to Canada by offering them a place to stay until they were on their own and, when possible, sponsoring their 'immigration'. She had cared for Mary's oldest child in her home for an extended period of time, when Mary, who was living in the United States, was pre-occupied with her studies. She had provided a home for various relatives who needed a place to stay while studying abroad, and she sent care packages to her sister Janet, who had returned to Dominica, whenever she heard of somebody travelling back to the island.

The significance of this moral aspect of the family's livelihood was apparent in the siblings' life stories. This was particularly clear in the life story of one of the brothers who had had an impressive academic career, but, according to family ideals, had not succeeded in leading a morally virtuous life because his first marriage had not worked out. Even though he had obtained a doctorate in psychology and had had an excellent career in his field, he therefore felt the need to explain the circumstances behind his failure to live up to family expectations:

> I was the first in the history of the family to get a divorce. That kept me married longer. I stuck it out for thirteen years. I should have divorced in the first year. I kept the marriage [going] for religion and family history. When I divorced and remarried one or two years later, I told friends that, if I had known what a different world it was, I would have done it sooner.

When his wife finally filed for divorce, he succeeded in having the marriage annulled, so that he and his new wife, who was also Catholic, could get married in church. But he also added: 'I wanted my nephews and nieces to understand that divorce is not easy; one must take marriage seriously'.

Inclusion and exclusion in the family network

The two intertwined ideals of educational achievements and moral values, which are central to the family's livelihood, provided a basic frame of reference in the life stories related by the first generation of siblings in the family network. The sharing of these values, and their being upheld in practice, defined the siblings as a family group and gave a particular identity to the family name. The siblings' travels to Great Britain, USA, Canada or within the Caribbean were, to a great extent, related to their desire to live up to the ambitious livelihood ideal that became an important part of this family's particular image. When they raised children of their own they imparted these family values to them, and to a large degree the life stories of the second generation of cousins revolved around the extent to which they had succeeded in honouring these values.

Some of those in the second generation who had grown up in Dominica said that they had experienced the wider family as an established upper middle-class group of professionals employed by the government, who were quite protective of the family name:

> I mix with anybody, but my family likes to see themselves as upper middle-class. In Dominica, it is the name – who your father was – and the name is handed down from generation to generation. And there is also land ownership. ['How did your family attain this class status?']
> It was mostly academic, their profession; their father had been a schoolteacher... All knew him in the village, and the brothers were all in the professions. It was not necessarily because of money, it was more the perception of a family name and a profession.
> ...
> They were very protective of the family name. I was a rebel, did my own thing. I was embarrassing; I wore braided jeans, jeans that were cut off. I made no shows, I went up in the mountains to fish, did trekking. I didn't necessarily fit into the ideas of how to behave.
> ['How would that be?']
> Working towards a serious profession like becoming a doctor. But I was not interested.... Another very big factor that I almost forgot is the religion. The Roman Catholic religion was pumped into us from an early age.

Those in the second generation, who grew up abroad, where the family had a less secure social position, experienced a struggle for upward social mobility. Some recalled that their parents had moved out of the immigrant, lower-class neighbourhoods as soon as they could afford to do so, often with financial assistance from their siblings. A move to such a neighbourhood was usually occasioned by the parents' wish to shield their children from potential problems associated with inner-city immigrant ghettoes, and to provide them with the better education that was available in suburban schools. Many in the second generation recalled having been strongly pressured to do well in school and get a 'proper' education in one of the professions. One cousin who had become a doctor joked that this had been the easiest way out when her father had given her the choice of becoming either the president of the United States or a medical doctor. Some of those who did not obtain an education within the professions felt that they had disappointed their parents. One person, who had had a respectable career within the fairly small avant garde art milieu of the North American city where he lived, thus contemplated moving to London, where this particular art form was part of a larger and more established milieu. This was not, he said, just in order to further his own career opportunities, but also to prove to his parents and the rest of the family that it was possible to do as well in the arts as in the recognized professions. Successful careers and social mobility were therefore measured not only in relation to the individuals' own life trajectories and the local environment in which they lived, but also to the social expectations of the family network. These expectations were impressed on succeeding generations through stories about the family achievements of the past and gossip about current family affairs. They were experienced more directly through visits from the family or trips to Dominica, where they encountered the high prestige associated with the family name.

The family played an even more important role as a frame of reference in relation to the upholding of moral values. Those who failed to live up to the family's moral standards – for example, by having children out of wedlock or divorcing – experienced such disapproval that they often chose to withdraw from the family. One person of the second generation noted:

> Once [my cousin] became pregnant and wasn't married, we didn't see her much.
> ['Was it shameful?']
> Very horribly. She was not excluded, but she knew about the disapproval.

People reacted differently to such exclusions from the family. Some explained that they began to look elsewhere for a community that could give them a sense of belonging, to replace that lost through rejection by the family. This was the case for another cousin, who recalled the painful experience of visiting Dominica with her small child, who had been born out of wedlock:

> When I went back to Dominica, when [my daughter] was 3, I was disgusted at [the] family. People did not relate to me, I felt that I saw just looks of disappointment. I felt isolated. These things were hushed up. I wasn't proud of what I had done, but mom was embarrassed. She supported me, but worried about what the neighbours, cousins, aunts, uncles might say. It made me feel rebellious, it made me realize that there was too much emphasis on values like job, money, the academic. Not enough on the creative. I felt creative; my accomplishments in the writing of poetry were not appreciated. All I felt was different. I associated with the Caribbean Indians, with Africa. I felt that the family did not think like me in terms of identity. I had stronger association with my African descent and Carib history. As a result, I wanted to do my own diploma in Caribbean history, and I have written a book about it.

In this statement, she described having rebelled against the family's values by becoming interested in Carib and African culture and history, an aspect of the family's background that is, generally speaking, not emphasized. It is noteworthy, however, that she reacted in terms of seeking an education in Caribbean history and writing a book about it, achievements that would be appreciated by the family and give her a certain amount of recognition. Several of the young people in the second generation had reacted in a similar way, so that after some years of rebelliousness against the family, they did, by and large, settle down, marry, and obtain an education or other kind of training that allowed them to pursue respectable careers.

Indeed, it is characteristic of the second generation that even those who were the most critical of the high expectations and social pressure that they had experienced in the family still expressed pride in it and its accomplishments. One person, who had had his share of problems fitting into the family, was therefore fiercely proud of it:

> Family is everything; it is wider than most think of it, it is not just the immediate family of husband, wife and children. The [family] name is so different, I am proud of it; it is not just any other name.
>
> . . .
>
> It gives a sense of belonging. I don't just belong to the immediate family. The parents are not there forever. I feel a closeness and longing to say I belong to that tribe. It is like saying you belong to the Ashanti tribe.

He described his situation as one of being 'out on a limb' because there were few relatives in his part of the world. He therefore made a concerted effort to keep in contact with the family. When his wife became pregnant, he sent the picture of the first scan of the baby to all the e-mail addresses in the family to which he had access. He explained: 'I don't want them to forget Jim is here!'

The family was important because it provided a source of identification that was different from the dominant one in the society where one lived. This source was grounded in Dominica where the family had risen to prominence, and in the strong family ideals that had created such a strong profile for the family in Dominica. The family thus gave a sense of identity to those who were living as more or less anonymous 'immigrants' in a Western society. Moreover, it provided a sense of belonging that was different from the racial or ethnic categorization to which family members were exposed in various migration destinations. A few of the younger family members had been involved in Caribbean organizations or Caribbean arts. Most, however, did not particularly identify with such transnational or diasporic forms of expression because they resented being categorized as ethnic or marked as different. For them the family was important because it constituted a unique group of people that provided a strong sense of belonging, at the same time cutting across ethnic, racial, national and territorial boundaries.

Life-story interviews with the third generation, most of whom had been born and raised outside Dominica, showed that they were still aware of the family's ideals. In this generation, however, these ideals mainly appeared in a much more moderate version that corresponds to the importance attached to education and individual development in middle-class life in Western societies. Most were quite conscious of the special importance of the professions to the family, and one explained that he had decided to become a doctor, because there were so many doctors in the family. Those in the third generation, whose grandparents were living in Dominica, visited the island periodically. Such vacations allowed them to become better acquainted with the wider family living in, or visiting, Dominica:

> ['Did you know anything about your Dominican family?']
> I didn't realize there were so many before I went there and spent the summer with my grandparents. Wherever I went I had to explain whose grandchild

I was. It was nice. I felt totally welcomed by everyone. Everybody has something for you, fresh mangoes, lunch.

In this case, Dominica and the family seemed to merge in the experience of one big happy family. While not everyone in the third generation had quite such pleasant memories of visiting Dominica, several described the experience of having been met by generous and welcoming people. In the third generation, where the family figured as a less imposing frame of reference in the life stories, the family was becoming the embodiment of togetherness and love.

Conclusion

In this study, I have taken as my point of departure a notion of livelihood that is given meaning and practised in a particular family network. In this way, I have sought to develop a framework of study that is defined by people's lives and livelihoods, the moves they entail, and the fields of social relations and sources of cultural identification that they engage and sustain. This ethnographic study of the cultural construction of livelihood in a large, global family network shows that movement in time and space does not necessarily imply the sort of spatio-temporal closure that is normally identified with migration as movement to, and incorporation within, the place of destination. It may just as significantly concern social mobility and individual development in relation to a social field of inter-personal relations, moral values and cultural identity, identified with the livelihood of a group of people. This field takes place in the sense that it touches down, and articulates with life, in specific locations, turning some of them in the process into places of significance in the lives of individual family members (Tuan 1974; Olwig 1997b). The field, however, still maintains a logic of its own that must be understood on its own terms.

This family network constitutes an extensive field of relations, both in the sense that it is not confined to one particular locality, and in the sense that its existence depends on considerable geographical mobility on the part of those who inhabit it. It was apparent that geographical proximity, in and of itself, had little to do with a person's relative position in the family. Indeed, some of those who were the least successful at living up to family ideals had tended to stay behind, mingling with the wrong set of people and acquiring a poor reputation. It was proximity to the moral and intellectual ideals that were central to the family's livelihood, rather than proximity in space, that enabled individuals to become important members of the family. Mobility played a central role here as a means of aspiring to these ideals. In other words, it provided a means of establishing a place for oneself within the family network: it was not an interruption that required a process of incorporation back into normal life again. The life stories thus revealed a different logic of incorporation than that associated with incorporation into a migration destination.

The family network that emerged out of these movements in space has been sustained and maintained by concrete ties between the various family members.

After the first movements abroad to unknown destinations, many of the later movements thus took place within the family network. The four sisters who moved to Canada to join a fifth sister, or the nephews and nieces who lived with aunts and uncles while pursuing higher education abroad, exemplify this. Furthermore, there has been a great deal of interaction within the family network in the form of the exchange of economic assistance, help and various goods, just as there is frequent communication through visits, telephone calls, letters and, in recent years, e-mails. The very act of communicating constitutes one of the most important means of sustaining the community. My interviews with people therefore seemed just to be part of the ongoing flow of information and exchange of stories about family members – indeed, it may be argued that the family lives largely through stories and gossip about various family members. These stories were told with reference to the ideal of high moral values and intellectual excellence that are essential to the kind of livelihood that has become an important defining characteristic of this family. This ideal is therefore not just a model *for* the family to admire and aspire to, it has also become established as a model *of* the family that is supposed to reflect its special achievements and identity (Geertz 1973). While many in the second generation were somewhat critical of this ideal, none were indifferent to it, and most had sought in various ways to accommodate themselves to it in the lives (and life stories) that they constructed for themselves. They did this, it seems, because they valued being part of the family and of the community of belonging and distinction that it constituted. Thus, the family gave family members a unique identity that negated their status as just immigrants from the Third World or members of predetermined ethnic groups.

While I have sought to demonstrate that the family, and the social relations and cultural values that it embodies, constitute an important context of life and livelihood, I do not wish to argue that the family constitutes the only, or necessarily the most significant, context of life for everybody. Quite the contrary, I wish to suggest that the family acquired its particular significance in relation to the different social, economic and cultural contexts of life in which individual family members found themselves. Such contexts might be the Dominican nation state where the family rose to prominence, major multi-cultural migration destinations where several family members congregated, or more isolated locations where individuals lived on their own 'out on a limb.' The meaning of the family as a source of belonging and identification also varied according to the specific arenas of work, ethnic organizations, religious communities or educational institutions with which individuals were involved. This network therefore provided only one of many contexts of life. Yet, it is one that was of some significance to everybody, and of a great deal of importance to most.

Although the culturally constructed model of a 'respectable livelihood' has its roots in the old colonial structure, it has now become an important basis of the independent nation state. Furthermore, it has become closely articulated with the mobile culture of the middle classes in Western societies who value education, personal achievement and social mobility (see, e.g. Ortner 1998a, b; Overbey and Dudley 2000). It is not just the middle classes who have desired a 'respectable livelihood': indeed, this kind of livelihood has become a general ideal of upward socio-economic mobility for people in the Caribbean. Although very few people in the Caribbean have succeeded as well as the family studied here, this has not led to a decline in interest in education – quite the contrary. As S. Gordon notes, concerning the development of a system of West Indian education in the nineteenth century: 'The few at all levels of the community who could see a chance of social betterment through the education offered gave it a status and allegiance beyond its merits' (1963: 3). I suggest that for the many who could not see much of 'a chance' of 'social betterment through the education offered' by the local society, migration provided a way out and a possible avenue towards educational achievement and socio-economic mobility abroad – whether or not this was a realistic opportunity. If this is so, a better understanding of the cultural construction of a 'respectable livelihood' in the Caribbean, and in post-colonial societies in general, may provide one important key to understanding the large-scale migration that has taken place from the Caribbean and other parts of the Third World to Western countries.

Notes

1 I have interviewed thirteen individuals in the first generation of siblings, including three spouses; twenty-seven in the second generation, including one spouse, and nine in the third generation. I have also interviewed an aunt of the first generation of siblings.
2 Briefly, I initiated every interview by asking the interviewee to relate his or her life story to me. Virtually everybody responded to this request by outlining the main events in their lives, although the length of this account varied from a few minutes to more than an hour. In the remainder of the interview, I asked interviewees to elaborate on various points in this life-story sketch and asked supplementary questions on certain issues that had come up in other interviews but which had not been touched upon in the initial life story related by the interviewee. The life-story interviews therefore permitted the study of individuals' movements through life; the socio-cultural order that they are seeking to establish in their lives, and their own particular understanding of themselves in this order. For a further discussion of the life-story method in anthropology, see Watson 1976; Little 1980; Langness and Frank 1981; Peacock and Holland 1993; Caplan 1997.
3 For further discussion of the Canadian domestic scheme, see Henry 1968; Douglas 1968.
4 According to Myers (1976: 106), in the period from 1955–60, 3,931 men and 2,365 women went to the UK from Dominica. He estimates the total number of Dominicans who had left for Great Britain by 1960 to be approximately 8,000, or 13 per cent of the Dominican population of almost 60,000 in 1960 (ibid.: 118).
5 According to Baker (1994: 187), the religious affiliation of the Dominican population was as follows in 1972: Catholics 85 per cent, Methodists 7 per cent, Anglicans 1.6 per cent. This has undoubtedly changed a great deal since then, as various Protestant churches have actively missionized on the island.
6 One of these eleven children died when an infant. In this study, however, I have included the father's oldest child, born to another woman, because she grew up with the family and is regarded as part of the group of siblings.
7 According to Gordon, 'the reward in respectable employment to be obtained from these qualifications is one that must recur in the chronicle of almost every family of any substance at all. It is one of the most remarkable facts of West Indian social history since emancipation' (Gordon 1963: 3).

References

Abrahams, Roger (1983) *The Man-of-Words in the West Indies*, Baltimore: The Johns Hopkins University Press.

Alexander, Henry Jacob (1973) *The Culture of Middleclass Family Life in Kingston, Jamaica*, University of Chicago: Ph.D. Dissertation.

Baker, Patrick L. (1994) *Centring the Periphery: Chaos, Order, and the Ethnohistory of Dominica*, Jamaica: The Press, University of the West Indies.

Brereton, Bridget (1993) 'The development of an identity: The black middle-class of Trinidad in the later nineteenth century' pp. 274–83, in H. Beckles and V. Sheperd (eds) *Caribbean Freedom: Economy and Society from Emancipation to the Present*, Kingston, Jamaica: Ian Randle Publishers.

Caplan, Pat (1997) 'Introduction' pp. 6–22, in *African Voices, African Lives: Personal Narratives from a Swahili Village*, London: Routledge.

Douglas, E. M. K. (1968) 'West Indians in Canada: The household-help scheme. A comment', *Social and Economic Studies* 17(2): 215–17.

Fleming, W. G. (1964) *Secondary and Adult Education in Dominica*, Toronto: Ontario College of Education, University of Toronto.

Frucht, R. (1966) *Community and Context in a Colonial Society: Social and Economic Change in Nevis, British West Indies*, Brandeis University: Ph.D. Dissertation.

Geertz, Clifford (1973) *The Interpretation of Cultures*, New York: Basic Books.

Gmelch, George (1992) *Double Passage: The Lives of Caribbean Migrants Abroad and Back Home*, Ann Arbor: University of Michigan Press.

Gordon, Derek (1987) *Class, Status and Social Mobility in Jamaica*, Mona: Institute of Social and Economic Research, University of the West Indies.

Gordon, Shirley (1963) *A Century of West Indian Education*, London: Longmans, Green and Co.

Gudeman, Stephen (1986) *Economics and culture: Models and Metaphors of Livelihood*, London: Routledge & Kegan Paul.

Henry, Frances (1968) The West Indian domestic scheme in Canada, *Social and Economic Studies* 17(1): 83–91.

Honychurch, Lennox ca. (1983) *Our Island Culture*, Roseau: The Dominica Cultural Council.

Langness, Lewis and Gelya Frank (1981) *Lives: An Anthropological Approach to Biography*, Novato, CA: Chandler and Sharp.

Little, Kenneth (1980) 'Explanation and individual lives: A reconsideration of life writing in anthropology', *Dialectical Anthropology* 5: 215–26.

Lowes, Susan (1995) ' "They Couldn't Mash Ants": The Decline of the white and non-white elites in Antigua, 1834–1900', pp. 31–52, in K. F. Olwig (ed.) *Small Islands, Large Questions: Society, Culture and Resistance in the Post-Emancipation Caribbean*, London: Frank Cass.

Myers, Robert Amory (1976) *'I love my Home Bad, But . . .': The Historical and Contemporary Contexts of Migration on Dominica, West Indies*, The University of North Carolina at Chapel Hill: PhD Dissertation.

Olwig, Karen (1985) *Cultural Adaptation and Resistance on St. John: Three Centuries of Afro-Caribbean Life*, Gainesville: University of Florida Press.

Olwig, Karen (1993) *Global Culture, Island Identity. Continuity and Change in the Afro-Caribbean Community of Nevis*, Reading: Harwood Academic Publishers.

Olwig, Karen (1995) 'Cultural complexity after freedom: Nevis and beyond', pp. 100–20, in K. F. Olwig (ed.) *Small Islands, Large Questions. Society, Culture and Resistance in the Post-Emancipation Caribbean*, London: Frank Cass.

Olwig, Karen (1997a) 'Toward a reconceptualization of migration and transnationalism', in Bodil Folke Frederiksen and Fiona Wilson (eds) *Livelihood, Identity and Instability*, Copenhagen: Centre for Development Research.

Olwig, Karen (1997b) 'Cultural sites: Sustaining a home in a deterritorialized work', pp. 17–38, in K. F. Olwig and K. Hastrup (eds) *Siting Culture: The Shifting Anthropological Object*, London: Routledge.

Ortner, Sherry B. (1998a) 'Generation X: Anthropology in a media-saturated world', *Cultural Anthropology* 13(3): 414–40.

Ortner, Sherry B (1998b) 'Identities: The hidden life of class', *Journal of Anthropological Research* 54(1): 1–17.

Overbey, Mary Margaret, and Kathryn Marie Dudley (eds) (2000) *Anthropology and Middle-class Working Families: A Research Agenda*, Arlington: American Anthropological Association.

Parkin (1979) 'The categorization of work: Cases from coastal Kenya', pp. 317–36, in Sandra Wallman (ed.) *Social Anthropology of Work*, A. S. A. Monograph 19, London: Academic Press.

Peacock, James L. and Dorothy C. Holland (1993) 'The narrated self: Life stories in process', *Ethos* 21(4): 367–83.

Philpott, Stuart B. (1973) *West Indian Migration*, London: The University of London Press.

Ranger, Terence (1983) 'The invention of tradition in colonial Africa', pp. 211–62, in E. Hobsbawm and T. Ranger (eds) *The Invention of Tradition*, Cambridge: University of Cambridge Press.

Richardson, Bonham (1983) *Caribbean Migrants: Environment and Human Survival on St. Kitts and Nevis*, Knoxville: The University of Tennessee Press.

Thomas-Hope, Elizabeth (1978) 'The establishment of a migration tradition: British West Indian movements to the Hispanic Caribbean in the century after emancipation', pp. 66–81, in C. G. Clarke (ed.) *Caribbean Social Relations*, Liverpool: Centre for Latin American Studies, Monograph Series No. 8.

Thomas-Hope, Elizabeth (1995) 'Migration in the post-emancipation leewards', pp. 161–75 in K. F. Olwig (ed.) *Small Islands, Large Questions: Society, Culture and Resistance in the Post-Emancipation Caribbean*, London: Frank Cass.

Thomas Hope, Elizabeth (1998) 'Globalization and the development of a Caribbean migration culture', pp. 188–99, in Mary Chamberlain (ed.) *Caribbean Migration: Globalised Identities*, London: Routledge.

Tuan, Yi-Fu (1974) 'Space and place: Humanistic perspective', *Progress in Geography* VI: 211–52.

Watson, Lawrence C. (1976) 'Understanding a life history as a subjective document: Hermeneutical and phenomenological perspectives', *Ethos* 4(1): 95–131.

Wilson, Peter (1969) 'Reputation and respectability: A suggestion for Caribbean ethnology', *Man* 4(1): 70–84.

Wilson, Peter (1973) *Crab Antics: The Social Anthropology of English-Speaking Negro Societies in the Caribbean*, New Haven: Yale University Press.

5 'You must win their affection . . .'

Migrants' social and cultural practices between Peru and Italy

Carla Tamagno

In this article, I explore local and transnational social networks as they are constituted and mobilized for a variety of livelihood goals. More specifically, I focus on networks that link family members in Peru – who are often migrants themselves – with their relatives abroad, and the kinds of networks that are developed and sustained at both ends of the migration continuum.[1] In doing so, I shall examine in particular the notion of *debes ganarte su cariño* – the need to win the affection of others – and ideas and practices of 'connectivity', 'being alert' and 'support' that are central to these family networks.

Poverty, social differentiation, accelerated recession and a general lack of work opportunities have forced many Peruvians, especially the young, to leave the country. According to Altamirano (1992, 1996), an average of 350,000 Peruvians emigrate every year. In Peru, impoverished would-be migrants use all their resources to establish links with networks that might facilitate their departure. When reaching migration destinations in North America and Europe, these migrants often sustain active social networks with family, kin and local communities in Peru. Their networking activities resemble what Glick Schiller and her associates have termed transnationalism, 'social fields that cross geographic, cultural and political borders' (Glick Schiller *et al.* 1992: ix). As transmigrants, they 'develop and maintain multiple family, economic, social, organizational, religious and political relations that cross borders [. . .]. At the same time they execute actions, make decisions and become involved in a field of social relations that link their countries of origin with their country or countries of settlement' (ibid.).

This way of thinking is useful when locating overseas migrants in transnational social fields, but it often leaves aside the analysis of the impact of their departure on the livelihood strategies of relatives who remain in areas of origin. This is important because the majority of overseas migrants leave their countries in search of better livelihoods, not just for themselves, but also for their relatives back home. Processes of connectivity involving flows and exchanges of information and goods, and communication between migrants and the families they leave behind transforms livelihood opportunities for family members back home and their visions of the sort of lives that they would like to live.

Recent critiques of the concepts of transmigration and transnationalism have argued that these concepts are centred on the crossing of national borders and therefore do not deal with the cultural and social meaning of movement in space as a phenomenon in its own right. Karen Fog Olwig suggests that the term 'transnationalism' is problematic because it implies a close relationship between place and nation, identifying movement in space as the crossing of national borders and the emergence of non-local relationships with the development of transnational relations (Olwig 1997: 57). She suggests that this close association between movement and international migration is not warranted, because many people engage in a wide range of movements that may be of central importance to their lives and livelihoods. She therefore calls for a return to basic ethnography that explores the geographic, social, cultural, economic or political nature of movements and their meaning in people's lives. In other words, she suggests developing an anthropology of movement (ibid.: 60). Along the same lines, other authors emphasize that, in order to avoid essentialist categories in migration and globalization research, it is necessary to focus on fluctuation, people's mobility and socially constructed processes of connectivity in which cultural phenomena are constantly being de-territorialized and re-territorialized (Kearney 1995; Gupta and Ferguson 1997; Mallki 1997). Based on these insights, this chapter takes as its point of departure a basic ethnography of the practices of connectivity that permit the cultural construction of social and transnational fields, or what I call 'cultural spaces'. Such cultural spaces are constituted by cultural beliefs and social practices, and are the products of human agency, which, as a consequence of global–local interactions, at times may be detached from place and territory.

The theoretical and methodological framework that has guided my understanding of the world of migration has been the 'actor-oriented approach' as developed by Norman Long and others. The central principle of this approach is that all individuals involved in social situations should be seen as actors who have their own understandings of the situation, their own perspectives of social change and their own strategies (Long and Long 1992, Long and Roberts 1997; Preston 1996: 302). In order to analyse such actors, we must first explore their livelihoods. A livelihood best 'expresses the idea of individuals and groups striving to make a living, attempting to meet their various consumption and economic necessities, coping with uncertainties, responding to new opportunities, and choosing between different value positions' (Long and Long 1997: 11). This approach takes into account the normative and cultural dimension of livelihoods, including lifestyles and the factors that shape them, and focuses attention on social situations and on how each actor creates her world(s) in her daily social life (Preston 1996: 302).

The actor-oriented approach thus allows us to understand the processes of social relations involved in the everyday lives of migrant families. In these processes, the flow of money and goods (including music cassettes, clothes, furniture and lifestyle magazines, exotic posters, photographs and amulets) between family members in Peru and in foreign migrant destinations carry a specific significance and specific values associated with migration, the world left behind and the world(s) encountered abroad. It is in these processes of social exchange that the cultural construction of transnational spaces takes place and that transnational lives are lived at home and abroad. I shall argue that the most important issue for the family members involved in a migration network spanning Huancayo, Peru and Italy is not the crossing of national and political borders by different family members, but rather the exploration, through movement, of livelihoods that will provide better opportunities not only for the migrants themselves, but more importantly for the family members left behind.

I begin my examination of these questions in an urban marginal neighbourhood of the city of Huancayo in Peru by presenting a case study of a Peruvian mother with daughters overseas.[2] I examine in particular the significance of the discourse of 'winning somebody's affection' as a strategic cultural practice that enables this woman, her daughters and their group of neighbourhood friends to establish and maintain social relations and wider social networks. Such networks, I argue, have allowed the inhabitants of the urban neighbourhood to face difficult situations and uncertainties in contexts of mobility, poverty, a lack of stability, and violence. In the second section, I focus on the various forms of 'connectivity' that exist between family members living in Huancayo and their daughters, who are currently working in Italy. These forms of 'connectivity' allow overseas migrants to keep in touch with those back home, and to strengthen their relationships through beliefs and social practices that contribute to the unification of transnational cultural spaces. Through processes of 'connectivity' involving telephone calls, the flow of goods (correspondence, parcels, cassettes, photographs, videos, etc.), money and cultural artefacts, dispersed family members maintain a strong presence in each other's lives. These transnational cultural spaces are strengthened by the use of various 'techniques of being alert' and of 'support', cultural livelihood practices that allow migrants to be alert and adjust emotionally and physically to new contexts in which symbols, goods and artefacts play a fundamental role. In the third section I analyse how the migrant daughters continue to be present in the lives and livelihoods of the family and the wider urban settlement by sending remittances and frequent information, and by communicating by means of telephone calls, correspondence and parcels. Through frequent communication with their daughters, those left behind have become linked to global worlds, which, among other things, has allowed them to rethink their future. Although physically distant, the daughters therefore play an important role in the definition and decision-making of family members back home, leading them to reconfigure their visions, aspirations and expectations.

Transnational migration and connectivity processes

Huancayo is located in the central area of Peru. As described in other contributions to this volume (see those by Paerregaard and Sørensen), large numbers of rural–urban migrants arrived in the city throughout the twentieth century, primarily from the communities of the Mantaro Valley and the southern provinces (mainly Huancavelica and Ayacucho). These migrants came in search of job opportunities, education and better living standards, and were employed in agriculture, industry, mining and trade (Long and Roberts 1984: 35; Smith 1989: 104). Between 1940 and 1961 the population of Huancayo nearly tripled. National and foreign investors arrived, set up industries in the region, and began to employ large numbers of manual workers. People were constantly arriving in and leaving Huancayo during this period, and the city became known for its openness to migrants (Long and Roberts 1984: 73–87, 142).

In the 1970s, as a result of the structural reforms introduced by the government,[3] light industry collapsed, its economic class only recovering through trading activities in the 1980s. However, this decade coincided with the emergence of political violence (1980–95). When the violence became more critical, the better-off families left Huancayo for Lima, and later, when they saw their investments endangered, for other countries. They were joined by migrants from various sectors of Peruvian society (see Chapter 6). However, yet others began to arrive in Huancayo, especially the so-called 'internally displaced population' from the southern provinces of Ayacucho and Huancavelica, where political violence increased (Tamagno 1998). With these arrivals, a total of sixteen registered urban marginal areas or so-called human settlements were created (Provincial Municipality of Huancayo, MPH 1996).

Justicia, Paz y Vida: A settlement in Huancayo

'Settlements' emerged in Peru when people took possession of private lands in the urban marginal areas by invading and expropriating private land. The first human settlements appeared in the early 1980s, in the form of slums in Lima and the provinces that were supported by governments of a populist tendency.[4] The taking over of land at the Settlement called 'Justicia, Paz y Vida', literally 'Justice, Peace, and Life' (JPV), was promoted by the Municipality of Huancayo (MPH), which was headed by the United Left during the 1980s. In the years of APRA populism in Peru (1985–90), the municipal governments were authorized to grant and expropriate lands on the basis of the 'social interest'. When in 1986 the Municipality of Huancayo became aware that a local landowning family was planning to convert its lands from agricultural to residential use, it summoned a meeting of its supporters and poor homeless families to prepare them to take them over.[5] By September 1986, around 2,400 families had registered for the 54 acres available, a number that could hardly be housed on the land. Following a change of mayor, however, the municipal government disregarded the settlement, and from that date on the leaders of the settlement began a long struggle for its recognition and legalization. Since that time right up to the present, 'Justicia, Paz y Vida' has constituted itself as one of the political arenas of greatest confrontations in Huancayo. In the years since its foundation, the leaders of the settlement have faced various attempts to evict them and bring them to court over land property rights and the payment of a fair price for the land.[6]

Visiting 'Justicia, Paz y Vida', one cannot help noticing the high level of organization of the settlement. The streets are straight and well-aligned, broad and unpaved, and are named after poets, writers and social activists and ethnic groups, such as Javier Heraud, Flora Tristán, Manuel Scorza, José María Arguedas, Maxim Gorki, Martin Luther King, Ernest Hemingway, the Insurgent, the Mochicas and the Quechuas. Almost all the houses are of the same size (between 100 and 150 m^2), with simple adobe walls painted white, or, if financed by state loans, made of cement. As you walk through the streets into the settlement, you will see a predominance of small shops selling food products and functioning on the side as bars where young and old meet to drink their '*calientitos*' in the evenings and share the day's gossip. In general, people are friendly and welcoming, and they know each other across neighbourhoods.

A great variety of trading activities take place at the entrance to the settlement from early every day. Residents located in that area have opened small shops in their houses or rented part of their lots to small businessmen, such as tyre-repair shops, welders, restaurants, shops selling a variety of products, hairdressers, hardware stores and bars. According to a survey of forty families conducted in 1998 in two sectors of the settlement,[7] 35 per cent of the settlers were active in informal trading. Many had their small shops within the settlement or in the regional fairs and markets (which mostly sold vegetables, fruits, trinkets and other goods easy to trade). Outside the small shops, others gather to wait for the manual labour contractors who come from various places in the valley or in the central jungle in vans or trucks to hire agricultural labour. Fifteen per cent were housekeepers who were also employed as seasonal agricultural labourers, and 22.5 per cent had temporary jobs in construction, agricultural labour, transportation, and so on. From 7 a.m. trucks offering services in the construction sector begin to arrive (loading sand, stones, bricks, etc.), also hiring many settlers or neighbours. The remainder of the population have other sorts of occupation.[8] It is common to see older children being left in charge of household activities, including caring for younger brothers and sisters, since many parents are absent from the settlement for long periods when migrating for seasonal work elsewhere. Our survey showed that teenagers attending school looked after 10 per cent of the households. It also indicates that 20 per cent of inhabitants return regularly to their rural communities of origin to supply the household with food products.[9]

Talking with neighbours of Sector X, it becomes apparent that few of them have family in Huancayo. Rather, most have close social relationships with friends and neighbours in the settlement. This was verified by the survey, which showed that 82.5 per cent of those interviewed had relatives outside the city of Huancayo, and 25 per cent of them had relatives overseas (in Europe, Japan and the United States).

Cultural practices in contexts of marginality, instability and post-violence

Camila[10] lives in 'Justicia, Paz y Vida'. She fled the violence of Huancavelica in the early 1980s and was among the initial leaders of the settlement process. Back in the 1980s she faced up to the police and the authorities when, time and again, they tried to force her out of her plot, until, as she puts it 'God remembered me' and helped her send her daughters far away to Italy for a good job as domestic workers. It is their remittances that allow her to continue educating her younger children and to obtain the standard of living she always wanted. Like many other Peruvian mothers, Camila is decisive, a real 'fighter', for whom her children are most important. She has therefore endured all types of personal sacrifices to ensure the well-being of her family. One day she told me: 'My daughters are everything to me and the best I have. I have given them all I have to give and I want the best for them'.

This woman and her group of friends arrived in Huancayo in search of better living conditions. One of their dreams was to have a piece of land of their own in the city. This became a reality, thanks to their struggle for land in the settlement. Their beliefs, discourses and use of social and cultural practices, I argue, have allowed them to face the continuous evictions, court hearings, abuse and general crisis experienced by most Peruvians during the political violence.

When I initially established contact with Camila, she stated that her daughters had been in Japan for a long time and that they never communicated. When, after some time, we became better acquainted, I learned that her daughters were actually in Italy and asked her why she had withheld this information. Camila replied that she just couldn't trust anyone; if people found out, they could harm her, out of 'jealousy and envy'. Given the history of political violence in the settlement, her fears were quite understandable.[11] For many years, Camila and her neighbours lived in uncertainty, absolute distrust and fear.

Camila and the lechugueras

Doing fieldwork in situations of marginality, violence and a lack of security posed very serious methodological challenges. It is necessary to be in close contact with the actors and 'win their trust', if not their affection. I entered Camila's world through an informal group of female neighbours who call themselves the *lechugueras* ('*lettuce women*'). This nickname stems from their meeting every evening in front of Rosa's house to 'chew coca leaves' which they call 'lettuce' because of the leaves' green and pleasant colour. Coca leaves are a link to their Andean origins. They meet, 'chew' and 'loosen up', share the intimacies of their daily lives, such as their personal problems, relationships with husbands or lovers, uncertainties as to how to educate their children, relationships with other neighbours, with their children's school, the problems of the settlement, novelties introduced from abroad and news from television programmes. They identify intimately with 'talk shows' (which are very much in fashion in Peru) and soap operas that represent dramatic situations in which they see their personal lives reflected. On other days they are moved by memories of their past experiences. In these situations they often emphasize their 'strength' and 'courage'.

For Camila and her friends Rosa and Juana and sometimes Aquino, the space of 'the *lechugueras*' is one of the pleasantest and most important in their lives. This is, they say, because they have been together ever since the formation of the settlement and have 'lived many things' that make them feel like 'sisters', 'family'. At the same time the group exerts various levels of influence and control over each other's lives. They would therefore not trust each other on issues that, they believed, might create jealousy among them.

For all of them mobility has been a constant feature of their lives, and '*winning the affection*' of the people with whom they interact has been fundamental. Camila has several relationships and migration experiences behind her. She grew up in Huancavelica. Her mother was left by three partners and was forced to leave Camila in the care of her grandmother. At the age of 15, Camila became pregnant from a relationship with a soldier and had her first son. She later became engaged to another man, with whom she had four more children. During their relationship, Camila worked as an agricultural labourer for five years, one of which was spent in the jungle. Occasionally, she did other people's laundry. Finally, when her second husband left her, she went to Huancayo to work as a domestic servant. Camila emphasizes that she always found people to support her because she '*won their affection*'.

Although she always worked hard, Camila nonetheless had difficulties making a living for herself and her children. To make ends meet, she sent her two daughters, Katty and Rita, to live with their father in the jungle when they finished school. Since their father had established a new family, he was unable or unwilling to provide for his daughters. They were sent to work, first as coffee-pickers in the jungle, then as domestic workers in Lima. The daughters recall this time as follows:

> We have endured all this for our mother. Although she worked day and night, the money was not enough to feed a big family, it just wasn't enough for all of us. We survived this period thanks to our mother's advice. Many times, when we had worked hard, suffered humiliations, swallowed our pride . . . the only thing that kept us going was remembering our mother saying, 'You must win their affection, you must be good workers, attentive, quick'. This is how it has been.

Like Camila and her daughters, each of the *lechugueras* has a particular history. For example, Juana travels to Jauja for the local festivities and the sowing and harvesting seasons, and she takes her friends along. When she returns, she always brings 'something' (often part of the crop) for her neighbours, who, she believes, have ill will towards her. Aquino sells her crops in Huancayo and Lima. She is an expert at convincing her customers to buy her produce and explains that she 'always gives them a little extra' to make them come back, 'to win their affection'. Rosa, the last *lechuguera*, is an orphan who always survived by 'helping others out' to earn their recognition and a little affection.

As we see in the life stories of the *lechugueras*, they have all developed particular strategies to relate to other people, and 'winning their affection' has been fundamental in surviving in the midst of difficult family situations and frequent moves. The common experiences of the *lechugueras* have united them and converted them into one of the women's most important social networks. Frequently, they do not see their own families, and they often say that they prefer to relate to friends rather than to their own families because in the latter there are more problems connected with envy and jealousy relating to competition for power and prestige.

For the *lechugueras* and their neighbours, the settlement in JPV has been one of the most important experiences in their lives. To acquire a plot and build a house of their own has been, as they say, 'God's blessing'. But if home ownership and recognition have been the most important objectives of the parents' generation, their children wish for more, for socio-economic mobility for the entire family, for higher status and social prestige. They are therefore concerned with the appearance of the house, its style of construction, household appliances and, ultimately, the relocation of the family home in a more prestigious neighbourhood.

Envy as a mechanism of social control

In the settlement, ideas of 'jealousy' and 'envy' are omnipresent and often expressed in gossip, rumour and insults, as well as in attitudes and interrelationships among neighbours. According to the *lechugueras*, feelings of jealousy and envy may lead other people to 'harm them' (for example, through witchcraft). For this reason, people 'take care' and 'protect themselves' in order to avoid becoming the object of envy, a position that may lead not only to 'failure' but also, in the last instance, to 'death'. Camila, Rosa, Juana and Aquino, therefore, do their utmost to avoid making enemies, attempting to get along with their neighbours by, as they say, 'winning their affection'.

At the same time, however, they keep a large, thorny, green plant known as *sábila* (*aloe vera*) tied with a red and white ribbon and a horseshoe at the back of their front doors. These are believed to protect them from the negative energies of those who may want to harm them. When things are not going well, the leaves become yellow and dry up. This is a sign alerting them to 'go and get advice' and to find out 'who can be causing the harm'. Then they proceed to clean the house and bathe in thistle water. Camila, for example, usually has a flowerpot with coloured flowers and leaves of male and female rue at the entrance to the house and a 'male garlic' plant (from the Amazon) on the table both to protect the house. These artefacts have an important meaning in the life of the *lechugueras* because they make them feel secure and protected from harm and from the ill will of other people.

One day Juana explained: 'It's always the same everywhere, that's why you shouldn't show that you have more than others, you must just take care always and make them love you. I am always bringing something for neighbours who I know don't like me. I also give them credit in my store, so I help them . . . .' Camila explained: 'It's like this, what can we do if the people are envious when they see you are making progress . . . .' And Rosa added: 'The people are too much, they are always talking, when you have something, they say you've stolen it or you're involved with cocaine or in some bad business. They're too much, they don't let you make progress.'

On another occasion, Camila remarked in secret (by lowering her voice) that she was careful not to tell others where her daughters were because she feared the envy and meanness of people:

> Few people know that my daughters are out of the country because people are mean, gossiping and envious; many times they have said bad things about me, and they can harm me just out of envy. One day my uncle's relatives talked about me to my sister-in-law, Inés, saying, 'How have those ignorant and starving *cholas* gone away? Probably stealing?' They said that; as you see, even our own family bears us ill will, so it must be worse with strangers.

Camila and her friends feel that having money makes them different from other neighbours and that this can provoke people's envy. They therefore pretend not to have any money. Camila receives remittances from her daughters regularly, but she spends it cautiously and does not boast about her money.[12] On the contrary, every time she buys something for her house, she keeps it wrapped in newspapers or in bags so that the neighbours do not realize she is improving her house.

'To win the affection' of neighbours and others seems to be embedded in a discourse of social control. This discourse is based on equality and regulates behaviour in the settlement. Social or economic progress is regulated by social practices of inclusion and exclusion. If a family makes progress but develops individualistic forms of behaviour instead of the behaviour associated with solidarity, then 'envy' and 'jealousy', expressed through gossip, rumour or witchcraft, will occur immediately. According to my observations, this is basically due to the fact that many inhabitants of the settlement originate in rural communities in which social relations are governed by *el uyay, el ainy* and *la minka* (various forms of reciprocal solidarity relations; see Paerregaard 1997).

In the lives of Camila, her daughters and the *lechugueras*, to win somebody's affection means to 'make others love you', to be accepted and acknowledged by others. It means gaining social prestige, but in a way in which a display of social differences is avoided. During the violence, this practice became an important survival strategy. Nowadays, in a context of poverty and post-violence, it means to share with the poorest, not feeling above them or demonstrating that you 'have more' than them. If you do, an undesirable exclusion will be provoked.

Connectivity and transnational cultural spaces

According to Camila, Rita and Katty's move to Italy was made possible by her ability to win the affection of others, especially Camila's younger brother Roberto, who loves her very much. He helped Camila for many years: for example, when he was still single he helped her out financially with the education of her children. Ten years ago, when he married Inés and they had a daughter, Katty and Rita became their nannies, and as soon as they left school in the afternoon, they went to play with the baby. Roberto's wife Inés is an independent professional and belongs to a well-established family in Huancayo. She has many relatives abroad, and a couple of her cousins own a company that arranges for Peruvians to travel for domestic work to Italy. When Inés agreed to help Rita leave the country, it was decided that Rita should go to Italy. The cost of the migration arrangements were guaranteed by Roberto and Inés, who used their own house to provide security for the USD 6,000 loan that financed Rita's journey, and which she managed to repay with interest after eight months working in Italy. As soon as the loan was returned, Rita facilitated Katty's migration.

In the first letter she sent from Italy, Rita wrote that her trip was 'an unforgettable experience'. She described how, at each stop, 'contacts' were waiting for her, asking her how the trip was and taking care of her in other ways. She stopped over in Spain and France before reaching Italy, where a network contact, Sara, was waiting for her. She took her to various Italian cities and taught her about Italian customs and how she was now expected to behave. For Camila and her daughters, their dispersal seems to have been countered by the distinct practices of 'connectivity' that they have developed to avoid losing contact. These practices include frequent telephone calls and sending letters and parcels, videos and cultural artefacts, and remittances – socio-cultural practices that allow them to be present in each other's lives and to help them adjust to and face problematic situations.

Letters, photographs and parcels

Letters, photographs and parcels sent and received by migrants and their dependents are valuable ethnographic sources. As Hammersley and Atkinson argue (1995: 159), letters, diaries and autobiographies are sources of information that allow the ethnographer to reconstruct the social life of the actors involved. While doing fieldwork in JPV, I became acquainted with Camila's world and her relationship with her daughters abroad through their letters. Sometimes I helped Camila prepare and send a parcel, and sometimes I accompanied her when she picked up letters and parcels from Italy. In this way I came to know about the experiences of her daughters in Italy and about the information that Camila relayed to her daughters, for instance about events in the family, news about friends and what went on in the settlement.

Camila taught me how to situate myself within the settlement, introduced me to her *caseras* and taught me how to *regatear* and over time we became friends.[13] Camila was herself friendly with all the women in the market, who helped her out when she was very poor. Many had given her credit, and she had a special affection for them. In return for her friendship, I helped her write letters to her daughters in Italy.

One day, when we had agreed that I should help her write a letter, she showed me 23 letters and several photograph albums sent to her by her daughters in Italy. The photographs showed her daughters in the streets of Milan, covered with snow, decorated for Christmas. There were also shots of them in various parks, squares and churches. Other photographs showed Rita's birthday being celebrated by her Latin American friends a few months after her arrival, and yet others showed the employers' houses. In the first letters, Rita related various anecdotes of her trip and of her adjustment to conditions in Italy. She wrote about the uncertainty and fear she felt in the beginning whenever she had to speak the language or was asked to carry out specific tasks. Six months later, Rita had adapted to the new conditions and wrote the following:

> Mom, now I have got used to being here, there's everything here, nothing is lacking: food is plentiful and everything is delicious. Now, I only have to clean the two living rooms and the bedrooms and serve young Santiago, who curses me when I don't understand him (but after your helpful advice, he's been more quiet). I'm also in charge of the laundry. I use a washing machine and the clothes come out dry (someday I will buy you one). I have to do all this. But, since I finish quickly, I help Karina (the cook). She is just like you and always gives me the best food [...] Mrs Marina (the owner of the house) already loves me because, she says, I am a good worker. I've told them that you taught me all that I know and they say: "Your mother must be a good woman". That is why she gave me the clothes I sent you. This is why I want you to buy them alpaca sweaters and send them to me. Could you also buy them some nice handicrafts from Peru (tell Pedro to choose them) and send them to me.[14]

When we went through this part of the letter, Camila was moved and made the following comment:

> I've taught my children to win people's love wherever they go; I've suffered so much in life, but there were always people who helped me because I won their affection. I've always been attentive to what they wanted [...] When I worked in the house of General Jauregui, his wife loved me very much, the same was true of the lady in La Punta, the same with Remolacha from the Amazon, that lady loved me so much... and even now she asks me to come and stay with her [...] I've learned to behave like this from my grandmother and my mother; it is the same with my daughters, and they will not suffer that much if they are like that.

To Camila's daughters in Italy, 'to win the affection' of their employers means to gain the trust and acceptance of the receiving society, to become a part of its process of interaction. When Rita got a job in the home of the Bocelli family, she was warned that poor Santiago (the elder son of the family) was bad tempered because he was confined to bed and could only move about in a wheelchair. But, with her mother's help and advice, her patience and ability for work, Rita 'won his affection'. Now he is her friend and he has convinced his father to guarantee Rita and Katty in the negotiations over their *soggiorno*. As such, 'winning affection' is their main cultural strategy of adjustment and adaptation to Italian society. The feelings generated by being accepted or rejected are fundamental to their well-being.

'Winning affection' is part of an accumulation of experiences and serves as an interaction strategy in unknown or difficult life situations. In other cases, however, this strategy may lead to distinct forms of exploitation and/or submission to a patron–client relationship (Long 1997: 10). For example, in the cases of Camila and her daughters, 'to win affection' means to be tolerant with employers, hardworking and honest, loyal and trustful, gentle, kind and educated. At the same time, however, as they become acquainted with their employers' way of life, customs and behaviour, they learn to relate to them. In doing so, they make use of different strategies that make their employers appreciative of them and considerate. By winning their employers' affection, they make themselves indispensable. As Camila's daughters relate, they have experienced 'humiliation', they have had to 'swallow their pride' in order 'to win the affection of employers'. These relationships have often implied various forms of submission and exploitation. But over time, the daughters have managed to make themselves 'indispensable'. This is also the case in Italy, where Rita and Katty have negotiated the protection of their employers in their legalization process, and, having obtained legal work permits, have managed to press for higher salaries.

Camila is in constant communication with her migrant daughters in order to help them cope emotionally with migration. In the letters I helped Camila write to Rita and Katty, Camila recommended: 'You should be patient, you should make people love you and you should gain their affection so they won't lay you off.'

She told them how the remittances had been invested:

> Now I've done what you told me, I have made myself look nice, I had my teeth fixed and I had a haircut; next time, I will send you a photograph [...] I have repaired the house as well because, with the rain, everything gets wet through the leaks. I am also having a new door made because there is a lot of robbery here in the settlement. Pedro told me to secure the house because they can steal our telephone [...] We have been thinking, with Pedro, that it might be a better idea to open a book store instead of a grocery, there's no other book store here. We try to find out what it will cost, but first we have to secure the house.

And finally she wanted to me write about each member of the family, describing their current situation and always emphasizing that all the family missed them and were expecting to be in touch with them soon. Feelings and messages were clearly intertwined. She wanted to keep her daughters in contact with Peru. Camila told me: 'My daughters will never forget their family, they will always be thinking about us because they know how much I have sacrificed for them; but it's always good to remind them'.

In the letters, Camila thus attempted to 'connect' her daughters with the rest of the family and used all the resources at hand for that purpose.[15] Continuous communication, so to speak, strengthens the 'transnational cultural space'.

But migration also strengthens Camila's self-esteem. Never before in her life has she been able to 'make herself beautiful', to 'shape up' and feel good about herself. The money her daughters send back has enabled her to have her teeth (or those she has left) fixed, to have her hair cut, to buy herself new clothes, and she has enjoyed indulging in the perfumes and lotions her daughters have sent. This has changed her life, and little by little she is not only experiencing herself as a new person, it also makes her feel connected to herself in a new way.

Techniques of alert and support

On top of the conventional ways of communication used by Camila and her daughters, Camila has other and more effective means of obtaining knowledge about her daughters, who, as she says, 'by being away and alone are exposed to greater danger'. One of these means is to *tirar el maíz*, to throw corn grains, and Camila frequently throws a handful of corn to 'see' how her daughters are doing in Italy. She learned how to throw corn from a friend more than fifteen years ago, but since her daughters migrated she makes frequent use of this belief-practice. It consists of identifying (according to her, 'seeing') a person's situation by examining the position of the corn grains after she has thrown them on to the table. When Camila occasionally 'sees' her daughters and perceives some danger, she phones to warn them, so that they are 'prepared'.[16]

Such beliefs and practices are deeply rooted in the settlement. When faced with any problems or if important decisions are to be made, people frequently consult individuals who know how to 'see'. Some throw corn grains, others coca leaves, tobacco or coffee, while yet others read cards or interpret dreams. I call these beliefs 'techniques of being alert', because I understand them as a set of cultural practices that lead various actors to be alert in specific situations. Through such consultations, people are led to think of potential problematic situations that may require certain precautions or other measures to avoid difficulties. Another widespread belief among people in the settlement concerns the protective power of amulets. Camila and her daughters are strong believers in such practices and artefacts. Together they form part of what I call 'techniques of support', that is, a belief in certain practices that offer emotional and affective security. Techniques of being alert and of support are only used in contexts of uncertainty and insecurity.

In September, Camila received a letter from Rita and Katty, who wrote, 'Mummy, now we are negotiating our *soggiorno* [residence permits], we need Susana's help so that everything goes right. Find her and tell her to make the best amulets for us. Tell her to make the one Rita asked for last time, she knows which. It is one of the most expensive ones, but it doesn't matter. We are sending you 2000 dollars; spend what is necessary and save the rest.

When, in accordance with Katty and Rita's wishes, Camila went to the jungle to look for Señora Susana, I decided to accompany her. We found her after half a day's journey. She read the cards to Camila and told her that her daughters' negotiations were going to be all right, though in Katty's case they might take a little longer than planned. This actually turned out to be the case. Susana also told us that Camila had to prepare the amulets properly and look after them for Rita and Katty. Only by being 'blessed' would they have the power to help their wearers in 'everything they wanted'. We therefore left without them, but later, when they were ready, Susana brought them to Huancayo herself. She gave them to Camila, who sent them to me in Amsterdam so that I could take them to Italy and give them to her daughters. They needed them urgently, she wrote, to aid them in negotiating their legal residence.[17]

What do these amulets mean in a transnational context? The psychoanalytical perspective tells us that migrants need to hold on to various elements of their native environment (familiar objects, folk music, memories and dreams in which aspects of the country of origin arise, etc.) in their struggle for self-preservation or in order to maintain the experience of 'being themselves' (see Gringberg and Gringberg 1984: 156). According to the Gringbergs, this is part of a 'transitional' 'non-human' space, in which material objects (artefacts, clothes, old furniture, amulets, etc.) that were valued by the migrants in their former environment continue to play an important role in the new context, and through which they experience a relief of tension (see also Denford, in Gringberg 1984: 98). In the case of Camila's daughters, however, I argue that the amulets also represent practices of connectivity to their home. First and foremost, they offer support that is fundamental for the maintenance of staying alert and being able to adjust to unknown or problematic situations. But they also connect people separated in space. Katty and Rita met Susana when they went to live with their father in the jungle. She always supported them and read cards to them on several occasions. At that time she told them that one day they would travel far away and earn a lot of money. This prophecy was hard to believe for two girls who had grown up in poverty, but it nevertheless came true. By continuously connecting with Susana, they make sure they retained the 'magic'.

Migration, networks and accumulated experience

They are still present

For Camila and her other children in Huancayo – Julia, Pedro and Leila – Katty and Rita are always present. Camila told me that, in a way, her relationship with her daughters had become closer since they left to work in Italy. Prior to their departure, even if they were in distant places such as Lima or the jungle, they seldom wrote her letters because they knew they could see her any time they wished and then speak to her face to face. Now that they are far away, they tell her everything in the letters, and Camila feels that she is taking part in her daughters' lives through the events that occur to them. They are in touch much more frequently than before, at least three or four times a month, through letters, parcels and telephone calls. They usually talk on the phone on Sundays, and through these phone calls, Katty and Rita receive information from their brothers about how things are going in Peru, how their family is doing, and other news of the settlement. On top of the phone calls, Katty and Rita write regularly to each of their siblings, recommending what Julia, Pedro and Leila should be studying or how they should use their spare time. Rita and Katty's younger siblings listen to their advice because they have experience of living in a more developed world. Rita and Katty also send parcels to their family with clothes and novelties, such as fashion magazines from Italy, tourist videos from Europe and photographs of holidays.

In their letters and recorded cassettes they tell all the siblings, 'We want you to enjoy, as we do, the best of Europe, and you must be up to date on what is going on here'. Through continuous communication they have therefore influenced their siblings in re-orienting their lives and their future. Rita has asked her 15-year-old sister Julia to study hard so that she might become a professional. She has also promised to help her financially with her higher education. During an interview Julia stated:

> I am making an effort because my sisters have told me to study English and computing, so that I may go to them and get a good job there. They tell me how things are over there and how you need to be well prepared to make good money. Everything has changed since my sisters went there. I don't miss them too much because we talk all the time. What I want to do is to finish school soon so that I can go with them to work and earn money.

Like Julia, Pedro, the oldest brother, is organizing his life according to his sisters' advice. He is 24 years old and has studied electricity at a technical institute, his studies being paid for by his uncle Roberto, with whom he works in computer systems. He is currently working to save enough money to join his sisters in Italy.

> My sisters have told me that if you know computing there (in Europe), you can make a lot of money. That is why, more than anything, I want to learn more. What I need to do is to learn English, they have told me to study and save all the money I can. They are saving money as well to be able to send me money for the airfare. I don't know when that will be, but I suppose it will be when we have saved enough and we have paid all our bills. We've also thought about helping our mother to set up a little business here at home. In helping her with this, I will be able to go without worrying and try my luck over there.

Pedro is perhaps the most important person for Rita and Katty, and when they call they always try to talk to him first, to suggest things he should do. In the end, he is the one who makes the important decisions in the family. In return, Pedro keeps them informed about key news in the country; he relates every piece of news or information he receives to his sisters, and over the phone they then form a common opinion on everything ranging from family problems, settlement problems, the national situation and politics, to fashion, music and religion.

Contact between the various family members has been strengthened by distance. For Pedro, having two sisters in Italy means being linked with the 'world'. He says that if it were not for them, he would not know anything about Europe or have other news of the world. Pedro has been following the news on the war in Bosnia, and his sisters keep him informed about the latest events. Pedro feels proud of them, and he is doing his best not to disappoint them and to help his family 'move forward'.

When analysing this case, the importance of the indirect presence of Katty and Rita in their family is obvious. It is they who make family decisions through the advice they give over the phone and in the letters and remittances that they send. For example, on one occasion they sent catalogues and magazines showing the styles, forms and fashion colours in European living rooms so that the family could order furniture made in a similar style. On another occasion they sent catalogues and magazines with models of modern European houses. A letter instructing the family about the models they liked followed the catalogues. In the same letter they suggested that the family hire the best architect in Huancayo, to design some decorative blueprints showed in one of the catalogue pictures.

In many ways, then, Pedro, Julia, Leila, and Camila have their lives planned according to the suggestions made by Katty and Rita. They are still present in the home in the settlement, and this presence is used to change the family's lifestyles, mobilize it socially and transform it so as to resemble Peru's upper middle class. While Katy and Rita will probably not be able to cross the social boundaries of Italian society, they want their family to have access to better conditions and to move up socially in their place of origin. To reach this goal they make use of mobile livelihood practices, such as 'winning the affection of others', which they developed in Peru and which they brought with them to Italy.

Conclusion

In this chapter, I have analysed the significance of entering the world of migration through the livelihood processes of various situated actors. I have argued that the main issue for Camila and her family may not be migration as such, but rather the nurturing and maintenance of the connectivity processes at stake. I have pointed to the important livelihood strategy of 'winning the affection of others', a strategy developed in times of violence and great instability in Peru, which seems to travel and fit well into an exploitative system of domestic work in Italy. I have also analysed some of the techniques of being alert and of support that are mobilized within the transnational cultural space, to the creation of which all family members contribute.

Connectivity practices are based on a constant flow of information, representations, understandings, images, discourses, beliefs and notions of belonging. The family in Peru is transforming its livelihood and planning the course of each family member according to what they learn from the daughters in Italy. As for the daughters, they also change their perceptions according to the information they receive from their country of origin, at the same time altering their perceptions of development through their contact with Italian values, styles and ways of living. Techniques of being alert and of support, such as throwing corn and seeking the protection of amulets as part of the process of regulating one's legal status, are part and parcel of this transnational system that connects people over large distances. In the present case, moreover, distance seems to have strengthened family bonds.

To the people involved, the crossing of national frontiers is relative. Greater importance seems to be attached to the crossing of social and economic borders that are directly related to family survival and well-being. As we have seen, money earned in Italy makes a whole world of difference to people in a human settlement in Peru. Here, some important gendered and generational differences nevertheless seem to be present. During the recent violent and poverty-ridden times in Peru, women have assumed the role of heads of households. In this process they have developed various practices to ensure their family's subsistence, of which 'winning the affection of others' is but one. To the generation of mothers who first experienced internal displacement and the struggle of settlement, the legalization of their plot of land has been their most important goal in life. Upward social mobility is the goal of their children, and they seem to believe that, in order to move up, you need to move out of the settlement and into one of the middle-class neighbourhoods of Huancayo. The question arises, however, how and to what extent local practices of winning other people's affection, processes of connectivity, and techniques of being alert and of support will continue to grow and evolve in this transnational socio-cultural space. Only time will tell. In the meantime anthropologists and other social scientists concerned with internal and international migration must work towards an ethnographic understanding of the social fields in which migrants are immersed. A focus on mobile livelihoods and the social networks involved in sustaining various forms of mobility seems a fruitful point of departure. A search for gender-specific coping strategies may complement our knowledge of migration in future studies.

Acknowledgements

An earlier version of this chapter was presented at the 'Advanced Research Seminar', at the University of Wageningen, on 26 February 1999, and at the workshop on 'Migration and transnational theory re-examined' in Santo Domingo, 22–24 April 1999. I would like to thank all my colleagues for their contributions. Special thanks go to Norman Long and Alberto Arce for their commentaries and valuable suggestions, which helped me to focus my ideas for the analysis of my field material. Special thanks is also owed to Ulla Dalum Berg. In addition, I would like to thank Karen Fog Olwig and Ninna Nyberg Sørensen for their accurate comments and suggestions on the final version of this chapter. I owe great thanks to Flor Grados Kroon and Ann Long for their unconditional support at all times. The chapter was translated by Ninna Nyberg Sørensen.

Notes

1 The essay forms part of the project 'Migrant Networks, Livelihoods and the Cultural Construction of Community in the Central Highlands of Peru'. The project is currently in progress and is part of the agreement between Wageningen University of Holland, University of Tel Aviv, Israel, and the Catholic University of Peru. The objective of the project is centred on the exploration of the socio-cultural, economic and political impact

of international migration and globalization on the livelihoods, life-styles and forms of organization of local populations in urban marginal sectors in the city of Huancayo.

2 The case is one of six case studies carried out between September 1997 and October 1998 in the city of Huancayo.

3 The military government of Velasco (1968–75) nationalized all private enterprises.

4 This designation corresponds to different government policies over the last two decades. The APRA government (1985–90) legalized land occupations and offered benefits to these populations. During Velasco's regime they were called 'new towns'. During Fujimori's regime they were called 'self-managed urban communities'.

5 MPH based its action on a 'Property Regime' article of the 1979 Peruvian Constitution, stating the possibility of expropriation based on social interest. This article was abolished by the Constitution of 1993. A Human Settlement Act was issued in the mayor's office in December 1986. This act declared that 'the expropriation of the 54 Has. Mejorada Estate in favour of the Human Settlement Justicia, Paz y Vida was executed on the basis of public use and need' (Resolution No. 932-86-A-MPH, my translation).

6 In 2000 the case was being evaluated by COFOPRI (Commission for the Formalisation and Regulation of Informal Urban Land Property, created in 1998). For a long time it seemed that ownership of these lands would pass to the Peruvian State, since the supposed owners did not have the original property titles. The Fujimori government nevertheless supported the negotiations of the present leaders of the settlement (to win the approximately 5000 votes of the settlers) in the April elections. The first land titles were nevertheless granted before the elections, on March 18, when the first 100 families bought their plots.

7 The survey was carried out in two sectors of the settlement. Survey data was processed in the Report of the NIRP Project during the early phases of my fieldwork in Huancayo. This report is for internal use only.

8 Only 3 per cent are professionals working in state institutions or universities, but they seldom participate in the social and organizational dynamics of the settlement.

9 Thirty-seven per cent originated in rural communities fairly close to Huancayo (the high zones and other communities of the Mantaro Valley) and 22 per cent in southern provinces such as Ayacucho and Huancavelica.

10 Camila and all other personal names referred to in the text are pseudonyms.

11 At various points in time, JPV was the centre of a struggle for supremacy between the guerrilla groups of the Shining Path and the MRTA (Tupac Amaru Revolutionary Movement), followed closely by state security.

12 When Rita, the first daughter to leave for Italy, had established herself after eight months, she sent between USD 100 and USD 150 a month. When her sister Katy joined her in 1998, they were able to send more money. For example, in one month in 1998, they sent USD 1,500 to have a telephone installed in Camila's house (until then, they communicated over Juana's phone). Later the same year, they sent USD 3,500 to be deposited in Camila's bank account, together with another USD 2,000 for which Camila was instructed to buy amulets for her daughters and presents for their employers. Compared to the Peruvian minimum wage of 320 Soles (equivalent to USD 90), these are substantial sums that allow Camila to live comfortably with her remaining children.

13 The term casera refers to a continuous relationship between vendors and buyers. Regatear means to bargain when purchasing goods. To be good at bargaining was important in earning the acceptance of the group of lechugeras, who are always looking for a bargain and for other ways to save money.

14 Camila did her best to repay the presents sent by her daughters in Italy, and on these occasions shipped the items they had requested.

15 Léon and Rebeca Gringberg have pointed out that the reactions and feelings of those who stay behind when others migrate depend on the quality and intensity of the relationships that link them together. In the case of close relatives, a feeling of loss and abandonment

is often inevitable (Gringberg and Gringberg 1984: 83). In the case of Camila, and of many other families, distance rather seems to strengthen family and social bonds.

16 When, occasionally, I watched Camila throwing corn grains, she used special 'consecrated' corns of different colours. For this practice she usually chooses twelve white, twelve black and five of different colours (grey, red, yellow). The person in question and her/his relatives are represented by the coloured grains; white grains represent positive energy, black grains negative energy. If one of the coloured grains is surrounded by black ones, that person, according to Camila, is in danger of being surrounded by evil. Camila will then suggest that the person in question think hard. Which could be the problematic situation; who could be the person wishing evil?

17 Katty and Rita had decided to present themselves to the Questura de Milano (Police Office in charge of issuing residence permits) to negotiate their legal residence permits to work in Italy. The Italian government had passed an 'Amnesty Law' for all the illegal migrants who had arrived up until March 1998 to submit their applications by December 15 to obtain their soggiorno.

References

Altamirano, T. (1992) *Exodo: Peruanos en el Exterior*, Pontificia Universidad Católica del Perú: Fondo Editorial.

Altamirano, T. (1996) *Migración, el Fenómeno del Siglo: Peruanos en Europa, Japón y Australia*, Pontificia Universidad Católica del Perú: Fondo Editorial.

Glick Schiller, N., Basch, L. and Blanc Szanton C. (eds) (1992) *Towards a Transnational Perspective on Migration: Race, Class, Ethnicity and Nationalism Reconsidered*, New York: New York Academy of Sciences.

Gringberg, León, and Rebeca Grinberg (1984) *Psicoanálisis de la Migración y del Exilio*, Madrid: Alianza Editorial.

Gupta, Akhil, and James Ferguson (1997) 'Culture, power, place: Ethnography at the end of an era', in A. Gupta and J. Ferguson (eds) *Culture Power Place: Exploration in Critical Anthropology*, Durham, N. C., and London: Duke University Press: 1–32.

Hammersley, Martyn and Paul Atkinson (1995) *Ethnography: Principles in Practice*, (2nd edn) London and New York: Routledge.

Kearney, Michael (1995) 'The local and the global: The anthropology of globalization and transnationalism', *Annual Review of Anthropology* 24: 547–65.

Long, Norman, and Ann Long (1992) *Battlefields of Knowledge*, London: Routledge.

Long, Norman, and Bryan Roberts (1984) *Miners, Peasants and Entrepreneurs: Regional development in the Central Highlands of Peru*, Cambridge: Cambridge University Press.

Long, Norman, and Ann Long (1997) 'Agency and constraint, perceptions and practice. A theoretical position', in *Images and Realities of Rural Life*. Wageningen Perspectives on Rural Transformations, Van Gorcum, The Netherlands: 1–20.

Mallki, Lissa (1997) 'News and culture: Transitory phenomena and the fieldwork tradition', in *Anthropological Locations: Boundaries and Grounds of a Field Science*, University of California Press: 86–101.

MPH (1996) *Informe de Saneamiento Urbano*, Municipalidad Provincial de Huancayo.

Olwig, Karen Fog (1997) 'Hacia una Reconceptualización de la Migración y la Transnacionalización', in *Las Migraciones Internacionales en el Caribe: Estudios socials*, July–September 1997, Year XXX, No. 109.

Preston, P. W. (1996) *Development Theory: An Introduction*, Oxford: Blackwell: 301–3.

Paerregaard, Karsten (1997) *Linking Separate Worlds: Urban Migrants and Rural Lives in Peru*, Oxford: Berg.

Smith (1989) Livelihood *and Resistance: Peasants and the Politics of Land in Peru*, Berkeley, Los Angeles and Oxford: University of California Press.

Tamagno, Carla (1998) *Abriendo espacios . . . tejiendo redes: Desplazamiento y Reconstrucción en la Región Central*, Master Thesis, Pontificia Universidad Católica del Perú.

6 Business as usual

Livelihood strategies and migration practice in the Peruvian diaspora

Karsten Paerregaard

It is getting chilly as the afternoon wind starts blowing in the Californian desert. Walking towards the car, Victor shakes himself because of the cold. He is on his way back to Bakersfield after visiting a couple of Peruvians who are currently working in the desert on labour contracts as shepherds. The landscape in early spring reminds him of the high plains of the Peruvian Andes, where he herded cattle as a child. Yet, for Victor that belongs to the past. He used to work as a shepherd himself in the United States, but ran away before his labour contract expired. After a couple of years as illegal immigrant, he decided to abandon his wife and children in Peru and marry a Mexican woman. They now live together in Bakersfield, earning a living as tailors.

In another corner of the world, Cecilia is preparing the bed for the old Catalan woman she nurses in Barcelona. Here the sun set several hours ago, but the lights and noise from the streets keep most Catalans awake till late. Cecilia, however, finds little amusement in Barcelona. Except for one hour when she goes out to buy groceries, she spends the entire day with the woman for whom she is caring, a job she got thanks to the Spanish immigration policy that grants a number of job permits annually to Latin Americans and a few other immigrant groups to satisfy the growing demand for labour in domestic service in Spain. Although Cecilia makes more money in Spain than she could in Peru, home sickness and memories of her family back in the city of Trujillo constantly remind her that her stay in Spain is only temporary.

It is now morning in Japan, and the first rays of sunshine are appearing over Isezaki, northwest of Tokyo. Antonio has just left the Peruvian restaurant where he spends most Saturday nights singing karaoke and enjoying the company of other Latin American immigrants. Yet, unlike Cecilia, nostalgia does not torment Antonio. He came to Japan in 1990 in the same way his father travelled to Peru sixty years earlier, that is, as a contract worker. Today he is out of work, but he has no plans to return to Peru. Antonio declares laconically, 'My destiny is much like that of my father, only the "other way round" '.

The aim of this chapter is to examine aspects of continuity and change in the migration practices and livelihood strategies of Peruvian migrants in the United States, Spain and Japan. In particular, I want to examine whether Peruvians reproduce or change former relations of inequality when they migrate transnationally in search of new livelihoods, and to explore to what extent transnational migration practices empower them as social agents. My argument is that the extended livelihoods that Peruvian migrants create when migrating transnationally are embedded in social relations of three different kinds:

1   Patron–client relations that have conventionally been used as a means to recruit rural labour for haciendas, mines and domestic service in Peru;
2   Migrant networks that grow out of the massive rural–urban migration that Peru experienced in the twentieth century and that today links almost every village in the Andean hinterland of Peru to the country's major cities, and also, in recent years, many regions to destinations abroad;
3   Ties of kinship and marriage between members of the same household or extended family; these make up one of the most important resources for the lower and middle urban classes in Peru in forming migrant networks and creating new livelihoods in other parts of the world.

In a historical perspective, clientelism has been used to recruit rural workers from regions with a surplus of labour to regions where there is labour shortage. Once migrants have established their own networks, however, they tend to develop other ways of mobilizing labour through the horizontal bonds of village and ethnic loyalties or narrower household and kinship ties. Yet, as I shall demonstrate in this chapter, most migrants draw on all three kinds of social relations in their pursuit of new livelihoods, and although clientelism is no longer a dominant form of labour recruitment in Peru, it continues to be an important means of mobilizing Third World labour for the First World.

The data discussed in this chapter deal with three migration flows that in very different ways illustrate the huge span of livelihood and migration experiences in the Peruvian diaspora. Yet, despite considerable historical and geographical variation, all three flows continue existing migration and labour recruitment traditions in Peruvian history. In particular, the dominant role that not only migrant networks and household ties but also patron–client relations continue to play in Peruvians' transnational livelihood strategies is evidence of the strong persistence of their migration practices.

My argument is that the migration processes we nowadays label as transnational to a large extent continue earlier population movements or are integral parts of larger migration systems. Although modern technology has intensified travelling and communication worldwide on an unprecedented scale, this should not lead us to neglect important dimensions of persistence in long-term migration processes or earlier precursors of present-day transnationalism. Migrant networks and transnational connections in the contemporary world often grow out of former migration practices, and migrants also tend to reproduce former hierarchical relations in the search for new ways of making their living.

On the wide, lonely plains of the rocky mountain

In 1969 the Peruvian government implemented a land reform that in a few years expropriated most of the big haciendas in the country, including many foreign-owned estates that were converted into state-owned cooperatives. When the American staff of the Cerro de Pasco company in the central highlands returned to the United States in the early 1970s, a link was formed between the peasant population of Peru's central highland and sheep-ranchers in California, Oregon, Nevada, Utah, Colorado, Idaho, Montana and Wyoming. Most of these ranchers are organized in the Western Ranch Association (WRA) based in Sacramento, which is in charge of recruiting foreign labour as shepherds. This recruitment has now lasted for three decades and brought several thousand Peruvians to the Rocky Mountain area to work on three-year contracts as shepherds on so-called H-2A visas. Many have returned on a third, fourth or fifth contract, while others such as Victor have decided to stay and become illegal immigrants in the United States.

During the first half of the twentieth century, the WRA and other American recruitment agencies mainly contracted Basque shepherds. However, as the Spanish economy began to prosper in the 1970s, they lost interest in working for American ranchers. Subsequently, Mexicans and Chileans were brought in, and when former American employees of the big estates and sheep ranches in Peru returned to the United States in the wake of the land reform, the WRA also began to recruit Peruvians. Within a few years Peruvians had exceeded Mexicans, Chileans and Basques in numbers, and today migrants from ex-haciendas and peasant communities in Peru's central highlands make up the chief source of labour for American sheep-ranchers.[1]

Peruvian labour migration to the United States meets different economic needs and links distinct life worlds in the First and Third Worlds. At one end of the migration network, the economic and political crisis in Peru generates a constant supply of rural workers in desperate search for alternative sources of income. At the other end, the sheep-ranching industry in the United States looks for cheap labour to perform work shunned by North Americans. The two ends are connected through a migration flow of Peruvian herders who travel repeatedly between the United States and Peru. In the North the ranch-owners, WRA and American immigration authorities control the flow of Peruvians entering and leaving the United States on H-2A visas; in the South an informal network of family and household relations assures the reproduction of the labour force and provides new recruits.

The networks that link shepherds to their families in Peru have developed as extensions of already existing kinship ties between villagers in the highlands and urban migrants in such cities as Huancayo and Lima (Long and Roberts 1978: 31–6). These bonds grow out of a century-long rural–urban migration tradition in the central highlands, generating a constant interchange of products and services between migrants and their native villages (Mallon 1983: 247–67; G. Smith 1989: 96–111).[2] Today, most villagers migrate to the mines, the jungle or the cities while still young to make money and expand their knowledge of the world. Some eventually return to their native villages, but many marry and settle elsewhere.

This blend of rural and urban worlds also characterizes shepherds' migration networks, which recruit migrants of very different social and economic backgrounds. Although most migrants were born in pastoral villages in the central highlands and have an intimate knowledge of shepherding, their experience as herders is often limited to their rural childhood. Indeed, many of the migrants recruited by the WRA have lived in Huancayo, Lima or other cities for many years working as schoolteachers or in factories or made a living in commerce. Some have studied in universities in Huancayo or Lima, and a few even have academic degrees.

New recruits are usually recommended by migrants who either have completed a contract or are currently working in the United States. As most migrants are cautious about proposing candidates outside the close circle of household and family ties, entering a migrant network is the most difficult part of obtaining a work contract in the United States. Thus, when I did fieldwork in the Peruvian highlands, I was struck to hear young villagers deplore the fact that they had no relatives or kin to recommend them for a first contract. When I asked one young man whether he wanted to go to the United States, he replied, 'Sure I want to, but I have no one in the family there to summon me!' Obviously, the potential number of new recruits is much higher than those currently working in the United States.

For herders already in the United States, the situation looks different. As the renewal of a contract with the WRA is contingent upon the employer's recommendation, the herders do their utmost to stay on good terms with the ranchers. This desire to win employers' confidence is supported by the expectations of the herder's family in Peru that he will help other male relatives get to the United States. In particular, those who have been away for long periods of time or who are reaching the age of retirement come under strong pressure to help their sons, brothers, cousins or brothers-in-law obtain a contract before they return to Peru. Young males in Peru, on the other hand, are expected to make use of these unique opportunities. One herder in the United States explained to me that he went on his first contract because he was recommended by a close relative. All his brothers and most of his brothers-in-law were already working there. The man recounted that several family members put pressure on him, arguing that 'If they can do it, you can too! Think of what they are doing for you so you can go too'. At the heart of the herders' migration practice, then, lies a cultural economy built on trust that not only urges Peruvians to continue working in the United States and to call upon new family members, but is exploited by American ranch-owners and the WRA as a means of disciplining the herders to endure the harsh working conditions of the mountains and the desert, and to deter them from running away.

Three migration histories

In what follows, I present three migration histories that illustrate in different ways how migrants design livelihood strategies and exploit the opportunities that labour migration to the United States offers them. While Victor, whom I presented in the introduction to this chapter, opted to stay in the United States and create a new life, Eugenio held on to his original plan of returning to his native village in Peru and investing his savings in agriculture. Finally, Leonardo, who is currently working on his sixth contract as a shepherd, still has to decide whether to stay in the United States or return to Peru.

Victor, 45, was born in a village close to Junín in the central highlands of Peru. He was brought up in Pachacayo, a sheep ranch that belonged to the American-owned Cerro de Pasco Mining Corporation before the land reform. Victor's migration experience began when he moved to Lima as a young man to be apprenticed to tailor. Later he started his own tailor's workshop, got married and had several children. However, Peru's economic crisis in the late 1980s had a disastrous effect on Victor's business, and in 1991 he decided to go on his first contract to the United States through a recommendation from one of his brothers. His initial plan was to return to Peru after one or two contracts and settle down with his family, but in 1994 he changed his plans, overstaying his H-2A visa and becoming an illegal immigrant. He later married a Mexican woman who had US citizenship, which allowed Victor to become a legal resident. The couple currently lives in Bakersfield, not far from the ranch where Victor used to work as a shepherd. Together they make a living by running a little tailor's workshop.

Eugenio, 42, comes from Chala, a small village northwest of the city of Huancayo. He has four brothers who have all worked or are currently working in the United States. Eugenio left on his first contract in 1981 at the age of 21 through a recommendation from his oldest brother. He spent three years working for a Mormon rancher in Utah, returning to Peru in 1984. He stayed in Chala for seven months and then left on another contract. This time Eugenio worked for a Basque rancher in California, which turned out to be a rather unpleasant experience. After returning home in 1988, he remained in Chala for a period of five years. By 1993, however, he had spent the savings from the first two contracts, so he decided to migrate for a third time. Three years later, in 1996, he came back to Peru again and stayed in Chala for four months before leaving on his fourth contract. When Eugenio returned to Peru in 2000, the dream of his life eventually came true, and he bought a used tractor for USD 18,000.

Leonardo, 51, was raised in Quishuar, a peasant community southwest of Huancayo. As a child he learned how to herd cattle and became familiar with the solitude of the mountains. Before coming of age he migrated to Huancayo with his father. In 1976 he was recommended by a cousin, who was already working on his second contract in the United States. Upon his return he married and had a family in Peru, planning to settle down and set up a business in Huancayo after another contract or two. However, over the following twenty years Leonardo returned for another four contracts to work for the same employer in Wyoming, with whom he built up a relationship of mutual trust. In 1998 the employer offered Leonardo a sixth contract, this time without the intervention of the WRA, and helped him obtain a permanent work permit in the United States. This allows Leonardo to travel back and forth and stay as long he likes, and it may allow him to bring his wife and children to the United States one day.

The livelihood experiences of Peruvian shepherds in the Rocky Mountain area are embedded in two kinds of social relations: the clientelistic ties that migrants establish with American ranch-owners, similar to the relations of exploitation that existed in Peru's highland haciendas before the land reform, and the close kinship and marriage bonds that these migrants draw on to recruit new members for their networks. However, although Victor, Bernardo and Leonardo were all contracted through extended family relations, and although all three entered into patron–client relationships with their American employers, their use of existing migrant networks and livelihood opportunities is very different. Victor broke out of the patron–client relationship that bound him to his employer in the United States, quit his job as a shepherd and became first an illegal, and then a legal immigrant. Bernardo and Leonardo, on the other hand, continued to return for new contracts, thus reproducing the same kinds of relations of inequality and exploitation that are used to recruit labour in rural areas back home. Whereas Bernardo decided to cease transnational migration after four contracts, settle in his native village again and invest his savings in agriculture, Leonardo is hoping that his practice of continuous migration will eventually allow him to settle in the United States with his family.

On the noisy, dirty factory floors of Japan

When Japanese contractors started to appear in Peru in the late 1980s to hire factory workers for Japan's 'bubble' economy, they re-activated a migration flow that had originally started in 1899. Ironically, it was Japanese contractors who had facilitated the migration of *dekasegi* workers to Peru to work in the plantations on the country's Pacific coast a hundred years earlier. This first act in the Japanese–Peruvian migration flow lasted forty years, only to be interrupted by World War II. In a broader historical perspective, the transpacific link consisted of the massive exportation of Japanese labour to the Americas that began with the recruitment of female migrants for the sugar plantations in Hawaii in 1868, and was later extended with the emigration of male workers to the United States, Canada, Mexico and southward to Peru and neighbouring countries (Gardiner 1981: 3).

The importation of *Nikkeijin*[3] (descendants of Japanese emigrants) from South America as temporary foreign workers was encouraged by a new immigration law passed by the Japanese government in 1990 to satisfy the urgent need for labour in the country's industry (Shimada 1994: 21–30; Sellek 1997: 182–6). While the employment of non-Japanese had been banned up to 1990, the law recognized the problem of the growing number of illegal workers in the Japanese industry and allowed a limited introduction of foreign labour.[4] In particular, the law favoured second- and third-generation descendants of Japanese emigrants (including their spouses) from South American countries, who were granted formal residence status, thus enabling them to work in Japan legally (Sellek 1997: 184, 189). Other *Nikkeijin* categories were also considered potential candidates for temporary work and residence visas. Sellek reports that 'As a result of the revised law, in Sao Paulo between 1988 and 1991, the number of visas jumped from 8,602 to 61,500, and in Peru about 15 per cent of Peruvian *Nikkeijin* are thought to have gone through the formalities of emigration' (ibid.: 189). Currently, the number of Peruvians in Japan is 53,000, of whom approximately 11,000 are illegal immigrants, an immigrant community exceeded in number only by the Koreans, Chinese, Brazilians and Filipinos (Foreign Press Center, Japan 1999: 7; Peruvian Consulate in Tokyo 1999).[5]

Although the return migration programme launched by the 1990 law was targeted at people of Japanese descent, non-Japanese Peruvians have also migrated to Japan to work in factories in large numbers. Until the visa exemption for Peruvians was abolished in 1994, many entered as tourists; others travelled with forged papers or as the adopted relatives of *Nikkeijin*.[6] Initially, migrants were mostly male (79 per cent of all Peruvians migrating to Japan in 1991 were men), many single and with university degrees (Fukumoto 1997: 357). However, in the mid-1990s many foreign workers were laid off because of the economic crisis, and although Japan's economy is slowly recovering, unemployment is still high by Japanese standards. Moreover, as female labour is traditionally paid less than male labour in Japan, the industry now prefers to hire women instead of men, which has prompted a growing number of Peruvian female *Nikkeijin* to migrate.

Most Peruvians in Japan came as contract workers. They were contacted in Peru by Japanese *contratistas*, who not only offered them a work contract with an employer in Japan but also arranged tickets, visa applications and accommodation in Japan. Many remained indebted to the *contratistas* for long periods after their arrival in Japan and had to pay back the loans at exorbitant rates of interest. Those who could afford it paid for the contract and the trip before migrating, but they were often cheated by the *contratista* running off with the money (Fukumoto 1997: 355–62). Yet others travelled to Japan on their own but were forced to ask local Japanese *contratistas* to help them find work and lodging when they arrived because they lacked the language skills to do it themselves. Indeed, in the early 1990s, before Peruvians had established their own immigrant community in Japan, the newcomers' dependence on the *contratistas* was reminiscent of the patron–client relations that had brought their Japanese ancestors to Peru originally. Not only did their future position on the Japanese labour market entirely depend on the brokers, but these brokers took care of almost all their needs, including accommodation, transportation, and even daily shopping. Furthermore, because only a few of the migrants spoke Japanese, they could only communicate with their employers and the local authorities through the brokers. One Peruvian *Nikkeijin* told me that, when he arrived in 1990, he was sent straight to Mooka in the department of Iberaki to work in a factory there. He recounts that 'There were no other foreigners and no one to talk to. The only person who knew us was the *contratista*.'

Today, more than 60 per cent of Peruvians engaged in Japanese industry are still contract workers employed by brokers. This places fewer responsibilities on the employer and allows for greater employment flexibility. Moreover, migrants are not merely paid less than their Japanese counterparts, but are less likely to be promoted and more vulnerable than native workers when companies have to lay off labour in times of crisis (Takenaka 1999: 1465). During the first years of immigration, many foreign workers were employed in the car industry and the electrical appliance industry. As the majority of Peruvian *Nikkeijin* had been self-employed in Peru before migrating, working on the factory floor was a hard and difficult experience for many (ibid.: 1466). Today most Peruvian immigrants work in smaller companies that provide spare parts or components for larger factories, which makes their position on the labour market even more unstable and insecure (Fukumoto 1997: 357). Thus, one Peruvian *Nikkeijin* in Isezaki in the department of Gunma told me that when he was fired in 1998 by the factory where he had been working for a number of years, his wife and son returned to Peru. He said, 'I was worried that the *contratista* would send me to Nagano for some weeks and then to some other remote place to work. I didn't think it would be good for my family to travel so much, so I sent them back to Peru'. However, he added, 'Two weeks after they returned to Peru, the *contratista* offered me a new job here in Isezaki'.

A decade after the *Nikkeijin* migration to Japan began, most Peruvians still have little interaction with Japanese society because of language barriers and their marginal position in the job market. Moreover, many foreign workers in Japan, including *Nikkeijin*, complain of discrimination and prejudice. One Japanese Peruvian explained to me: 'Here all Peruvians are *gaijin* [foreigners in Japanese], whether *cholos*, *negros* or *nisseis* [urbanized Indians, Blacks or *Nikkeijin*].' Indeed, the encounter with the country of their ancestors and the experience of being *gaijin* in Japanese society have radically altered the notion that many Peruvian *Nikkeijin* had of being Japanese and Peruvian before migrating.[7] As Takenaka points out, 'The transformation of Japanese Peruvians' ethnic identity first involved the denial of their Japanese identity in return migrating to Japan' (1999: 1466). Or as one Peruvian told me, 'I came to Japan in 1989. At that time we *nissei* felt different and somehow more privileged than all the illegal Peruvians. Today we feel much the same'.[8]

Over the past decade many *Nikkeijin* households have extended their close kinship and marriage ties across the Pacific toward members living scattered in Peru as well as Japan. In effect, most newcomers are now aided by relatives already in Japan, who arrange the necessary paper work and offer them economic support to travel. Transnational networks have also been created between *Nikkeijin* organizations in Peru and the emerging community of Peruvians in Japan that make it possible for immigrants to acquire Peruvian products, rent video copies of films with Spanish subtitles and Peruvian television programmes, and send remittances back to relatives in Peru. Moreover, a growing number of Japanese *contratistas* are being replaced by brokers of *Nikkeijin* origin, which improves migrants' positions in negotiating their work contracts.[9] However, because of the Japanese government's strict immigration policy and the lack of alternative job opportunities for immigrants, the emergence of transnational networks and the formation of a Peruvian community in Japan are not likely to alter immigrants' position in the Japanese labour market or change the clientelistic relationship between Peruvians (particularly those of non-Japanese descent who are illegals) and the *contratistas*. For most *Nikkeijin* it is still extremely difficult to escape patron–client relationships with the brokers who facilitated their migration and helped them find work in Japan.

Three migration histories

Although Peruvians in Japan are subjected to the same structural constraints, the three following migration histories suggest that the strategies that migrants pursue and the tactical manoeuvres they engage in to achieve their goals vary greatly. While Antonio, whom I introduced at the start of this chapter, has opted to stay in Japan, Marco decided to return to Peru. He later re-migrated to California, where Peruvian *Nikkeijin* have established their own migrant community separate from other Peruvian and Latin American immigrants. By contrast, Roberto, who is a Peruvian of non-*Nikkeijin* origin and is therefore living in Japan illegally, is planning to go to Italy, where his wife and daughters are working.

Antonio is painfully aware of the irony of his family history. His father and mother left Japan in 1934 on the same boat that brought the parents' of former President Fujimori to Peru. They came from Fukushima in Northern Japan and were hired by a Japanese *contratista* to work in Peru's sugar plantations. The father managed to pay back his *enganche* debt within a couple of years and was then successful in saving enough capital to buy land in Huaral, north of Lima. After finishing school, Antonio got a good job at the office of Nissan's Peruvian branch in Lima. However, as he wished to make a career in the car industry and his father knew of a Japanese *contratista* looking for workers from Peru, Antonio decided to try his luck in Japan. To his regret, he ended up as a factory worker in Japan's 'bubble' economy together with thousands of other *Nikkeijin*, not as a white-collar worker as the *contratista* had promised. The *enganche* practice has changed little since his father migrated to Peru almost seven decades ago. Today, after five different factory jobs in Japan, Antonio has retired at the age of 48. He added bitterly, 'They only want young people today, preferably women'. Still he plans to stay in Japan together with his three children, who migrated from Peru during the 1990s.

Marco, 41, is the grandson of two Japanese emigrants who came to Peru in 1914 in search of a better future. He was born in Lima, where he went to school and later studied to be a psychologist. Although Marco never graduated, he later got a job as a schoolteacher. However, Peru's economic crisis in the late 1980s forced him to find new ways to make a living, and in 1989 he emigrated to Japan on a work contract arranged by a Japanese broker. Although he had several remote relatives in Japan, he never felt at home there, and after two years working in factories he returned to Peru in 1991. The same year he re-emigrated, this time to California, where his *Nikkeijin* wife has a sister. Today he lives in Los Angeles with his family, making a living as a gardener. He explains that most Peruvian *Nikkeijin* in California work as gardeners 'because that's what is expected of Japanese migrants here'. His family is scattered on both sides of the Pacific. His oldest brother lives in Japan, where he works as a factory worker, while two younger sisters are still in Peru.

Before migrating, Roberto, 46, worked as a truck driver in Peru. In 1990 he decided to emigrate after being laid off. One year later he travelled to Japan on a tourist visa, which he overstayed, becoming an illegal immigrant. Unlike Peruvian *Nikkeijin*, Roberto cannot obtain a work permit or permanent residence in Japan legally because he is not of Japanese descent. Yet although he lacks legal identity papers, he has had little trouble finding work. He says that it is always possible to find *contratistas* who are willing to hire illegal workers: 'They pay you less and you are always in danger of being caught by the police, but it is still worth it'. He says that the hardest thing about being an illegal is that he has not seen his family for eight years. However, Roberto does not plan to stay in Japan for long. His wife and two daughters travelled to Italy in 1999, and Roberto hopes to follow them within a short time. Although he knows little about Italy or Europe in general, he is looking forward to being united with his family. He asserts that 'In Italy we can all get work as domestic servants taking care of old people. I hope I'll have a better life there than here'.

Antonio, Marco and Roberto were recruited into Japanese industry in the early 1990s through the same *enganche* system. Patron–client relationships (made necessary by Japanese immigration policy and cultural prejudice against foreigners) have restricted all three of them in changing jobs, integrating into Japanese society and ascending in the social hierarchy. Yet, although they faced the same structural constraints, their livelihood and migration experiences turned out very differently. Antonio sardonically observes the irony of his father's and his own experiences with the *enganche* system, but he has adopted a new identity as a *gaijin* or 'guest worker' in Japan and plans to stay there. Marco, on the other hand, decided to break out of the patron–client relationship that coaxed him into going to Japan and to return to Peru. Instead of transforming himself into a conventional return migrant, however, he engaged in a second migration attempt to the United States, this time through his kinship and marriage network rather than the patron–client relationships that enticed him and thousands of other Peruvian *Nikkei* to toil on Japanese factory floors in the early 1990s. Today, the same *Nikkei* background has helped Marco find work as a gardener in Los Angeles. Unlike Antonio and Marco, Roberto cannot claim any ethnic capital in Japan, where only Peruvians of *Nikkei* origin are allowed to work legally. Although the option of making a living as an illegal is not only extremely limited but also very risky, Roberto regards his last eight years in Japan as highly profitable. Yet, he plans to continue his migration trajectory by travelling to Italy, where he expects to be reunited with his wife and children and find work as a domestic servant, this time by making use of his Peruvian background.

In the timeless, grey sitting rooms of Catalonia

Until recently, scholars agreed that most population movements take the form of labour migration and that most migrants are men. However, since the mid-1980s the idea of migration as a largely male phenomenon has been seriously questioned, and a growing number of researchers now regard women migrants as agents who are playing 'an increasingly important role in all types of migration in all regions of the world' (Campani 2000: 147). In this new feminization of migration, 'it is not the case that women migrants migrate primarily as dependants or for family reunification. Instead, women migrants are more often than not a main source of family support and see their role in terms of a family strategy' (Anthias 2000: 24). This change in the gender pattern of international migration is caused partly by already existing processes of rural–urban migration and the presence of a huge sector of unemployed or underpaid female labour in the Third World, and partly by changes in the economies of the First World, where the incorporation of women into national labour markets has created a growing demand for domestic service (Phizacklea 1998: 32–4).

The visibility of women in transnational migration is particularly salient in Southern Europe, where economic prosperity in the 1980s and 1990s has prompted many women to take jobs outside the family and thus created an urgent need for imported female labour to do domestic work.[10] Moreover, the growing flow of female labour into Spain, Italy and Greece during the past fifteen years demands attention because it is occurring at the same time as Spaniards, Italians and Greeks have stopped migrating to Northern Europe for work. Indeed, Southern Europe's sudden change from being emigrant societies to being host countries for foreign immigration has happened so fast that most governments still are struggling to develop coherent immigration policies (King 2000; King and Black 1997; Anthias and Lazaridis 1999; Petrillo 1999; Escrivá 2000). Meanwhile, the number of both legal and illegal immigrants continues to increase, and today Spain has a foreign population of 850,000, Italy one of around one million, and Greece of half a million (Anthias and Lazaridis 2000: 2). Anthias and Lazaridis note that much of this migration is illegal and that 'many of these migrants are women, coming in as domestic maids or as "cabaret" artists'. They also point out that these 'women usually are found in the lowest levels of the employment hierarchy in the service industry' (ibid.: 4), and that many 'are on short-term contracts or are undocumented, subjected to the vagaries of their employers' (ibid.: 6).

Although immigration to Spain is low compared to immigration to Italy or Greece, it has caused much political attention among native Spaniards because of the high number of illegal immigrants concentrated in a few national groups (Arango 2000: 259–61; Driessen 1998). Thus the country's foreign labour force is composed to a large extent of Moroccans working mostly in agriculture and construction, Latin Americans – mainly Dominicans and Peruvians working in Madrid and Barcelona as domestic servants – and to a lesser extent of other African and Asian nationals. This specialization in livelihoods within the migrant labour force is clearly reflected in the gender composition of the three immigrant groups: 83 per cent of the Moroccans are men, while 80 per cent of the Dominicans and 65 per cent of the Peruvians are women (King and Rodríguez-Melguizo 1999; Ribas-Mateos 2000: 177, 181).[11]

The Foreigner Law adopted by Spain in 1985 not long after the country entered the European Common Market reflects the country's strong historical links with its ex-colonies by granting Latin Americans and citizens of other countries that have a Spanish colonial past special rights to apply for residence and work permits (Escrivá 2000: 202). In response to the growing inflow of illegal migrants, the Spanish government established a system of annual regularization of foreign workers in 1991 that grants a limited number of one-year work permits to immigrants from outside the EU. Initially, these permits were restricted to specific occupations and geographical areas and were mainly reserved for Moroccan workers to satisfy the need for seasonal labour in agriculture. A similar quota system has been applied by different Spanish governments since 1993 in granting a growing number of work permits to the domestic industry (Arango 2000: 264–73). This development has confirmed the privileged status of Dominicans and Peruvians especially in Spanish immigration policy.[12]

Although the presence of Peruvians in Spain is far from new, their role in the country's recent transformation from an emigrant to an immigrant society calls for attention. During the 1950s and 1960s, it was mostly sons from Lima's middle- and upper-class families who travelled to Spain to study medicine or law at the country's universities.[13] Since the late 1980s, however, the migration flow has been dominated by poor working-class women from Peru's urban shanty towns (mostly in Lima and the northern coast towns such as Trujillo) migrating in search of work. In the late 1980s and early 1990s, many of these female immigrants took over the positions that Philippine and Portuguese workers previously occupied as domestic servants in Spanish upper-class families. More recently, this immigration has been fuelled by an urgent need for imported female workers to replace younger generations of Spanish women, who increasingly prefer to take work outside the home. Peruvians now constitute the second largest immigrant group in Spain (Escrivá 2000: 207), and Peruvian women 'are preferred to other foreigners because they often have training or knowledge of the health professions, they behave respectfully toward the elderly and they have Spanish skills' (Escrivá 1997: 54).[14]

Women's role in modern Peruvian migration history dates back to the early twentieth century, when young girls from Peru's Andean hinterland started to migrate to Lima and other cities in search of work as domestics. Most of these women were drawn to Lima through already existing rural–urban migrant networks before coming of age. They had little or no education, and many were unfamiliar with the Spanish language (their mother tongue being Quechua). In the 1950s some of these rural–urban female migrants were brought to the United States by their Peruvian or American employers, who were then moving to Miami and other North American cities.

Although women continued to play a dominant role in Peruvian population movements in the 1990s, the social and political context of recent migration flows towards Southern Europe differs from that of previous migration movements to North America in the 1950s and 1960s. Unlike the latter, which developed as extensions of ongoing rural–urban migratory processes in Peru and were spearheaded by rural women who had little or no educational training and were brought to the United States as legal workers by their employers in Lima, the pioneers of contemporary migration to Spain and other Southern European countries are women from Peru's urban working classes, who are often trained in health, education and similar fields, and who rarely have previous experience as domestic servants in Peru. Most of them have travelled illegally and only recently started to form legal and more stable migrant communities in major cities in Spain and Italy (Escrivá 2000: 222). Escrivá describes this form of movement as 'solo' or 'autonomous' migration, because the women act on their own initiative and migrate alone (ibid.: 213, 216, 222). However, she also contends that 'women's migration may be part of a family strategy to survive or to maintain and increase their social position and improve their living condition' (ibid.: 213) and adds that 'There is a linkage of female migration, not so much to expectations of climbing a career ladder, but to the career and survival of others: children, parents, brothers and sisters, even husband' (ibid.: 215). In other words, most of these women are what has been called 'target migrants' (i.e. they migrate for shorter periods of time with the aim of making money), whose principal objective is the welfare of others rather than their own immediate needs, such as obtaining legal residence, changing social status or improving their living conditions in the host country.

Despite the fact that migrant women with previous professional training experience a downward process of deskilling by taking domestic work, which in Peru is considered work for rural women from the Andean hinterland and is thus poorly paid, domestic work has become 'accepted as one of the best forms of employment' (ibid.: 216). Moreover, the loss of status and downward occupational mobility in Spain is experienced as the very condition of migration because of the rigid immigration policy pursued by the Spanish government, which leaves Peruvian women with no other opportunity than domestic service, in particular the caring of old people.[15] Recent transnational migration to Southern Europe, then, has spurred these young, semi-professional urban women to engage in livelihoods conventionally reserved for rural uneducated women and to assume the pioneer role formerly occupied by female migrants from Peru's Andean hinterland. It has also pushed them into an occupation that is still dominated by clientelistic relationships, not only in Peru but also in Mediterranean countries. Thus, the domestic servant industry in Spain 'is a sector without the same legal rights enjoyed by other workers', where live-in servants are submitted to 'quasi-servile relationships' (Escrivá 2000: 216), and 'suffer isolation in the work place' (ibid.: 209).[16] The vulnerable position of many Peruvian women in Spain is underscored by their lack of legal rights as temporary migrant workers and thus dependence on their employers to renew their work permits.[17] As Anthias points out, 'Few domestic maids have a migration status separate from their work entitlement on entry as domestic workers, and they are therefore vulnerable; if they leave their employer, they could be deported' (2000: 26).

Three migration histories

The following three migration histories reflect the range in livelihood experiences of migrant women in the 1990s, who migrated at a time of economic crisis in Peru and immigration control in Europe. Vanesa, who left Peru in 1991, belongs to a group of migrant pioneers who spearheaded Peruvian migration to Europe. Today she lives with her husband and child in Barcelona and claims that she has no wish to return to Peru. Cecilia, on the other hand, whose migration experience in

Barcelona was presented briefly in the introduction to this chapter, came to Spain in 1994. Although she wants to return to Peru, the situation there obliges her to stay in Spain and send money back to her family. By contrast, Amelia, who travelled to Spain a few years after Cecilia, decided to quit her job in Barcelona and return to Peru.

Since Vanesa, 28, went to school in the city of Trujillo on the northern coast of Peru, she had dreamt of migrating to *progresar* (make progress). After graduating she got work as a nursing assistant in a hospital in Trujillo. In 1991 she decided to go to Spain, where a couple of remote cousins were living. Three months after her arrival, Vanesa overstayed her tourist visa and joined the growing community of illegal immigrants in Barcelona. There she found a job as domestic servant in the home of a Catalan family and rented a room with a female relative of Telmo, her boyfriend back in Trujillo. In 1992 Telmo followed her. Today he works in a factory making what he considers a reasonable salary, while Vanesa has three part-time jobs as a cleaner for retired Catalan women. They live in a rented flat together with Marc, their two-year-old child, who was born in Spain and is thus a Spanish citizen. Vanesa claims that she sees no future in returning to Peru. She says, 'I have to look forward and think of the future of my son. And as long as I'm in Spain I can support my family in Peru. Telmo has a good employer, and I can always make money as domestic. So why go home?'

Cecilia was 23 years when she came to Spain in search of work in 1994. Before migrating, Cecilia had studied to become a nurse in Trujillo and worked as a laboratory assistant. However, because of her low salary Cecilia decided to emigrate. The decision was taken together with her two older sisters, who had already made arrangements to travel to Japan. They agreed to go abroad for a period of three years each to save money to support their parents and to pay for the studies of their two younger brothers in Peru. In Spain, a cousin who was already working in Barcelona helped Cecilia find a retired Catalan lady who was looking for a domestic servant to nurse her. Cecilia then returned to Peru and applied for a work permit at the Spanish embassy, which she was granted after a two-month waiting period. This allowed her to travel to Spain again, this time legally, with a one-year permit to do domestic work. Although the woman Cecilia looks after treats her well, she suffers from solitude and homesickness. Most of the time Cecilia thinks about her family in Peru. She says, 'I'm concerned about my younger brothers in Peru. I hope they will be able to study and find work. That's why I send all my money back to them. I don't feel well here and I want to go home soon'. She adds that 'In Spain I work to forget myself'.

Amelia, 56, has spent most of her life in Peru, where she grew up and spent her youth in Mendoza, a provincial town in the northern department of Amazonas. At the age of 17 she got a job as teacher in the local school, a profession that became her livelihood after she moved to Lima ten years later together with her parents and nine siblings. The family's move to Lima was part of an extensive rural–urban migration network that has pulled thousands of mendozinos to Lima in the past three decades. In 1995 Amelia travelled to Spain to visit her four siblings living in Barcelona. Initially, she planned to stay for a short time, but when an old Catalan woman offered her a job as a domestic servant, Amelia decided to stay. Although the employer first contracted Amelia to clean and cook, she soon learned to appreciate her company and hence decided to hire another immigrant from Ecuador to do the domestic work. In effect, Amelia was promoted to be the employer's personal companion. However, in spite of this improvement in her working conditions, Amelia quit the job after two years and returned to Peru. She asks, 'Why should I continue to work for the lady? She needed me more than I needed her. She keeps writing, asking me to come back. But I have my pension as a schoolteacher in Peru, and I can always go back to Barcelona and get another job'.

Although Vanesa, Cecilia and Amelia all migrated to Spain to work as domestics, none of them had any previous experience in this field; indeed, they all have a background as semi-professionals in Peru (Vanesa as a nursing assistant, Cecilia as a laboratory assistant and Amelia as a schoolteacher). Similarly, they all travelled to Spain on their own initiative with the help of relatives (Vanesa's remote cousins, Cecilia's close cousin and Amelia's siblings). However, despite these similarities, and although all three women have experienced the same legal obstacles and restrictions in the job market in Spain, their situations today are very different. Vanesa, who was granted legal residence in Spain shortly after her arrival and is therefore allowed to take any job she wants, works for several employers and feels content with the salary she makes. She is now well settled in Spain with her husband and son and has no wish to return to Peru. Cecilia, on the other hand, continues to work for the same employer and has little hope of changing her job or improving her living conditions in the near future. By contrast, Amelia, who currently lives in Peru on the pension she receives as retired schoolteacher, expects to obtain permanent residence and permission to work in Spain within a year or two, which will allow her to return to look for work as domestic whenever she wants.

Conclusion

There is ample proof in the social science literature that the current transformation of local–global relations entails uprooting, migration and hybridization in the First as well as the Third Worlds (Appadurai 1991; Kearney 1996; Rouse 1991) and that these changes enable people to create transnational links and communities (Basch *et al.* 1994; Guarnizo and Smith 1998). Yet, migration processes in the contemporary world are far from being always synonymous with globalization, transnationalism, diasporization, etc. As Portes, Guarnizo and Landolt point out, 'if all or most things that immigrants do are defined as "transnationalism", then none is because the term becomes synonymous with the total set of experiences of this population' (1999: 219). In order to define more precisely what these terms mean, we need to know how and to what extent population movements that are labelled transnational migration in the current literature differ from other forms of migration (previous international migration practices, rural–urban migration, labour migration, etc.). Likewise, we need to explore the specific circumstances that make people engage in global mobility, choose places of destination and establish transnational connections. Finally, we need to examine ethnographically the implications of transnational migration for everyday lives and livelihood activities (Mahler 1998: 81–2).

Peruvian migration history encourages us to be cautious in theorizing transnationalism as a recent phenomenon. While it is true that contemporary migration processes are fuelled by technological developments in means of transportation and communication, this should not lead us to ignore central aspects of persistency and continuity in global population movements or forget that these are often extensions of existing rural–urban migrant networks or inversions of former international migration processes. Similarly, the data suggest that recent attempts to define transnationalism as an independent social movement of Third World migrants ('transnationalism from below') that can be distinguished from other, more dominant and elitist transnational currents ('transnationalism from above') run the risk of examining migration processes in isolation from the structural constraints and power relations that shape these movements. Thus, it is evident from my material that patron–client relationships, legitimized and reinforced by migrants' own rural–urban networks and kinship and marriage bonds, still play a crucial role as mechanisms in recruiting migrant labour in contemporary Peruvian migration processes. Although labour migrants today pursue different strategies and are met with different structural constraints than their predecessors in Peruvian migration history, many of them submit themselves to patron–client relations similar to those that were used to recruit labour for the haciendas and mines in the highlands and coasts of Peru and to do domestic work for middle- and upper-class families in Lima. However, the nine migrant histories presented here also indicate that there is space for individual agency in transnational migration processes and that migrants may to some extent influence the course of their own lives and thus empower themselves by pursuing their own strategies and engaging in tactical manoeuvres.

Notes

1 Peruvians in California report that the WRA also tried to import shepherds from Mongolia. However, they stopped the recruitment because of language difficulties.
2 For a further discussion of rural–urban migration in Peru, see Paerregaard 1997.
3 Generally, *Nikkeijin* refers to all descendants of Japanese who emigrated abroad between 1968 and 1973. However, 'in the context of the issue of foreign migrant workers in Japan, the term *Nikkeijin* refers specifically to South American Japanese descendants up to the third generation and their spouses, mainly those from Brazil and Peru' (Sellek 1997: 178).
4 Most illegal workers take so-called 3D jobs ('dirty, dangerous and difficult'), in Japanese 3K jobs (*kitanai* [dirty], *kitsui* [tedious], and *kiken* [dangerous]), which are shunned by younger Japanese workers (Fukumoto 1997: 355; Sellek 1997: 182). In 1990 the number of illegal workers was estimated to be 30,000, a mere drop in the ocean of Japan's total work force of over 65 million (Shimada 1994: 24–5). In 1999 the number of foreign workers was estimated to be 271,000 (Foreign Press Center of Japan 1999: 59).
5 Other immigrant groups come from Pakistan, Bangladesh, Iran, Thailand and Malaysia (Sellek 1997: 182).

6 Peruvian *Nikkeijin* recount that, in the heyday of immigration in the early 1990s, flights arrived at Tokyo's airport full of Peruvians who all happened to be 'brothers or sisters'. Many entered with forged passports or *koseki*, Japanese family registers, which they had purchased from Japanese families in Peru (Takenaka 1999: 1461). Some non-*Nikkeijin* even underwent eye surgery before leaving Peru in order to look more Japanese and thus avoid being detected as illegal immigrants in Japan (Fukumoto 1997: 358). Fukumoto estimates that more than 50 per cent of all Peruvians in Japan are *falsos Nikkei*, that is, fake nikkei (ibid.).

7 Sellek suggests that 'At first glance, the position of *Nikkeijin* in Japan is comparable to, for example, the *Aussiedler* (ethnic Germans) living in parts of East Europe' and continues: 'Similarly, certain European states, notably Italy, Portugal, Germany and Spain, permit Latin American descendants of European immigrants to take up employment'. However, Sellek concludes, 'the *Nikkeijin* do differ from these other ethnic immigrants (. . .). The *Nikkeijin* generally have had less contact with relatives in Japan than has been the case with Latin Americans of European origin' (1997: 203).

8 Takenaka reports that the 'ethnic denial' experienced by Peruvian *Nikkeijin* in Japan has been transmitted to Lima through personal communication and the ethnic media. As a result, 'Japanese Peruvians in Lima, regardless of their migratory experience, have come to perceive a greater distance from the Japanese. They have learned that the image of "good, old Japan" that has served as the principal identity of the community no longer exists. The Japanese simply have ceased to be the reference group for the community' (1999: 1466).

9 However, the replacement of Japanese brokers by *Nikkeijin*, is also used by many employers to lay off migrant workers in times of crisis.

10 Anthias and Lazaridis state that 'There are at least 6.4 million women in Europe who are not full citizens of the countries where they live. It is estimated that there are more than one million domestic workers who are dependent on the goodwill of their employers' (2000: 17).

11 A similar feminization of Peruvian immigration can be observed in Italy, where 70 per cent of Peruvians are women (Campani 2000: 150).

12 In 1998 the total number of permits that the Spanish government granted to immigrants from non-EU countries was 28,000 with 9,154 in agriculture and catering, 1,069 in construction, 16,836 in services, and 941 in others (Escrivá 2000: 205).

13 One of the oldest Peruvian organizations in Spain is the Centro Peruano in Barcelona. Formed in 1963 on the initiative of Peruvian migrants who came to Spain to study and later decided to stay, this organization still plays a dominant role in the Peruvian community in Barcelona. The current president is a lawyer who migrated to Spain in 1978. His father, who came to Spain to study medicine in the 1950s, was also president of the organization for a number of years.

14 In recent years, a growing number of Peruvian migrant men have also been hired to nurse elderly Spaniards and Catalans.

15 Ribas-Mateos, who studies Filipino and other immigrant groups in Spain, suggests that the country in particular attracts female migrants from the Third World because of its immigration policy and need for domestic workers (2000: 181). She remarks that 'it is interesting to see how men are over-represented in Filipino migration to other countries in contrast to Italy and Spain. It is the demand for live-in maids, as well as the quota system from the Spanish government, which determine this feminized flow from Asian and Latin-American countries' (ibid.).

16 Campani argues that 'one of the key reasons for the high demand for domestic helpers in Southern Europe is the increasing rates of professional activity and mobility among Southern European women themselves, combined with the deficit in social services to support working women' (2000: 150). She adds that 'This archaic relationship of master-servant can also be interpreted as the product of an over-rapid and incomplete "modernization", without the progressive interiorization of the values of what one

might term the "social democratic" model of the industrial or post-industrial society'
(ibid. 151).
17 Lazaridis reports that in parts of Greece it is not unusual for employers to keep the
passports and other documents of their Filipino domestic servants to prevent them from
running away (2000: 63). A Peruvian woman who came to the United States in 1939 told
me that this practice was also common in Miami when Peruvian and America families
began to bring in Andean women as domestic workers in the 1950s and 1960s.

References

Anthias, Floya (2000) 'Metaphors of home: Gendering new migrations to southern Europe',
in F. Anthias and G. Lazaridis (eds) *Gender and Migration in Southern Europe: Women
on the Move*, 15–48, Oxford: Berg.

Anthias, Floya, and Grabriella Lazaridis (1999) 'Introduction. Into the margins: Migration
and exclusion in southern Europe', in F. Anthias and G. Lazaridis (eds) *Into the Margins:
Migration and Exclusion in Southern Europe*, 1–12, Aldershot: Ashgate.

Anthias, Floya and Gabriella Lazaridis (2000) 'Introduction: Women in the move in southern
Europe', in F. Anthias and G. Lazaridis (eds) *Gender and Migration in Southern Europe:
Women on the Move*, 1–14, Oxford: Berg.

Appadurai, Arjun (1991) 'Global ethnoscapes: Notes and queries for a transnational
"anthropology"', in R. Fox (ed.) *Recapturing Anthropology: Working in the Present*,
191–210, Santa Fe: School for American Research Press.

Arango, Joaquín (2000) 'Becoming a country of immigration at the end of the twentieth
century: The case of Spain', in R. King, G. Lazaridis and C. Tsardanidis (eds) *Eldorado
or Fortress? Migration in Southern Europe*, 253–76, London: Macmillan Press.

Basch, Linda, Nina Glick Schiller and Christina Szanton-Blanc (1994) *Nations Unbound:
Transnational Projects, Postcolonial Predicaments, and Deterritorialized Nation-States*,
Langhorne, PA: Gordon & Breach.

Campani, Guivanna (2000) 'Immigrant women in southern Europe: Social exclusion,
domestic work and prostitution in Italy', in R. King, G. Lazaridis and C. Tsardanidis (eds)
Eldorado or Fortress? Migration in Southern Europe, 145–69, London: Macmillan.

Driessen, Henk (1998) 'The "New Immigration" and the transformation of the European–
African border', in T. Wilson and H. Donnan (eds) *Border Identities: Nation and States
at International Frontiers*, 96–116, Cambridge: Cambridge University Press.

Escrivá, Angeles (1997) 'Control, composition and character of new migration to south-west
Europe: The case of Peruvian women in Barcelona', *New Community* 23(1): 43–57.

Escrivá, Angeles (2000) 'The position and status of migrant women in Spain', in F. Anthias
and G. Lazaridis (eds) *Gender and Migration in Southern Europe: Women on the Move*,
199–226, Oxford: Berg.

Foreign Press Center of Japan (1999) *Facts and Figures of Japan*, Tokyo: Foreign Press
Center/Japan.

Fukumoto, Mary (1997) *Hacia un Nuevo Sol: Japoneses y sus Descendientes en el Perú*,
Lima: Asociación Peruano Japonesa del Perú.

Gardiner, Harvey (1981) *Pawns in a Triangle of Hate: The Peruvian Japanese and the
United States*, Seattle: University of Washington Press.

Guarnizo, Luis E. and P. Michael Smith (1998) 'The locations of transnationalism', in
M. Smith and Guarnizo (eds) *Transnationalism from Below: Comparative Urban and
Community Research* 6: 64–102, New Brunswick: Transaction Publishers.

Kearney, Michael (1996) *Reconceptualizing the Peasantry: Anthropology in Global Perspective*, Boulder: Westview Press.

King, Russell (2000) 'Southern Europe in the changing global map of migration', in R. King, G. Lazaridis and C. Tsardanidis (eds) *Eldorado or Fortress? Migration in Southern Europe*, 1–26, London: Macmillan Press.

King, Russell, and Isabel Rodríguez-Melguizo (1999) 'Recent immigration to Spain: The case of Moroccans in Catalonia', in F. Anthias and G. Lazaridis (eds) *Into the Margins: Migration and Exclusion in Southern Europe*, 55–82, Aldershot: Ashgate.

King, Russell, and Richard Black (eds) (1997) *Southern Europe and the New Immigrations*, Brighton: Sussex Academic Press.

Lazaridis, Gabriella (2000) 'Filipino and Albanian women migrant workers in Greece: Multiple layers of oppression', in F. Anthias and G. Lazaridis (eds) *Gender and Migration in Southern Europe: Women on the Move*, 49–80, Oxford: Berg.

Long, Norman and Bryan Roberts (1978) 'Introduction', in N. Long and B. Roberts (eds) *Peasant Cooperation and Capitalist Expansion in Central Peru* 3–43, Austin: University of Texas Press.

Mahler, Sarah (1998) 'Theoretical and empirical contributions toward a research agenda for transnationalism', in M. Smith and Guarnizo (eds) *Transnationalism from Below: Comparative Urban Community* Research 6: 64–102, New Brunswick: Transaction Publishers.

Mallon, Florencia (1983) *The Defense of the Community in Peru's Central Highlands: Peasant Struggle and Capitalist Transition, 1860–1940*, Princeton: Princeton University Press.

Paerregaard, Karsten (1997) *Linking Separate Worlds: Urban Migrants and Rural Lives in Peru*, Oxford: Berg.

Petrillo, Agostino (1999) 'Italy: Farewell to the "Bel Paese"?', in G. Dale and M. Cole (eds) *The European Union and Migrant Labour*, 231–62, Oxford: Berg.

Phizacklea, Annie (1998) 'Migration and globalization: A feminist perspective', in K. Koser and H. Lutz (eds) 21–38, *The New Migration in Europe: Social Constructions and Social Realities*, London: Macmillan Press.

Portes, Alejandro, Luis Guarnizo and Patricia Landolt (1999) 'Introduction: Pitfalls and promise of an emergent research field', in Special Issue on Transnational Communities, *Ethnic and Racial Studies* 22(2): 217–237.

Ribas-Mateos, Natalia (2000) 'Female birds of passage: Leaving and settling in Spain', in F. Anthias and G. Lazaridis (eds) *Gender and Migration in Southern Europe. Women on the Move* 173–98, Oxford: Berg.

Rouse, Roger (1991) Mexican migration and the social space, *Diaspora* 1(1): 8–23.

Sellek, Yoko (1997) 'Nikkeijin: The phenomenon of return migration', in M. Weiner (ed.) *Japan's Minorities: The Illusion of Homogeneity*, 178–210, London: Routledge.

Shimada, Haruo (1994) *Japan's 'Guest Workers': Issues and Public Policies*, Tokyo: University of Tokyo Press.

Smith, Gavin (1989) *Livelihood and Resistance: Peasants and the Politics of Land in Peru*, Berkeley: University of California Press.

Takenaka, Ayumi (1999) 'Transnational community and its ethnic consequences: The return migration and the transformation of ethnicity of Japanese Peruvians', *The American Behavioral Scientist* 42(9): 1459–74.

7   The moving 'expert'

A study of mobile professionals in the Cayman Islands and North America

Vered Amit

On a number of occasions during the course of fieldwork in Grand Cayman between 1993 and 1996, British expatriates told me that they had left Britain seeking 'adventure', a chance for something 'different', to live abroad for a while.[1] These were not youths with little investment or few social obligations seeking a travelling interlude between school and work. They were, for the most part, middle-aged, middle-ranking professionals: nurses, teachers, draughtsmen, archivists, etc. How, I wondered, could people leave long-standing jobs, property and familial relations to take up well paid but insecure contractual employment and temporary work permits in a locale about which, in most cases, they knew little or nothing for a purpose so frivolous as a little adventure? The term must, I thought, be code or even cover for more substantial motivations: capped salaries, career stalemates, and family difficulties. And indeed these kinds of factors, to a greater or lesser extent, also often appeared to be in attendance. But I think I missed the point.

More recently, I have started to interview consultants based in Canada whose work requires frequent travel across large distances to a succession of different clients.[2] When I started this new project, I assumed that the pressures of economic restructuring – fragmentation of production, the globalization of marketing and distribution networks and transnational corporate structures – had made it difficult or even impossible for this class of professionals to avoid travelling in the course of their work. In the context of the structure of contemporary global economies, the choice of a particular career had *inter alia* imposed the necessity of travel. But so far I am discovering rather more frequently a reverse direction of choices, that is to say career paths chosen or explicitly structured to allow for regular travel. This even when other less peripatetic work opportunities have been available and even in cases where there has been an acknowledgement that the social and emotional costs of such frequent movement can be high. My expectations of new forms of transnational sociability arising in the wake of occupational itinerancy have been stymied by portrayals which have stressed social distance and circumscription as necessary features of mobile professionalism. Was this portrait an 'official' representation, I asked myself, masking the development of more rounded, complex associations? Surely, people wouldn't willingly leave family, friends and consociates behind so frequently for such canalized, 'thin' forms of social interaction? But I think I missed the point again.

The point is that neither these itinerant Canadian consultants nor the British expatriates I met were seeking community through travel; if anything they were actively seeking escape from it, or in the words of my Caymanian-based informants: a little adventure. But why should this have surprised me? Is not this an exceedingly common feature of global travel? After all the *sine qua non* of tourism, the most common basis for contemporary travel, is the opportunity which it provides for a similar if less consequential extrication from the embeddedness of everyday life, a chance to temporarily escape the myriad activities, roles, obligations, expectations, representations, peers, intimates, adversaries and other consociations that impossibly complicate our usual routines. As well, while many forms of business mobility do not require the frequent absences experienced by the peripatetic consultants in my own study, a host of more occasional occupational travellers still experience a similar if more cursory canalization of social life through movement. Surely I am not the only university scholar who has found the relatively restricted range of roles and expectations associated with occasional conference going a welcome temporary relief from teaching, parenting, neighbouring and a host of other ongoing involvements.

What is noteworthy about the two groups of mobile professionals I am concerned with here is not their anticipation of travel as disjuncture, a common enough expectation, but their apparent willingness to reconfigure their lives so thoroughly in terms of it. In this chapter I will argue that their respective openness to disengagement and movement arises in the context of an increasingly common identification of spatial with occupational mobility. In one instance of this convergence, the world's borders are viewed as easily traversable for the Western youth or professional who is adventurous and willing to take advantage of the availability of short-term contractual employment and temporary work visas dispersed across a global marketplace. Labour migration and tourism are thus deliberately confounded. In another instance, professionalism is identified with constant motion and a disembedding of work roles from other social relationships, modelling carefully calculated footlooseness as a standard of successful adaptation to high modernity. Apparently opposed orientations – an escape from the usual routines of career and home on the one hand and a primary preoccupation with career development on the other – both draw on a common process of economic abstraction (Carrier and Miller 1998). In this chapter I consider the dismay with which expatriate professionals in the Cayman Islands have come to realize that in embracing this process, they have assured their own dispensability. I contrast their consternation with the more triumphant tone of several North American-based consultants who, in spite of their self-assurance, appear to have accepted conditions of similar structural insecurities. That they have done so with such apparent willingness is testament to the reinvigorated hegemony of Western conceptions of individuation, now interpreted in neoclassical economic terms as the progress of 'flexibility'.

Competing visions of connection and disjuncture

Over the past decade, anthropologists too have eagerly sought out movement, eager to establish their scholarly credentials as *au courant* chroniclers of a contemporary, interconnected world in motion. In the course of these efforts, we have, however, to some extent continued to be captive of long-standing paradigms within our discipline. On the one hand, we have been anxious, even to the point of redundancy, to renounce and distance ourselves from some earlier representations of collectivities as highly bounded, rooted and dehistoricized. In reacting to this representational excess, we have sometimes moved towards an obverse but equally problematic credulity in the apparently porous nature of political borders. In common with theorists in cultural studies, anthropologists have welcomed concepts of borderlands or borders as metaphors for processes of deterritorialization and cultural connection and as vehicles for arguing that pastiche, hybridity and boundary transgressions are ordinary processes of cultural production. Or as Renato Rosaldo puts it in justifying his argument for an ethnography focused on border zones: 'All of us inhabit an interdependent late twentieth century world marked by borrowing and lending across porous national and cultural boundaries that are saturated with inequality, power and domination' (1989: 217).

While many of the writers on transmigration – an approach which has dominated the American literature on transnationalism and has been most commonly identified with Basch *et al.*'s *Nations Unbound* (1994) – have made an effort to move beyond these free flowing metaphors of deterritorialization towards a more empirically rigorous political economy, here again the emphasis tends to be on the permeability of political borders. Specifically, the emphasis is on the transnational connections created when migrants continue to maintain a foothold in their country of origin even as they participate in nation-building projects in another state. Or, as Luis Guarnizo argued in a more recent publication, being a transnational 'implies becoming habituated to living more or less comfortably in a world that encompasses more than one national structure of institutional and power arrangements, social understandings, and dominant political and public cultures.' (1997: 310). This duality constitutes, he suggested, a 'transnational habitus' linking two states – in his example the Dominican Republic and the United States – as a *single* sociocultural, economic and political field (ibid.: 311).

This embrace of the unbounded nature of nations, collectivities or social fields has not apparently loosened the paradigmatic hold of the notion of collectivity or community. In fact, if anything, as place has lost its privileged role as an epistemological anchor, the capacity of community to locate the anthropological subject has become even more critical. Given the potential contradiction between these two thrusts respectively towards boundlessness and the circumscription implied by the notion of collectivity, it is not surprising that Benedict Anderson's concept of 'imagined community' has become such a popular analytical vehicle, applied to an ever wider range of socially recognized identities. While Anthony Cohen's work in the 1980s began the process of moving the concept of community away from a structural designation to an emotive and symbolic vehicle, he still anchored this sense of belonging most firmly in the local, in daily social processes of every-day life, in boundaries 'constituted by people in interaction' (1985: 13). As the concept has become a more ubiquitous vehicle to represent deterritorialization, it has been stripped of much of its social and interactive content so that it looks increasingly like little more than a categorical referent, the possibility of attribut-ing social connection without the complications of place, commonality or even regular interaction (see Gupta and Ferguson 1997). But the increasing lightness of community has, if anything, excited rather than dampened enthusiasm for the explanatory power of this concept.

A partiality for attributions of collectivity to processes of deterritorialization may be understandable in terms of anthropological traditions, but it also incorpo-rates a fundamental contradiction between the tendency to treat the very possibility of collective transnational connections as axiomatic and the simultaneous effort to problematize the territorial, cultural and social underpinnings of these links. Occasional invocations of displacement and flux notwithstanding the most strik-ing aspects of these representations of deterritorialized relations are their persistent subtext of unity and stability. Migrants operate in a single continuous field, man-age to maintain spatially dispersed family and economic relationships over time; national borders become porous sites of ongoing syncretism, and communities continue to be imagined effectively. Ironically, as border crossing is increasingly adopted as a key metaphor for the post-modern human condition, the very scale of the transitions and obstacles involved in the movement of persons across borders becomes minimized. This tendency to treat borders and boundaries as fundamen-tally porous is not, however, easily reconciled with a 'world of many more and in some cases stronger states' (Wilson and Donnan 1998: 2); a world in which the movement of labour continues to be subject to harsh and often harsher restrictions even while capital flows ever more freely.

It seems somewhat premature therefore to assert the permeability of borders or the capacity for social connections to be reconstituted across them before we give at least equal attention to the disjunctions which they impose and indeed are intended to. Some ten years ago, Arjun Appadurai noted that the relationship between the global flow of people, technology and money was 'deeply disjunctive and profoundly unpredictable', even as each acted 'as a constraint and a param-eter for movements in the other' (1990: 298). This disjunction is itself part of a process which James Carrier and Daniel Miller have referred to as economic abstraction.

> The core of economic abstraction is the process that Karl Polanyi (1957a) described as 'dis-embedding'; that is, the removal of economic activities from the social and other relationships in which they had occurred, and carrying them out in a context in which the only important relationships are those defined by the economic activity itself. In essence, economic activity becomes abstracted from social relations.
>
> (Carrier 1998: 2)

This orientation, Carrier argues, occurs at both a practical level, that is, the ways in which people organize themselves to carry out economic activities, and at a conceptual level, that is, the ways in which people envision their economic lives (ibid.). He reserves the notion of virtualism for the process in which the latter form of abstraction progresses to the point where it is taken as real rather than a model and an effort is made to make the world conform to it (ibid.). As Carrier notes, one of the forms of practical abstraction that has characterized the changing organization of Western capitalism has been the rise of the 'market-driven, flexible firm', and with it a demand for market-driven, flexible workers. In this chapter I would like to examine the way in which this shift in the organization of employment has been associated with the successful rise of a model of disembedded economic agency, asserting an unencumbered movement of individuals between places and organizations. It is a model that has been so successful that certain classes of professionals actively seek to organize their lives in terms of it.

Contract and consultancy

At the turn of the millennium, experts move transnationally through circuits shaped by the restructuring of production and labour which has taken place over the last decade in the Western economies which still dominate the export of these specialist services. The increasing fragmentation and dispersal of the operations and holdings of large, particularly transnational corporations has created a need for an array of specialized services to cope with the ensuing administrative and developmental challenges (Sassen 1994). The result has been a marked expansion of the business service sector which includes lawyers, accountants, advertisers, computer analysts, and more who provide services to these firms. But, as Saskia Sassen has noted, large corporations have not been the only users of these services. Smaller firms and governments all over the world have responded to the opportunities afforded by the greater diversity and availability of these business services, and their patronage has in turn reinforced the development of this sector (ibid.).

The growth of the business service sector is, however, by no means simply a factor of the need for more specialized expertise. The expansion of this sector has also been driven by the increasing tendency among many firms to contract out work that would once have been performed 'in-house' by their direct employees. The result has been a transfer of jobs from producer to service industries, particularly the business, engineering and management industries (Clinton 1997: 3). It is instructive to note that in the United States between 1972 and 1996, the two most rapidly growing categories of business services were personnel supply and computer services, expansions catalysed respectively in the one case by the onus towards 'flexible labour' or contracting out, and in the other by the need for very particular skills in the wake of rapid technological development (ibid.: 4).

On the face of it, these two forms of labour restructuring appear to have rather different impetuses and very different outcomes. Contracting out is first and foremost oriented towards rendering labour more disposable and hence cheaper. In contrast, the expansion of freestanding consultancy services reflects heightened demands for an ever more diversified and specialized range of skills to meet recent technological, communication and marketing shifts, demands that today even large corporations would have difficulty meeting entirely in-house. The former structural shift is oriented towards rendering particular labour categories dispensable even while the latter can incorporate professionals as valued employees of new forms of service corporations. However, systematically distinguishing the effects of these two types of workforce restructuring is easier said than done because both, even while generally working in opposite directions of valorization, rely on converting salaried jobs into purchasable services. Saskia Sassen has argued that the differentiation of the business services sector is a factor of an increasing occupational and educational polarization in this sector between highly educated and highly paid workers on the one hand and low paid and often manual workers on the other (1994: 120). Yet, this rather simplistic dichotomization of occupation and education may in fact be helping to obscure the degree to which labour restructuring has reconfigured the old wage/salary distinction. Whereas the relative insecurity of hourly wages could once be generally associated with low skill, blue collar occupations while more highly skilled, white collar workers and professionals enjoyed longer term and more secure salaried positions, the effect of contracting out has been to extend the conditions of waged labour up the occupational and educational ladder. Today, an increasing number of administrative support and professional workers are working on short-term contracts and are in effect receiving little in the way of commitment from their employers beyond their hourly rates. Among more highly skilled and educated workers, the inherent vulnerability of these waged work conditions can be masked by the gloss of glamour imparted by high pay, the prestige associated with particular occupations, and the appropriation of the consultant label.

Tanya[3] was a professional on salary with the environmental section of a large, Montreal-based Canadian engineering and consulting company. Her work involved consultation on a variety of infrastructure development projects dispersed over a far-flung swathe of sites all over the world. Each project entailed the assembly of a new team comprising a mixture of professionals who like Tanya were salaried employees of the same firm as well as independent consultants who were hired on a temporary contractual basis. On the largest project Tanya had ever worked on, a feasibility study for a major new road development in the Caribbean, her firm eventually offered the project directorship to an independent consultant with particular experience in this field. Tanya, the salaried employee, thus becomes subordinate to a consultant working on contract. Over the years that Tanya had worked for her employer, a number of her former salaried colleagues had moved out on their own and were now operating as independent consultants working on contract, sometimes for projects run by their former employer. When Tanya was offered a new job by a similar Ontario-based firm, she discovered that most of the former employees of the division she was now to manage had shifted into contractual work, much of it for their former employer. How many of these shifts were altogether voluntary is not clear to me, but it is apparent that the relative prominence of independent consultants can vary greatly. High demand for the skills of a particular consultant can have the practical effect of ensuring a steady even high income, without changing the intrinsic structural vulnerability of their 'independence'. It is an insecurity that appeared to weigh negatively in the balance when Tanya considered her options, even during a period of increasing dissatisfaction with her work situation.

The continuum of prestige associated respectively with salaried and contractual work also appeared in the accounts of Monica, a Seattle based management consultant specializing in high technology who was a salaried employee of a large multinational consulting firm, and her spouse Richard, a systems analyst working for a somewhat smaller multiestablishment firm when I asked them about the relative status of independent consultants *vis a vis* salaried professionals in the same field. Richard replied:

> It really depends. I would think size of the job would be a factor. The task that has to be done. I can't see a whole bunch of independent consultants and a rag tag bunch of programmers coming into a Fortune 500 company and getting the same sort of job of a company like Sierra or a Cambridge or a System House in particular.[4] They [the Fortune 500 company] can say we've got a set of resource people to draw upon that are educated and know the methodology, they talk the same language, they carry the same banner, kind of thing, going in as a cohesive team. I think an independent consultant probably makes more than some of us in a salaried position in a consulting firm, but they won't get the same work. I don't think we'd be stepping on each other's feet.

Monica added:

> A lot of times the independents are subcontracted by larger companies again, due to resource shortages. That's never by choice. If they're subcontracted, it's either because they have specific knowledge in an area that that company doesn't know, or because that company just doesn't have the resources to put in. But the companies would definitely prefer to put in their own people because for them, it's expensive to pay a subcontractor versus paying their salaried people. In terms of status, I'd have to say that probably if you're from a larger consulting company, it's perceived that you're a better quality consultant than an independent with the exception of some of the people who've really made a name for themselves and they can go in and charge probably the highest rates possible. But for the people just in the databases that you can sort of draw on and say 'Here's a C++ programmer', I think those people are considered to be sort of one step down from the company's point of view, from the client's point of view.

Monica and Richard appeared reasonably confident about the prestige conferred by their salaried positions within large consulting firms and equally confident that demand for their own specialized expertise in information technology would remain high for some time. Freelance work, even at a higher pay, did not appear to pose much attraction. At the same time, they were far from enthusiastic about the separations which could be imposed by the peripatetic nature of their field. While their choices of employment had been, at least in part, driven by their desire to avoid the necessity of frequent travel, both found themselves spending extended periods of time away from their Seattle base and each other, at the sites of their respective clients. According to Monica:

> I think the companies do try to be sympathetic, but on the other hand, if the choice is, well you know, you can take the less interesting work locally or you can travel, then they're sort of putting you in a difficult position, I think, because you sacrifice either your personal life or you sacrifice your career. So it becomes not much of a choice. It kind of [and she laughed] either way you go, you're going to lose somewhere.

Yet, Monica and Richard have taken the initiative to change jobs several times in the course of their careers, changes which involved long-distance moves across Canada and between Canada and the United States. Some of these job changes like their move from Eastern Canada where they had been educated to the British Columbia Lower Mainland where Monica had been raised, were spurred by a desire to live in a particular locale. Yet, when only a few years later Monica decided to change jobs because of a dissatisfaction with management changes, she opted to take up a position which required relocation to Seattle, even when she had been offered reasonably comparable jobs in Vancouver. Richard arranged for a transfer between the Vancouver and Seattle offices of the same company. They left friends and family behind. As Canadians, their migration to the United States was facilitated by provisions of the North American Free Trade Agreement, NAFTA allowing certain categories of foreign professionals to be awarded temporary work permits with relative ease. Both Monica and Richard relied on their employers to handle the process of applying on their behalf first for NAFTA and then subsequently other types of temporary work visas. If they decide to stay in the United States, they will eventually have to arrange permanent residence (i.e. 'green card'), a process sufficiently complex, time-consuming and expensive that they expect to have to depend on their employers yet again to handle this application. In due course they expect to change their employers repeatedly. Within their fields, Monica claimed, it was fairly common for professionals to change jobs every year and a half to two years.

> But I think for consultants as a whole, even the ones who go into industry and don't want to travel any more, it doesn't mean that they'll stay at the job for twenty years. I don't think that's the mind-set at all. I don't think that any consultant really takes it for granted that you're going to have a twenty-year career path and stay with a certain company. So even if they go somewhere else and don't want to travel, they might stay with that company for a few years and go to a different company. I think they're pretty much ready to change all the time.

It is a change in the nature of employment that Monica and Richard allowed had affected the more general labour market encompassing a wide gamut of workers. Consultants had simply 'adapted to that change better than maybe some other people in other industries.' And indeed a little over a year later, Richard changed jobs again.

Distinguishing stable, salaried employment from contractual work becomes a rather ambiguous exercise in the face of this expectation and enactment of occupational transience. Monica and Richard were after all, employed on temporary work visas allowing employment in positions they did not intend to maintain very long. And given their apparent willingness to change locations along with their jobs, their desire to avoid too many travelling assignments appeared to be a very limited circumscription of the impact of mobility on their personal lives. Twenty years older than Monica and Richard, Tanya who was dubious about the precariousness of independent consulting had also been much more cautious and hesitant about changing jobs and residential locale. Yet, she had eagerly embraced an existence of almost constant motion. Over the course of only one year, Tanya had travelled to clients in Dominica, Thailand, the Philippines, visited friends in Vietnam, then onto a new project in Senegal, back again to Dominica, Thailand and the Philippines before completing the year with a project of several months duration in Jamaica. She punctuated these trips with visits, rarely more than a few weeks in duration, back to Montreal, her home base as well as to New England where she had family and friends. It was a way of life to which Tanya had deliberately and enthusiastically subscribed. Indeed one of the primary criteria in Tanya's search for a new job had been the desire to continue this level of transnational work and travel.

Tanya's son had already grown up and left home before she embarked on this circuit of travel, but Margaret, a consultant in the related field of urban planning and economics, had initiated a similarly mobile career when her daughter was still very young and even though her husband, a managing partner with a large consulting corporation, was also engaged in frequent journeys. Unlike Tanya, Margaret had welcomed the opportunity for venturing into independent consulting. Thus, in the late 1980s, in partnership with two other women, she had been able to establish a small consulting firm which specialized in 'international work'. She and her husband took turns remaining in Canada to care for their daughter. 'It's the modern career', pronounced Margaret. She was shocked that more people were not taking up these kinds of opportunities for movement. 'When you get paid in US dollars and you get flown around the world, I don't understand why you'd want to do a project in Chilliwack', she said, referring to a somewhat non-urbane and peripheral town in the Lower Mainland of British Columbia, the region in which she resided. The key to success in this way of life, Margaret contended, was scrupulous self-discipline and a measure of professional sang-froid. Relationships with other consultants were kept deliberately 'casual'. She and her partners had intentionally kept some distance from the large consulting firms in order to maintain their independence and had carefully avoided nurturing too strong a friendship with clients.

> I think you often find that when you're exposing a lot of difficulties that your client has on delivering on policies, it's often difficult if you've got too close of a relationship with a client. I think you've got to keep a professional role. You can be charming but you still have to be professional.

A common orientation underpins the different career choices of these four Canadian consultants, a vision of career as ineluctably shaped around mobility and a willingness, even insistence on maintaining a level of social disengagement sufficient to enable frequent moves between firms, projects, colleagues and places. Their commitment to movement and disembedding is hardly absolute, and they vary in their respective attraction to different conditions and types of mobility. Monica and Richard are quite willing to change employers and places of residence but they do not welcome travel to assignments which involve separation from each other. Tanya is less keen to change employers and residences although she has done both, but she finds the constant variation of places, new clients and colleagues entailed in her work on a constant succession of far-flung projects exciting and engrossing. On each project, she plunges into an intense but temporary sociality with clients and colleagues. A similar fascination with the escape from the local offered by 'international' work animates Margaret's career choices, but she has opted for the independence of her own firm as well as limiting her travel, when possible, to six months of the year in order to make time to be with her daughter. She identifies professional autonomy with careful limits on social familiarity. Yet, in spite of these variations and the limits on their capacity to entirely control the circumstances of their movements or the attendant social costs, they do not see their motile lifestyles as the simple dictate of a restructured labour market. They could surely, they noted, have made other choices of employers, locations or projects that would not have entailed such frequent or disparate moves. They, therefore, appear inclined to view their orientation towards mobility as an exercise of relatively free agency, one that signifies them as more up-to-date or cosmopolitan than the kind of sedentary people who, as Margaret put it, would prefer dull Chilliwack to the excitement of globetrotting.

Cayman adventures and their consequences

The sense that travel could offer an escape from the staleness and stalemates of a sedentary life also figured prominently when a number of expatriate professionals I met explained their motivations for taking up temporary contracts in Grand Cayman. But unlike the transnational consultants referred to above, for these would be adventurers in Cayman, movement had not been enlisted in the development of careers so much as marketable skills enabled them to act on longing for movement and/or change. James had arrived in Grand Cayman from England in 1982. He had seen a job in Cayman advertised in a computer press, but this was the first he had heard of this Caribbean island. 'I came not really knowing if I would be living in a mud hut or in comfort'. He had come, he explained, for 'the adventure aspect of it, the sun, sea, sand, to see the world.' For James this was his first extended period outside England. 'If Cayman had not been as good, I would have probably dotted around the world.' As it was, conditions were sufficiently good that James stayed on. James had met his wife Joan, another British expatriate, while she was visiting a relative living in Cayman. Eventually, Joan herself had migrated to Cayman. She explained that 'I had a very good job in England, but I had gone as far as I could go in this job and I couldn't go any further. Life was pretty stale. I was looking for a change, for adventure, something different. I was sick of not earning much money, of not being able to travel . . . Having a relative here gave me access to living here for a while without a work permit.' Joan was then able to find a job as a midwife in a Caymanian hospital.

Joan and James referred me to their friends Anne and Greg. Anne, a nurse, and Greg, a teacher, were also British expatriates in their 30s who had met and married in Grand Cayman. Like James and quite a few of the other expatriate professionals I spoke to, Anne had been drawn to the Cayman Islands by a job she saw advertised in London. The job had captured her attention because it called for a nurse with a background in community health, her speciality. She was interviewed for the job in London and then hired. At that time she was single. She was looking for a change in scenery, but like James she did not even know where the Cayman Islands were. She had to look them up. This was the first time she had worked outside England. She had longed to travel overseas for some time, but family commitments had previously prevented her from acting on that desire. When she accepted the offer of a job in Cayman, she had had no particular long-term plans. She figured that Cayman might be a stopping off point to somewhere else. It was only a two-year contract, the salary was very good, and she had 'nothing to lose'. 'It was a safe way to take my first step overseas.' She had thought that this experience would allow her to decide which way to go. It would either bolster her courage about living away from England or else demonstrate to her that she was going to be too homesick for this to be feasible. In the end, however, she had not actually committed herself to either option. After three years, she and Greg had left Cayman. They embarked on a year's travel abroad, and because they had bought a round-the-world ticket, the final destination had to be their point of embarkation, Cayman. What they had intended as a quick return visit and vacation ended up being extended when Greg was offered a new two-year contract in his old teaching job. So they stayed on again although Anne had experienced difficulty in finding employment. Anne said that she and her husband were feeling pretty open-minded about what was going to happen when Greg's contract expired again.

In contrast to these two young couples, Mark, a somewhat older British expatriate, had been rather more careful and deliberate in planning his escape when he too had responded to an advertisement for a job in Cayman. He had left behind a wife, a house and children on the Isle of Man where he had been employed for eighteen years. 'I was either going to be there until I retired, or else I moved . . . I had just finished six years straight as the chairman of our professional body. I was looking for something to fill that place.' The job in the Cayman Islands had appealed to him because it provided a 'challenge' and it paid well enough to help provide for his family and property on the Isle of Man. His wife, who was also employed on the

Isle of Man, stayed there. 'She's from the Isle of Man. But if my job here finishes, I've got a home to go back to . . . I couldn't get my job back there. If she came out here, the chances of her getting her job back was slim. It would have been quite a risk for both of us to give up our jobs.' Such risk mitigation notwithstanding, Mark had still been jarred by the inherent insecurity of the contractual nature of the jobs available to expatriates.

> You live on a knife-edge, of never knowing when you're going to be turned down [for a renewed work permit/contract]. It does cause anxiety. It goes in waves. Six months after you've been here and the novelty wears off and you realize you only have eighteen months left in your contract and you have to apply a year in advance and you think that's not very much time left.

In 1995 when I interviewed him, he had been living in Grand Cayman for four and a half years. He was into his third contract and was sure there was enough work in his field to keep him occupied in Cayman for a lifetime, but he was not at all confident that his work permit would continue to be renewed. 'When you get to the point when you could apply for status, they tend to turn down your work permit. It's silly because they don't have to give you status [even after you are eligible]. If someone objects to your work permit, you get turned down.' Like most of the large foreign workforce in the Cayman Islands, Joan, James, Anne, Greg and Mark were employed on temporary, albeit renewable contracts and associated work permits.

Since the early 1970s, the basis of the Cayman Islands economy has been comprehensively transformed from a small-scale maritime economy dependent on the remittances of merchant seamen to a major offshore financial and tourist centre. Per capita incomes are now among the highest in the Western hemisphere, levels of consumption and education have risen dramatically. While the Cayman Islands remain a British colony with ultimate constitutional authority still vested in the Crown, the islands are now, for the most part, operationally and financially independent of the United Kingdom. They are, however, if anything even more heavily dependent on the custom of foreign patrons, particularly American ones, as investors in and consumers of the finance and tourist industries that utterly dominate the economy. There is virtually no local manufacturing, and a small agricultural sector supplies only a fraction of the foodstuffs consumed on the islands. Almost all consumer items are imported, and the tax that is levelled on imports provides a principal source of public revenue in a jurisdiction with no direct personal or corporate taxes. But the transformation of the economy has also created new labour demands that cannot be met by the indigenous workforce. As a result, Cayman has, like a number of other smaller Caribbean islands (McElroy and De Albuquerque 1988), shifted from being an exporter to a net importer of population. In 1994, a little over forty per cent of the workforce comprised foreign workers. The most important sources for this imported workforce are Jamaica, Honduras, North America, the United Kingdom and Ireland. Foreign workers are distributed in every sector of the economy, including the civil service, health, educational, social service and construction sectors, as well as a significant portion of the workforce in the two primary industries of finance and tourism. While imported workers account for most of the domestics employed on the islands, the expatriate workforce is, for the most part, highly skilled, with skilled workers and professionals accounting for 42.0 per cent and 17.4 per cent respectively of all work permit holders (Shah 1995: 510–11).

As Cayman has become more dependent on foreign workers, legal and social distinctions between new arrivals and indigenous residents have become more sharply drawn. It has become increasingly difficult for expatriates to acquire permanent residence status. Foreign workers' residence in Grand Cayman where most Caymanians and expatriates are located, is overwhelmingly tied to temporary work permits. Even the British governor is employed on a temporary work permit. Work permits range from a few months to three years in duration but are frequently renewable, and foreign workers can change jobs with the appropriate issuance of new work permits. Employers are, however, legally required to give preference to qualified Caymanians not only when first filling a vacancy, but at each instance of contract renewal.

Thus, in 1995, after thirteen years of employment in the Caymanian civil service, James had been informed that his latest contract would not be renewed because he was about to be replaced by qualified Caymanians. He was hoping to find another computing job in Grand Cayman but was also considering employment prospects elsewhere. Tensions between indigenous Caymanians and expatriate workers were, according to James, a constant subject of conversation among the latter and had been so for years. James and his wife did not think there was anything expatriates could do to change their tenuous status in the Cayman Islands. 'Most expats realize that we're guests here, that our work permits will eventually expire if Caymanians are there to replace us', explained Joan, whose job as a nurse had also been taken over by a Caymanian. James added:

> Some expats just want to come here for two or three years. Others like us would like to make our home here. We would dearly love tenure here. Every year that topic comes up ... We can't vote, we don't have elected members that have expat's interests in mind, no representation, therefore [we] can't change it. If you try and change it, then you come up against the victimization part again, and eventually you will suffer for it.

If all else failed, John supposed they could return to Britain, but he was also equally willing to move to another country if a good job opportunity presented itself. 'We would go wherever work is. We don't feel very tethered.' But Joan was getting worried that her husband would have 'trouble getting a job in England if we stay here too long. He's getting close to 40, and that's the cut off.' Similarly, Mark was concerned that at 48 'you think, if I stay here for four more years, who wants to employ a 52-year old?' Commenting on the termination of James' contract, Mark remarked with more than a trace of bitterness: 'This does seem to be a taking situation. They want you until they've used up what you've got, and then they just replace you, and you're discarded'.

Yet, was not this kind of exploitation, the inherent disposability of foreign labour, always an explicit aspect of the conditions under which Mark and James, their expatriate friends and family members had been employed? After all, from the outset they had been recruited to fill positions only on a limited term contractual basis. Why then this sense of betrayal, of dismay at the vulnerability that attends even renewable short-term contracts. I cannot speak for these professionals, but I suspect that their consternation derives from the unwelcome realization that when Caymanian officials and employers said 'temporary', 'employed only until . . .', they actually meant it. When foreign professionals are being actively and determinedly courted to come to the Cayman Islands, recruited in their home countries, wooed with high tax free salaries, the occasional fringe benefit, the delights of a warm and attractive locale, it seems hard to imagine that alongside that valourization of skills and experience is an intrinsic definition of the person that provides them as structurally dispensable. Easier surely to see temporary contracts as bureaucratic formalities, easier to assume that how long you work and stay in the Cayman Islands, given the demand for your skills, will be your choice, and a shock to discover that it is not. And fast on the heels of this discovery comes the realization that national, regional and highly local boundaries continue to be crucial features of the global organization of labour, that there may be no going back to the job or employment market you 'escaped' from, that here too the choice may not be yours. Your job may no longer be there to go back, you can be deemed too old, your experience elsewhere may not be judged as valid as local careers, and so on. And in the course of these realizations, the dream of unfettered mobility, of the transnational portability of skills, of the potential for greater agency embedded in the proliferation of contractual work across borders and across job categories can stand revealed as highly contingent.

Conclusion

In the dialogue I have contrived between the situation of expatriate professionals in the Cayman Islands and highly mobile consultants in North America, there seems to be a potentially significant lesson that the former could suggest to the latter. In Western economies, amidst the celebration of expertise, invocations of 'brain drains' and a global competition for scarce and specialized skills, of the increasing polarization of rewards between elite professionals and the larger mass of workers, it can be difficult to believe that the demand for knowledge now so highly esteemed might diminish. An interpretation of 'flexibility' as the interaction of agency with mobility and expertise does not necessarily connote acceptance of chronic insecurity. Monica could not easily envisage her sector of employment being touched by an economic downturn.

> I think especially if we [Monica and Richard] stay very technology focused as we are now, I don't think so because even in a down-turn economy people are actually probably going to implement more systems than they normally

would. So I think it's kind of like banking. You're pretty safe either way. I think so.

Yet, as the global value attributed to professional credentials of a certain sort rises, as major consultancy firms assume the transnational scale and proportions of the corporations they often serve, and as individual experts become ever more itinerant, the chances rise that the seemingly powerful transnational consultant is him or herself actually employed on a temporary work visa or has been hired on a temporary contractual basis. And there is historical precedent to suggest that when the conditions of intellectual supply shift, restrictions on the transnational movement of knowledge workers can quickly follow suit.

Like their American neighbours, Canadian federal and provincial governments have recently been trying to encourage the import of highly skilled workers by introducing provisions such as an easing of employment restrictions upon the spouses of specialists hired on temporary visas. This is hardly, however, the first instance in which Canada tried to meet shortages of professional credentials through transnational recruitment. In the 1960s and 1970s, during a period of dramatic expansion of Canada's higher education system, thousands of American and British academics were hired. By the mid-seventies, as the newly expanded system succeeded in producing an abundance of Canadian PhDs, immigration rules, still in place today, were introduced that made it difficult if not impossible to hire foreign scholars. But this early generation of imported foreign intellectuals were from the outset offered much more secure immigration and employment status than many of their late twentieth century professional counterparts. Thus when the immigration boom came down – at the urging of Canadian academics – those foreign scholars already hired remained in post because they held tenured university jobs and permanent residence status. It is hard to believe that the temporary contracts, however lucrative, and quickly obtained temporary work visas which are spurring a good part of the contemporary transnational traffic of knowledge workers would offer equal protections, should there be similar shifts in the demand for particular credentials. To have convinced notably well credentialed and educated specialists – and not a few academic pundits – that in assuming the waged and/or guest worker status once associated with economic marginality, these 'experts' have become somehow *more* not less valourized, more successful, not less secure, is a powerful indication of the extent to which a model of employment around the concept of flexibility has become successfully generalized and normalized.

To the extent that this model advances the disembedding of work from other social relations, it is not surprising that the mobility it encourages is also more likely to be associated with disjunction than the kinds of images of continuity and collectivity which anthropologists have tended to attribute to other transnational interpolations of work and movement. Accordingly, there are British professionals using the availability of contractual work in a distant Caribbean locale they know little or nothing about to escape the mire of local routines and attachments. There are Canadian consultants linking mobility with transience and social compartmentalization as a standard of their own commitment to cosmopolitan professionalism.

These then are mobile livelihoods pursued as opportunities for and capacities for disengagement.

Notes

1 This research was supported by a grant from the Social Sciences and Humanities Research Council of Canada. Fieldwork was conducted at intervals between 1993 and 1996.
2 This study was supported by a grant from the Concordia University General Research Fund. Research is still ongoing.
3 Throughout this chapter, aliases are used in place of the actual names of informants in order to protect their confidentiality.
4 These are all large, American headquartered consulting companies.

References

Anderson, Benedict (1991) *Imagined Communities: Reflections on the Origin and Spread of Nationalism*, Revised Edition, London & New York: Verso.

Appadurai, Arjun (1990) 'Disjuncture and difference in the global cultural economy', in Mike Featherstone (ed.) *Global Culture: Nationalism, Globalization and Modernity*, London, Newbury Park & New Delhi: Sage Publications.

Basch, Linda, Nina Glick Schiller and Cristina Szanton Blanc (1994) *Nations Unbound: Transnational Projects, Postcolonial Predicaments and Deterritorialized Nation-States*, Basel, Switzerland: Gordon and Breach Publishers.

Carrier, James G. and Daniel Miller (eds) (1998) *Virtualism: A New Political Economy*, Oxford & New York: Berg.

Clinton, Angela (1997) 'Flexible labor: restructuring the American work force', *Monthly Labor Review*, August: 3–27.

Cohen, Anthony (1985) *The Symbolic Construction of Community*, Chichester, Sussex: Ellis Horwood Ltd. & London & New York: Tavistock Publications.

Guarnizo, Luis Eduardo (1997) 'The emergence of a transnational social formation and the mirage of return migration among Dominican transmigrants', *Identities* 4(2): 281–322.

Gupta, Akhil and James Ferguson (1997) 'Beyond "Culture": Space, identity and the politics of difference', in Akhil Gupta and James Ferguson (eds) *Culture, Power, Place: Explorations in Critical Anthropology*, Durham & London: Duke University Press.

McElroy, Jerome L. and De Albuquerque, K. (1988) 'Migration transition in small northern and eastern Caribbean states', in *International Migration Review* XXII: 30–58.

Rosaldo, Renato (1989) *Culture and Truth: The Remaking of Social Analysis*, Boston: Beacon Press.

Sassen, Saskia (1994) *Cities in a World Economy*, Thousand Oaks, London, New Delhi: Pine Forge Press.

Shah, Ryhaan (ed.) (1995) *Cayman Islands Yearbook 95 & Business Directory*, Grand Cayman: Cayman Free Press.

Wilson, Thomas M. and Hastings Donnan (1998) 'Nation, state and identity at international borders', in Thomas M. Wilson and Hastings Donnan (eds) *Border identities: Nation and State at International Frontiers*, Cambridge: Cambridge University Press.

8 Irse pa' fuera

The mobile livelihoods of circular migrants between Puerto Rico and the United States

Jorge Duany

Migration has traditionally been considered as a single, one-way, and permanent change of residence. The dominant narratives on international migration typically focus on the relocation of surplus workers from poorer to richer countries, as well as on their impact on the host society, particularly the United States (see Pedraza and Rumbaut 1996; Portes and Rumbaut 1996). However, an axiom of international migration is that every flow of people generates a corresponding counter-flow. For instance, historians have documented the massive reverse movements from North America to southern and eastern Europe – especially Italy and Poland – in the late nineteenth century and the beginning of the twentieth (Hoerder 1985; Rosenblum 1973). Contemporary patterns of return migration have also been studied in Central America, the Caribbean, Southeast Asia, West Africa, and other regions of the world (see Cordell *et al.* 1996). Less well known is the propensity of some groups of people – such as Mexicans, Puerto Ricans, Dominicans, and Jamaicans – to move back and forth, or circulate, between their places of origin and destination. Such two-way, repetitive, and temporary moves do not fit easily within conventional models of migration. As Douglas Massey *et al.* (1998) point out, current thinking on transnational migration remains largely framed within nineteenth century concepts and methods.

Circular migration (also known as commuter, swallow, or revolving-door migration) is an increasingly common feature of international population movements. Although back-and-forth movements have long characterized many migrant streams, the current magnitude of circulation is unprecedented. Constant border crossing in both directions has been well documented among recent migrants from Mexico, Central America, and the Caribbean to the United States (Basch *et al.* 1994; Duany 1994; Hernández Cruz 1985, 1994; Martínez 1994; Massey *et al.* 1987; Rouse 1991; Schiller *et al.* 1992; Smith and Guarnizo 1998). Among other factors, the geographic proximity of countries such as Mexico, the Dominican Republic, Puerto Rico, and El Salvador to North America facilitates circular migration. Although economic, political, and cultural penetration by the United States entices people to move there, migrants often return home when socio-economic conditions abroad become less attractive – only to move back again when the local situation is unsatisfactory. Moreover, growing access to mass transportation and communications has increased the likelihood that people will engage in repetitive moves across national frontiers throughout their life cycles.

In this essay, I will argue that the emergence of 'mobile livelihoods' helps to explain large-scale population movements in multiple directions (Olwig and Sørensen 1999). By mobile livelihoods, I mean the spatial extension of people's means of subsistence across various local, regional, and national settings. Circular migration is only one, albeit an important, form of physical and socio-economic movement that reflects mobile livelihood practices. People who frequently cross geopolitical frontiers also move along the edges of cultural boundaries, such as those created by language, citizenship, race, ethnicity, and gender ideology. Thus, the development of mobile livelihoods has serious implications for the construction of labour markets, discourses of citizenship, language policies, and national identities. The concept of mobile livelihoods is especially pertinent to Puerto Ricans, who are US citizens by birth and therefore circulate more easily between their country of origin and the US mainland than other groups.

Nation on the move

Researchers on Puerto Rican migration traditionally assumed that it was a permanent relocation of low-wage labour from the periphery to the core of the capitalist world system (see History Task Force 1979; Sánchez Korrol 1994; for literature reviews, see Baerga and Thompson 1990; Duany 1994–95). Moreover, some scholars believed that large-scale migration from Puerto Rico to the United States had effectively ended after the great exodus between 1945 and 1965 (Hernández Alvarez 1967; Massey *et al.* 1998). The number of returnees began to surpass those leaving for the United States in the early 1970s, especially as a result of minimum wage hikes on the Island and the industrial restructuring of New York City, the traditional centre of the Puerto Rican diaspora (Meléndez 1993a; Santiago 1993; Tienda 1989). But mass emigration resumed during the 1980s, at the same time that return migration continued unabated, foreign immigration increased, and circular migration emerged as a significant phenomenon. Between 1991 and 1995, net migration from Puerto Rico to the United States was estimated to be 168,475 persons, compared to 116,571 in the 1980s (Autoridad de los Puertos 1996; Rivera-Batiz and Santiago 1996). In 1994–95 alone, 53,164 persons emigrated from the Island, while 18,177 immigrated (Olmeda 1997). In short, contemporary Puerto Rican migration is best visualized as a transient and bipendular flow (a 'revolving-door' movement), rather than as an irrevocable and unilateral displacement.

The massive reverse movement of people from the US mainland to the Island has been well documented since the mid-1960s (Bonilla and Campos 1986; Bonilla and Colón Jordán 1979; Cordero-Guzmán 1989; Enchautegui 1991; Hernández Alvarez 1967; Muschkin 1993). Return migrants to Puerto Rico were part of a large-scale two-way traffic of labour, capital, goods, and information that accelerated after World War II. This transnational flow preceded by several decades the current trend toward the globalization of financial and labour markets, facilitated by the lack of formal political barriers between Puerto Rico and the United States. Technically, Puerto Rico is an 'unincorporated territory' of the United States, neither a state of the union nor a sovereign nation, but a dependent country with limited autonomy under the current Commonwealth status. As they move between the Island and the US mainland, Puerto Ricans need not carry travel documents or apply for visa permits; the frontier between the two places is more cultural than juridical. But more than simply returning to their homeland (like many other migrants had done before), Puerto Ricans have traced a complex circuit, often involving frequent moves in multiple directions, not necessarily beginning or ending in the same points.

The circular flow between Puerto Rico and the United States challenges conventional views of population movements as linear and irreversible forms of mobility, as permanently disconnected from their sending communities, or as prone to inevitable assimilation into the host societies (see Hernández Cruz 1994; Rivera-Batiz and Santiago 1996; Torre *et al.* 1994). Such mobile livelihoods subvert dominant discourses of racial, ethnic, class, and gender relations, as well as legal concepts of state and nation, including sedentary notions of place, community, and citizenship. Among other results, the large-scale circulation of people, ideas, and practices frequently fractures hard-line positions on national identity, based on clearly bounded territories, languages, or cultures (see Gupta and Ferguson 1997; Kearney 1995; Olwig and Hastrup 1997; Schiller *et al.* 1995). Elsewhere, I have argued that Puerto Rico has become a 'nation on the move,' especially through the relocation of almost half of its population to the United States and the constant flow of people between the Island and the mainland (Duany 2000). The Spanish folk term for this back-and-forth movement is extremely suggestive: *el vaivén* (literally meaning fluctuation). *La nación en vaivén*, the nation on the move, might serve as an apt metaphor for the fluid and hybrid identities of Puerto Ricans on and off the Island.

Circular migration implies a broader definition of cultural identity among Puerto Ricans in the United States and in Puerto Rico itself. First, it poses the need for functional bilingualism in both places in order to maintain communication between those who stay and those who move frequently in either direction (Flores 1993; Urciuoli 1996). Rather than being Spanish or English monolinguals, growing numbers of Puerto Ricans are found somewhere along the bilingual continuum. In her study of El Barrio of New York City, Ana Celia Zentella (1997) documented that migrants redefined 'Puerto Ricanness' to incorporate monolingual English speakers as well as code switchers. Although Island-based Puerto Ricans still perceive the so-called *Nuyoricans*[1] as culturally different, the increasing number of people with mainland experience and bilingual skills may well challenge the public perception that moving abroad necessarily implies becoming more American and somehow less Puerto Rican.

Second, circular migration further erodes conventional definitions of citizenship and nationality based on place of birth or residence. Puerto Rican migrants have developed 'dual home bases,' one in the United States and another in

Puerto Rico, which allow them to maintain strong psychological attachments and social networks on the Island even when living abroad for long periods of time. As Marisa Alicea (1989, 1990) has argued, frequent movement within extended households and communities, spread widely across space, has become a common experience for Puerto Ricans over the last five decades. Such dual or multiple residences allow circular migrants to combine various sources of support from work, family, and the state. Thus, it is increasingly difficult to draw the line between the Island and the diaspora, inasmuch as a large proportion of Puerto Ricans spends part of their lives at both ends of the migratory circuit. Mobile livelihoods create a porous border zone between communities on and off the Island, which migrants continually traverse and transgress, sometimes several times a year.

Some scholars and journalists have argued that circular migration has a negative impact on human capital among Puerto Ricans (Tienda and Díaz 1987; see also Meléndez 1993b). The lack of attachment to local labour markets may confine circular migrants to unskilled blue-collar and service jobs because they cannot accumulate experience and skills either in the United States or in Puerto Rico. Moreover, circular migration can lead to disruptions in schooling and job training as well as in family life (Rivera-Batiz and Santiago 1996: 62). From this standpoint, frequent movement between the Island and the mainland is one of the main reasons for the socio-economic problems of Puerto Rican migrants. However, other scholars approach circulation as a flexible survival strategy for Puerto Rican families on and off the Island (Ellis *et al.* 1996; Hernández and Scheff 1997; Rodríguez 1993). In response to shifting economic circumstances in the United States and Puerto Rico, people may seek better employment opportunities elsewhere and maximize their resources by moving constantly. From this perspective, circular migration constitutes a spatially extended livelihood practice. Until now, the academic controversy over Puerto Rican circular migrants has not been settled because of lack of adequate data, research designs, and conceptual approaches.

This essay addresses the following issues: What is the actual extent of circulation between Puerto Rico and the United States? What kinds of people are likely to commute between the Island and the mainland? How does circular migration vary from one community to another and over time? How do circulating Puerto Ricans construct and maintain transnational ties to their places of origin and destination? What are the repercussions of circulation for national identity in Puerto Rico? To what degree do multiple movers contribute to a transnational socio-cultural system? Finally, how does the Puerto Rican experience compare with other contemporary cases of border crossing? My main thesis is that massive migration – both to and from the Island – has undermined dominant discourses of the nation based exclusively on territorial, linguistic, or juridical criteria. Thousands of Puerto Ricans have developed mobile livelihood practices that encompass places in the mainland as well as in the Island. Those who live abroad, speak English, and participate in US politics must be included in any public and academic discussions on the future of Puerto Rico.

Rethinking Puerto Rican circulation

Circular migration has been a hotly debated but little researched topic among Puerto Rican scholars. José Hernández Alvarez's (1967) pioneering work underlined one of the distinctive traits of the Puerto Rican diaspora since the 1960s: the constant flow of people in both directions for various periods of time – what has come to be known as 'circular migration.' As researchers began to reconceptualize the flow between the Island and the mainland, they used the term 'circulation' to capture the restless movement of labour as well as capital (Ashton 1980; Bonilla and Campos 1986; Conway *et al.* 1990; Ellis *et al.* 1996; Rodríguez 1988). The term served to emphasize the increasing tendency of Puerto Ricans and other groups to engage in repeated and temporary moves between various localities (Olwig and Sørensen 1999).

Juan Hernández Cruz (1985) was one of the first social scientists to systematically analyse the return movement to the Island as part of a circular flow produced by the increasing integration between the US and Puerto Rican economies. Other scholars have referred to the migrants as 'commuters' (Fitzpatrick 1987; Santiago 1993; Torre *et al.* 1994), as 'swallows' (Segal 1996), or, borrowing the literary image coined by Luis Rafael Sánchez (1994), as metaphorical passengers in the 'airbus' (*la guagua aérea*). More recent essays have expanded the range of possible terms to refer to this movement as revolving door, multiple, frequent, repetitive, recurrent, intermittent, seasonal, cyclical, or recycling migration (Hernández and Scheff 1993, 1997; Segal 1996). Many of these terms also appear commonly in studies of Mexican migration to the United States (Durand 1994; Martínez 1994; Massey *et al.* 1987).

Although scholars disagree as to the precise terminology, magnitude, and impact of circular migration, partly due to different sampling frames, most convene that the Puerto Rican diaspora has become a sustained bilateral movement of people. Estimates of the volume of circular migration between the Island and the mainland range from 10 to 45 per cent of the total flow, depending on various definitions, sources, methods, and approaches (Ellis *et al.* 1996; Hernández Cruz 1985; Ortiz 1994; Rodríguez 1994). According to the 1990 Census, 130,335 people commuted between the Island and the mainland – more than 23 per cent of those who left Puerto Rico – during the 1980s (Rivera-Batiz and Santiago 1996). Regardless of the exact number, back-and-forth movement has become a key feature of contemporary Puerto Rican society.

Recent thinking on transnationalism, hybridity, and translocality is very relevant to the Puerto Rican diaspora. Current notions such as 'divided borders' (Flores 1993), 'transnational circuits' (Rouse 1991, 1995), 'hybrid cultures' (García Canclini 1990), 'deterritorialised nation-state' (Basch *et al.* 1994), and 'translocal nation' (Laó 1997) are useful to revisit the Puerto Rican experience in the United States and Puerto Rico. Applying such notions must take into account that Puerto Rico is not a sovereign state, and therefore the analytical distinction between state and nation must be made carefully. For example, government authorities do not police Puerto Ricans moving back and forth between the Island and the mainland, unlike those who cross international frontiers. However, the subjective experience of migration for many Puerto Ricans as a dual process of deterritorialization and reterritorialization has been well established in the literature (see Rodríguez 1989; Sánchez Korrol 1994). As Puerto Ricans commonly say, moving to the United States involves *irse pa' fuera*, literally 'going outside' – their Island-country, that is.

The Puerto Rican diaspora has usually been interpreted as a unique, special, or anomalous case because of the Island's dependence on the United States, the legal nature of the migrant flow, and the free movement of labour and capital in both directions (see Bonilla and Campos 1986). Indeed, some people believe that Puerto Rican migration to the United States should be considered as an internal population movement, similar to, say, the relocation of residents of New York to Florida, rather than as an international migration (see, for example, Ashton 1999). From a different perspective, Puerto Ricans have been characterized as 'colonial immigrants' similar to Africans and West Indians in their English, French, and Dutch metropolises (Grosfoguel 1994–95; Rodríguez 1989). Although Puerto Rican migrants are not technically 'international' because they do not cross a formal political frontier between the Island and the mainland,[2] they are 'transnational' in the sense that they move from one national culture to another. Differences in geography, climate, religion, race relations, and other customs are sufficiently large to create symbolic frontiers between the United States and Puerto Rico, similar to those with Mexico or the Dominican Republic. The similarities and differences between the transnational practices of Puerto Ricans and other migrant groups (such as Mexicans) merit further reflection. As detailed later, this essay will use the same instrument, sampling method, and procedure as prior and current studies conducted by the Latin American Migration Project in Mexico, the Dominican Republic, and Paraguay (see Mexican Migration Project 1999).

Many of the findings and interpretations of transnational migration are applicable to the Puerto Rican case. For example, dense family networks characterize the transnational circuit between Puerto Rico and the United States as much as they do in the case of Mexico (Massey *et al.* 1987; Rouse 1991). Moreover, moving between the Island and the mainland entails crossing significant cultural, linguistic, and geographic frontiers (Massey *et al.* 1998: 70). For instance, Puerto Ricans moving to the United States have to learn some English, while those returning home must maintain their competence in Spanish. In turn, studying Puerto Rican circular migrants may help to reconceptualize current population movements, if only because most Puerto Ricans consider their nationality to be Puerto Rican rather than American. In Michael Kearney's (1991: 53) terms, Puerto Rican migrants cross 'borders' – understood as geographic and cultural contact zones – but not 'boundaries' – the legal spatial markers of nations. Thus, a transnational approach to the circulation of people between Puerto Rico and the United States should prove fruitful for both theoretical and empirical reasons.

From this standpoint, revisiting the Puerto Rican case shows that border crossing is hardly confined to movements across state frontiers. Rather, people may create fluid fields of social, economic, and political relations in various settings – local, regional, national, and transnational. Constant movement in multiple directions suggests the spatial expansion of personal and familial livelihood practices to geographically distant but socially connected areas (Olwig and Hastrup 1997; Olwig and Sørensen 1999). Under such shifting conditions, it is difficult to 'site' Puerto Rican culture in a particular landscape, either in the Island or in the US mainland. The frequent mobility of the Puerto Rican population tends to collapse conventional distinctions between points of origin and destination, between places of birth and residence. Consequently, examining recent transnational flows to and from Puerto Rico can contribute to contemporary debates on the relation among peoples, cultures, places, and identities (see Gupta and Ferguson 1997). In particular, circular migrants test the limits of spatially localized images of life, work, and homeland.

The remainder of this essay will empirically substantiate the mobile livelihood practices of circular migrants between Puerto Rico and the United States. To begin with, many Puerto Ricans continue to move back and forth between the Island and the mainland, for relatively long periods of time. Second, mobile livelihood practices are more common in communities with recent histories of migration to the United States than in those with more established migrant traditions. Third, circulating Puerto Ricans have geographically broadened their subsistence strategies to a larger number of destinations than in the past. Fourth, circulation between the Island and the mainland is more common among men, older people, better educated, and relatively skilled workers. Fifth, frequent movement is associated with having many relatives living in the mainland. Finally, circulation tends to improve a person's occupational and educational status, as well as English language skills.

Studying circulation[3]

Sample

Four communities were surveyed in Puerto Rico during July and August of 1998. (One community was partially surveyed between July and September of 1996).[4] A variety of *municipios* – the basic administrative units of local government on the Island, roughly equivalent to counties in the US mainland – was sampled to provide a basis for comparison and generalization. The communities were chosen to represent a range of population sizes, regions, ethnic compositions, and economic bases. The sample covered communities in the *municipios* of San Juan, Cataño-Guaynabo, Cidra, and Loíza; it thus included the Island's largest urban centre, two contiguous urban fringes within the San Juan metropolitan area, a medium-sized town in the inner highlands, and a small town on the northeast coast. By local standards, Loíza is a predominantly black community and Cidra is primarily white, while racial mixture is more common in San Juan and Cataño-Guaynabo.

The sample size ranged between 100 and 200 households for each community, for a total of 650 households or 2,989 individuals. Each community was censused on a house-by-house basis and households were selected using simple random methods. To qualify for an interview, household heads had to be born in Puerto Rico

Table 8.1 Characteristics of the sample[a]

	Cataño-Guaynabo (N = 863)	Cidra (N = 615)	Loíza (N = 607)	San Juan (N = 904)	Total (N = 2,989)
Sex					
Male	48.1	47.8	44.0	46.1	46.6
Female	51.9	52.2	56.0	53.9	53.4
Median age (number of years)	35	38	36	41	37
Median education (number of years of schooling)	11	12	11	11	11
Birthplace					
United States	5.6	6.5	7.2	8.3	6.9
Puerto Rico	89.1	88.0	91.4	82.8	87.5
Other countries	0.5	0.5	0.2	1.4	0.7
Unknown	4.9	5.0	1.2	7.4	4.9
Employment status					
Unemployed or out of the labour force	70.6	74.7	57.7	68.1	67.7
Employed	29.4	25.3	42.3	31.9	32.3
Current occupation[b]					
Managers and administrators	1.0	1.6	0.1	2.5	1.7
Professionals and technicians	14.8	34.9	14.9	19.7	19.4
Administrative support and sales workers	36.9	22.2	9.5	34.5	25.4
Craft and repair workers	27.1	25.4	11.6	22.7	20.8
Operators and labourers	5.4	5.6	53.1	8.9	20.6
Service workers	14.8	10.3	9.5	11.3	11.5
Agricultural workers	0.0	0.0	0.1	0.5	0.6

a In percentages, unless otherwise indicated.
b Of all employed persons with a known occupation.

or in the US mainland of Puerto Rican descent. The main characteristics of the sample are summarized in Table 8.1.

Instrument

The instrument for this study was an adapted version of the ethno survey designed by the Mexican Migration Project (MMP) at the University of Pennsylvania and the University of Guadalajara. Developed by Douglas Massey and his colleagues, the ethno survey was originally employed to collect information on migration between

Mexico and the United States (Massey *et al.* 1987; Massey and Zenteno 1998; Mexican Migration Project 1999). The questionnaire followed a semi-structured format to generate a flexible, unobtrusive, and nonthreatening interview schedule. Although identical information was obtained for each person, question wording and ordering were left to the interviewers' judgment.

The Puerto Rican version of the MMP instrument contained 14 tables with variables arranged in columns and rows referring to persons, events, years, and other categories. The first tables recorded the social, economic, and demographic characteristics of the household head, the spouse, their living and nonliving children, and other persons residing in the household. The following tables gathered information on each person's first and last trips within Puerto Rico and the United States. Next, the instrument focused on the household head and his or her spouse's business ownership and labour histories, beginning at age 15 or the first job, whichever came first. Another table recorded the migratory experiences of the head's relatives and friends in the United States. Finally, detailed information was compiled about the head's most recent trip to the United States, including social ties with US citizens of various ethnic origins, English language ability, and job characteristics.

Procedure

Four local research assistants, supervised by a field coordinator, conducted interviews in Spanish, with the household head serving as the principal respondent for all persons in the sample. The questionnaires were applied in three phases. In the first phase, interviewers gathered basic data on all members of the household, including age, birthplace, marital status, education, and occupation. The interview began by identifying the household head (as defined by the respondents) and systematically enumerating the spouse and children, whether or not they lived at home. If a son or daughter was a member of another household, this fact was recorded as well. A child was considered to be living in a separate household if he or she was married, maintained a separate house or kitchen, and organized expenses separately. After listing the head, spouse, and children, other household members were identified and their relationship to the head was clarified.

An important task in the first phase of the questionnaire was the identification of people with prior migrant experience in either Puerto Rico or the United States. For those individuals with migrant experience, interviewers recorded the total number of trips within Puerto Rico, as well as information about the first and most recent trips, including the year, duration, destination, occupation, and wage. This exercise was then repeated for the first and most recent migrations to the United States.

In the second phase, interviewers compiled a year-by-year life history for all household heads and their spouses. This section of the questionnaire focused on business formation, labour, migration, property, and housing. In the third and final phase, interviewers gathered further information about the household head's last trip to the United States, including the kind and number of relatives and friends living there, social ties with US citizens of various ethnic origins, English language ability, and job characteristics. If necessary, households were revisited to complete or clarify information.

Moving between the island and the mainland

Table 8.2 summarizes the total number of trips made by all persons in the sample.[5] More than 77 per cent had never moved to the US mainland, nearly 20 per cent had travelled once, and 3 per cent had completed two or more trips. (The latter is used as the operational definition of multiple movers or circular migrants in this paper).[6] Of those who had been abroad, 13.4 per cent were multiple movers. This figure is slightly higher than some earlier estimates of circular migrants (Conway *et al.* 1990; Ellis *et al.* 1996; Ortiz 1994; Rodríguez 1993) and is much lower than others (Hernández and Scheff 1997; Hernández Cruz 1985; Rivera-Batiz and Santiago 1996). Thus, the circulation of people between Puerto Rico and the United States is a substantial but minor component of a much broader migrant stream.

Migration rates ranged from a low of 18.3 per cent in Cataño-Guaynabo to a high of 27.6 per cent in Loíza, with San Juan (21.9 per cent) and Cidra (25.1 per cent) falling in between. The mean number of trips taken by *loiceños* doubled that of residents of Cataño-Guaynabo. Moreover, Loíza had the highest incidence of multiple movement (5.9 per cent), while San Juan had the lowest (2 per cent); Cidra (2.3 per cent) and Cataño-Guaynabo (2.7 per cent) had intermediate proportions. Not surprisingly, Loíza has the highest unemployment and poverty rates in the sample, whereas Guaynabo has the lowest (US Department of Commerce 1993). Thus, the findings confirm that the volume of Puerto Rican migration, particularly circular migration, varies from one *municipio* to another. As Massey *et al.* (1998) propose, people are more likely to move abroad if they come from a community with a high prevalence of out-migration, because they are better connected socially to people who have been abroad. For members of such a community, mobile livelihoods may be an expected part of life.

Furthermore, the proportion of household members still on their current trip to the United States varies from one *municipio* to another. San Juan and Loíza have relatively high per centages of persons living abroad (39.6 and 37.7 per cent,

Table 8.2 Number of trips to the United States (in percentages)

	Cataño-Guaynabo	Cidra	Loíza	San Juan	Total
No trips	81.7	75.0	72.3	78.1	77.3
One trip	15.6	22.8	21.7	19.9	19.6
Two or more trips	2.7	2.3	5.9	2.0	3.0
Still on current trip	26.1	23.4	37.7	39.6	32.3
Mean number of trips	0.22	0.27	0.44	0.25	0.29

Table 8.3 Year of first and last trip to the United States (in percentages)

	Cataño-Guaynabo		Cidra		Loíza		San Juan		Total	
	First	Last	First	Last	First	Last	First	Last	First	Last
1940–49	5.1	4.5	5.3	5.3	0.6	0.6	7.7	5.7	4.8	4.0
1950–59	19.1	15.9	19.7	17.8	11.3	6.5	25.8	25.3	19.2	16.7
1960–69	15.9	15.9	23.7	22.4	16.7	14.3	20.1	19.1	19.1	17.9
1970–79	26.8	24.8	18.4	18.4	26.8	23.8	14.4	15.5	21.3	20.4
1980–89	24.8	25.5	17.8	19.1	28.6	32.7	20.6	19.6	23.0	24.1
1990–8	8.3	13.4	15.1	17.1	16.1	22.0	11.3	14.9	12.7	16.8
Median year	1973	1977	1971	1972	1978	1981	1968	1969	1973	1976

respectively), while Cataño-Guaynabo and Cidra have much lower proportions (26.1 and 23.4 per cent, respectively). Altogether, about a third of all household members were living in the mainland at the time of the ethno survey. This figure is much lower than the 45 per cent obtained for Mexicans interviewed in the Mexican Migration Project (1999).

Table 8.3 compares the dates of departure for the first and last trips to the United States from the four Puerto Rican communities. About a third of the residents of San Juan made their first trip in the 1940s and 1950s, while over half of Loíza's residents made their first trip in the 1970s and 1980s. Proportionally more *loiceños* made their last trip during the 1990s than from other *municipios*. The median year of first departure ranged from 1968 in San Juan to 1978 in Loíza, with intermediate years in Cidra (1971) and Cataño-Guaynabo (1973). The median year of last departure ranged even more widely, from 1969 in San Juan to 1981 in Loíza. Hence, out-migration proceeded first from San Juan, then from Cidra and Cataño-Guaynabo, and finally from Loíza. According to the ethno survey, more people left the Island during the 1980s than any other decade. This phasing of migrant flows is probably related to the exhaustion of various development strategies employed by the Puerto Rican government since the onset of the industrialization programme in 1947 (Dietz 1986; Pantojas-García 1990).

Of the four areas under study, San Juan has a much longer history of out-migration. This finding is related to the incidence of internal migration from other *municipios* to San Juan, as witnessed by its high proportion of residents born elsewhere (32.3 per cent). Historically, the capital city has served as a stepping-stone to the US mainland. Furthermore, many migrants who were born outside San Juan have resettled there upon returning to the Island (Hernández Alvarez 1967). Hence, the capital also has the highest proportion of residents born in the United States (8.3 per cent). In any case, multiple movement is more common among communities with recent migrant traditions than among those with well-established histories of migration to the mainland.

The duration of residence in the United States also varies among the four *municipios*. Overall, the average stay abroad increased slightly between the first and most recent trips – from 136.7 to 137.4 months. Residents of San Juan tended to remain abroad much longer than those from other places – over 14 years and a half. In contrast, residents of Loíza stayed in the mainland for only nine years on both occasions. Except for residents of San Juan, migrants spent roughly the same or more time in their first and last trips. Many Puerto Ricans are apparently postponing the return to the Island, instead of shortening their stay in the United States. This trend may be related to continuing economic difficulties on the Island, especially after the elimination of section 936 of the US Internal Revenue Service, which provided tax exemption for American corporations operating in Puerto Rico.

Much has been written about the increasing dispersal of the Puerto Rican population in the United States. Analysis of recent census data has suggested a movement away from traditional areas of settlement in large urban centres of the northeast and Midwest and toward smaller cities of the northeast and Southeast, especially in states like Florida and California (Rivera-Batiz and Santiago 1994). However, when one compares the place of destination for the first and last trips among multiple movers, their concentration in New York City and other cities on the northeast coast remains extreme (Table 8.4). Nearly one-third of all multiple movers travelled to New York City on their first journey to the United States, as did one fourth on their second journey. On their first trip abroad, the migrants' secondary concentrations were Buffalo, Philadelphia, and New Haven. On their most recent journey, they went more often to Boston, Hartford, and Providence. Thus, the evidence provides modest support for the hypothesis that Puerto Ricans are more likely to move to different metropolitan areas than in the past. However, the back-and-forth movement tends to follow the traditional clustering of Puerto Ricans in New York City and other centres of the diaspora.

The data also suggest strong linkages between particular *municipios* in Puerto Rico and certain cities in the United States (Table 8.5). For instance, the leading

Table 8.4 Major metropolitan areas of destination for multiple movers on first and last trip to the United States (in percentages)

	First trip	Second trip
Boston, MA	6.2	10.9
Buffalo, NY	10.8	4.7
Chicago, IL	6.2	4.7
Cincinnati, OH	0.0	3.1
Hartford, CT	3.1	6.3
Los Angeles, CA	3.1	1.6
Miami, FL	3.1	1.6
New Haven, CT	7.7	6.3
New York, NY	32.3	25.0
Philadelphia, PA	10.8	9.4
Providence, RI	0.0	6.3
Syracuse, NY	1.5	4.7
Other places	15.0	16.0

Table 8.5 Major metropolitan areas of destination on first and last trip to the United States, by community of origin (in percentages)

	Cataño-Guaynabo		Cidra		Loíza		San Juan		Total	
	First	*Last*	*First*	*Last*	*First*	*Last*	*First*	*Last*	*First*	*Last*
Allentown, PA			3.4	3.5					0.7	0.7
Boston, MA	1.8	1.8	2.3	2.3	28.9	31.0	4.0	4.0	11.8	12.4
Buffalo, NY	4.4	1.8	1.1	1.2	5.7	4.4	2.0	3.0	3.7	2.8
Chicago, IL	5.3	5.4	23.9	23.3			7.1	6.0	7.4	7.2
Cleveland, OH						0.6	3.0	3.0	0.7	0.9
Greensboro, NC			3.4	3.5					0.7	0.7
Hartford, CT			13.6	12.8	0.6	0.6	1.0	1.0	3.1	3.5
Los Angeles, CA	1.8	0.9	1.1	1.2	3.8	3.8			2.0	1.7
Miami, FL	6.2	6.3			1.3	0.6	5.1	5.0	3.1	2.8
New Haven, CT					8.2	7.6			2.8	2.6
New York, NY	62.8	64.9	22.7	25.6	29.6	25.9	60.6	58.0	43.1	42.0
Newark, NJ			11.4	11.6	2.5	1.9			3.1	2.8
Philadelphia, PA	9.7	9.0	1.1	1.2	9.4	9.5			5.9	5.7
Springfield, MA			6.8	7.0					1.3	1.3
Syracuse, NY					3.8	5.1			1.3	1.7
Worcester county, MA	2.7	3.6							0.7	0.9
Other places	5.4	6.3	8.9	7.2	6.5	8.7	22.1	20.0	8.8	7.0

destination for residents of Loíza is now Boston, while New York City dominates the traffic of people from Cataño-Guaynabo and San Juan. For residents of Cidra, Chicago, Hartford, and Newark are important secondary destinations; residents of Loíza travel more frequently to Philadelphia and New Haven. Migrants from Cataño-Guaynabo also move to Philadelphia and Miami, while many *sanjuaneros* settle in Chicago and various places not contained in metropolitan areas. Each of the *municipios* has tended to form its own 'daughter communities' (Massey *et al.* 1987) in the United States, especially in New York City, Chicago, and Boston. In sum, each sending community has developed a distinct migratory circuit that connects it to several points of the diaspora.

Table 8.6 compares the socio-demographic characteristics of multiple, one-time, and non-movers. To begin, men were more likely than women to move once or more frequently. On average, multiple movers were five years older than one-time movers and 13 years older than non-movers. The median education of recurrent and one-time migrants was one year higher than for non-migrants. A higher per centage of multiple movers than of the rest of the sample was born in Puerto Rico rather than abroad. More than half was unemployed or outside the labour force, especially housewives and retired persons. Of those who worked, the vast majority were operators, labourers, craft and repair workers. Thus, the data suggest that circulation is most common among middle-aged men with a high school education and a blue-collar job.

Table 8.6 Sociodemographic characteristics of non-movers, one-time movers, and multiple movers[a]

	No trips	One trip	Two or more trips
Sex			
Male	45.2	50.8	56.0
Female	54.8	49.2	44.0
Median years of age	35	43	48
Median years of education	11	12	12
Birthplace			
Puerto Rico	92.0	91.2	97.7
United States	7.3	8.1	2.3
Other countries	0.7	0.7	0.0
Employment status			
Unemployed or out of the labour force	69.4	62.4	55.7
Employed	30.6	27.6	44.3
Current occupation			
Professionals and technicians	20.2	20.9	12.9
Managers and administrators	1.4	2.5	0.0
Administrative support and workers	29.0	18.4	16.1
Craft and repair workers	18.6	16.6	22.6
Operators and labourers	18.4	26.4	45.2
Service workers	11.5	14.7	3.2
Agricultural workers	0.9	0.0	0.0

a In percentages, unless otherwise indicated.

Table 8.7 compares multiple movers' occupations during their first and last trips to the United States. Note that the proportion of persons who were unemployed or out of the labour force decreased considerably between the two trips. The main change (from 31.4 to 8.6 per cent of the total) occurred among students and other persons under 15 years of age who did not study or work during their first trip, and were working during the second trip. Among those who were employed, the proportion in white-collar and skilled occupational categories increased significantly, especially among craft and repair workers and administrative support workers. Inversely, the proportion of agricultural and service workers decreased substantially. The evidence suggests that moving back and forth between the Island and the mainland tends to improve the occupational status of Puerto Ricans.

The social networks of household heads who had moved to the United States are summarized in Table 8.8. Multiple movers had proportionally more relatives – such as parents, older siblings, uncles, aunts, nieces, and nephews – living in the United States than one-time migrants. Only on one count – cousins – did one-time movers have more relatives abroad than multiple movers. Moreover, multiple movers had developed close relations with Nuyoricans at work and at home, as well as one-time movers. However, multiple movers had proportionally fewer friends

Table 8.7 Employment status and occupation for multiple movers during first and last trip to the United States (in percentages)

	First trip	Last trip
Employment status in the US		
Unemployed or out of the labour force	50.0	36.2
Employed	50.0	63.8
Occupation in the US		
Professionals and technicians	2.9	5.4
Managers and administrators	0.0	0.0
Administrative support and sales workers	0.0	8.1
Craft and repair workers	11.4	21.6
Operators and labourers	25.7	27.0
Service workers	17.1	5.4
Agricultural workers	42.9	32.4

Table 8.8 Social networks of household heads who moved to the United States (in percentages)

	One trip	Two or more trips
Mother resides in the US	17.8	21.3
Father resides in the US	9.7	27.7
Older sibling resides in the US	55.7	72.3
Uncle or aunt resides in the US	21.8	25.5
Cousin resides in the US	54.6	51.1
Niece or nephew resides in the US	57.8	66.0
Has one or more friends in the US	75.7	47.1
Related to Nuyoricans at work and at home	44.8	44.1

abroad than those who had moved only once. Hence, the data show that recurrent migration is associated with close-knit kinship networks in the United States. Such social ties help migrants to secure jobs, housing, financial and emotional support for the transition between life on the Island and in the mainland. Family obligations are also one of the major reasons why people – especially women – move back and forth, in addition to looking for a job, improving one's economic situation, studying, and retiring.

The frequency and meaning of mobile livelihood practices differ significantly by gender. Prior studies have characterized female circulation between Puerto Rico and the United States as 'tied-circulation,' because it depends largely on others' decisions to move, especially male partners, parents, and other relatives (Conway *et al.* 1990; Ellis *et al.* 1996). Most Puerto Rican women do not migrate to work outside the home or search for employment. Rather, they move to 'attend to their home or family group' (Olmeda 1997) – that is, to sustain the mobile livelihoods of transnational households. Circulating women do much of the unpaid labour – such as baby-sitting and taking care of the sick and elderly – required to maintain kinship networks across wide distances. Female mobility tends to concentrate in certain critical points of the life cycle, such as marriage, divorce, and retirement (Alicea 1989, 1996; Rodríguez 1994).

Table 8.9 reports language use among migrant heads of households while they were living in the United States. As expected, multiple movers had a larger per centage of persons who spoke English frequently or always at home, at work, among friends, and in the neighbourhood. The results confirm that multiple movers use English more commonly and in more situations than those who move only once. As argued before, circular migrants need to be fully bilingual in English and Spanish to succeed in the United States as well as in Puerto Rico. This pattern has long-term effects on Puerto Rican cultural identity, although the ethno survey did not specifically inquire about this topic. Among other consequences, it may contribute to erode the long-standing assumption that being Puerto Rican is equivalent to speaking Spanish. In New York City, the Puerto Ricanness of English-speaking children raised in the mainland is rarely questioned, as it is on the Island; family origin and cultural traditions are the key markers of identity for most migrants (Zentella 1997). Perhaps circular migration will expand the monolingual Spanish definition of Puerto Rican culture on the Island as well.

In sum, the results of this study question many commonly held beliefs about Puerto Rican circular migration. To begin with, most Puerto Ricans do 'commute'

Table 8.9 English language use among household heads who moved to the United States (in percentages)

	One trip	Two or more trips
Spoke English at home		
Never	57.8	56.7
Sometimes	28.9	20.0
Frequently	6.3	16.7
Always	7.0	6.7
English at work		
Never	19.5	20.0
Sometimes	44.5	23.3
Frequently	9.4	23.3
Always	26.6	33.3
Spoke English among friends		
Never	39.8	36.7
Sometimes	43.8	26.7
Frequently	14.1	33.3
Always	2.3	3.3
Spoke English in neighbourhood		
Never	23.4	23.3
Sometimes	57.8	40.0
Frequently	10.9	23.3
Always	7.8	13.3

regularly between the Island and the mainland but remain settled in one of the two places. Those who circulate do so mainly between their communities of origin on the Island and a few cities of the north-eastern United States, such as New York City, Boston, Philadelphia, Hartford, New Haven, and Providence. Certain kinds of people are more likely to move frequently, such as middle-aged, better-educated men employed as blue-collar workers. Contrary to a popular assumption, back-and-forth movement usually has a positive effect on a person's occupational status. Multiple movers have a larger network of relatives in the United States, are more proficient in English, and use it in more situations than those who have travelled abroad only once. Thus, the mobile livelihoods of many Puerto Ricans expand their economic opportunities, social relations, and cultural practices.

Conclusion

Much of the current knowledge on international population movements is based on the premise that people move only once, in a single direction, and settle permanently in another country. Over the last decade, scholars have contributed to rethinking transnational flows of people that do not conform to the classic pattern of international migration (see Massey *et al.* 1998; Schiller *et al.* 1995; Smith and Guarnizo 1998). People often return home after spending some time abroad and, less frequently, move again to the first or a different destination. The strategy of recurrent migration from Mexico to the United States has been well documented, especially among seasonal farm workers since the beginning of the twentieth century (Massey *et al.* 1987). In the Mexican Migration Project database, nearly 44 per cent of all migrants had made two or more trips to the United States. Among Puerto Ricans, circular migration has been notable at least since the 1960s. According to the findings reported in this essay, about 13 per cent of those who have moved abroad had made multiple trips. Compared to frequent movers from Mexico, those from Puerto Rico are more likely to be legal, female, older, educated, unemployed, skilled, and long-term migrants.

Overall, the results of this study suggest a major reassessment of Puerto Rican circular migration. On average, circulators between the Island and the mainland are better educated than non-migrants and are more likely to be employed than one-time migrants. Admittedly, multiple movers are more concentrated than non-migrants and one-time migrants in unskilled blue-collar jobs. But most people's occupational status improved between their first and last trips to the United States. Hence, circular migration tends to increase the human capital of Puerto Ricans, contrary to earlier writing on this topic. Moreover, recurrent migrants display a higher degree of bilingualism and a larger number of relatives abroad than one-time migrants. To be successful, mobile livelihoods require dual language skills and far-flung social networks.

The finding that frequent mobility among Puerto Ricans tends to improve their socio-economic position runs against much of the conventional wisdom on circular migration. A recurrent problem with prior work on this topic was that it did not distinguish clearly between the causes and effects of circulation. Hence, it was difficult to know if people moved frequently in search of a better livelihood or if, alternatively, the spatial expansion of their means of subsistence led them to move constantly. The results of this study provide empirical support for the second proposition. That is to say, many Puerto Ricans move back and forth between the Island and the US mainland because their subsistence strategies have broadened geographically to include several labour markets, multiple home bases, extended kinship networks, and bilingual and bicultural practices as a result of transnational migration. When economic opportunities are unequally distributed in space – as they are in the case of Puerto Rico and the United States – many people develop mobile livelihood practices through circulation and other forms of physical, social, and economic mobility.

In closing, let me underline three main consequences of circular migration for Puerto Ricans on the Island and in the diaspora. First of all, the results of this study suggest that circulation by itself cannot account for the continuing poverty and deprivation among Puerto Ricans in the United States (see Meléndez 1993b; Tienda 1989). Rather, the fluidity of Puerto Rican population movements is a productive survival strategy for many households on and off the Island, in view of the incapacity of labour markets to absorb additional workers, especially in the declining manufacturing sector (Ellis *et al.* 1996; Rodríguez 1993). Circulation is a way of mobilizing personal and family resources spread widely in space and transcending geo-cultural boundaries. It constitutes, in the terms proposed by the editors of this volume, a set of mobile livelihood practices in two or more localities (Olwig and Sørensen 1999). For most people, multiple movement is a form of acquiring skills and education and improving their occupational status. The bilateral displacement of Puerto Ricans is one of the key transnational links between their communities in Puerto Rico and the United States, especially along the north-eastern seaboard. More than for other migrants, the daily lives of circular migrants depend on dense and multiple social networks across national frontiers (Schiller *et al.* 1995).

A second implication of circular migration between Puerto Rico and the United States is the mobilization and flexibilization of cultural identities beyond neatly bounded categories of language, territory, or citizenship. Circular migrants have to acquire bilingual and bicultural skills to survive in both a Puerto Rican and an American setting. In developing dual or perhaps multiple 'home bases' (Alicea 1990), they also defy standard criteria to assign permanent residence to a single place over prolonged periods of time. US citizenship appears as a practical convenience, rather than an emotional identity marker, for those who travel frequently between the Island and the mainland. That such a large proportion of Puerto Ricans have lived abroad, many more than once; that most have relatives and friends in the United States; and that they maintain close ties to Nuyorican communities suggest that Puerto Rico itself has been thoroughly transnationalized over the last five decades through massive migration, circulation, and other social processes. For many Puerto Ricans today, the Island no longer represents a separate national entity, an exclusive homeland, but rather one point in an extensive migratory circuit, a pole in a geographic and cultural continuum of interrelated places of residence and work.

My final point regards the comparative significance of circulation among Puerto Ricans and other migrants. Contrary to my original expectation, recurrent migration is much more common among Mexicans, many of whom are undocumented, than among Puerto Ricans, who are US citizens. Returning to Kearney's (1991) intriguing distinction between borders and boundaries, Mexicans cross legal boundaries more frequently than Puerto Ricans cross the cultural border to the United States. Traversing formal geopolitical frontiers may actually *increase* the likelihood of moving back and forth, at least between bordering regions such as western Mexico and the southwestern United States. In any case, the mobile livelihood of many Puerto Ricans on and off the Island undermines the highly localized images of space, culture, and identity that have dominated nationalist discourse and practice in Puerto Rico and elsewhere. Although much work remains to be done on this topic, *irse pa' fuera* represents a radical decentring of the Puerto Rican nation.

Acknowledgements

This paper was written while I was a visiting scholar at the Population Studies Center of the University of Pennsylvania during June and July of 1999. I want to express my gratitude to Douglas S. Massey and Jorge Durand for inviting me to collaborate with the Latin American Migration Project at Penn. I am also thankful to Mariano Sana and Nolan Malone for their help in processing the data. I appreciate the useful comments and suggestions on earlier drafts of this paper by Ninna Nyberg Sørensen, Karen Fog Olwig, and Douglas S. Massey. Finally, I would like to acknowledge the efforts of the project's interviewers in Puerto Rico: Sonia Castro Cardona, Diana Johnson, Moira Pérez, and Rafael Zapata.

Notes

1 As popularly used in Puerto Rico, 'Nuyorican' refers to all Puerto Ricans born or raised in the United States, not just in New York City. Here I will use the term in the wider sense of the Puerto Rican diaspora, without intending any negative connotations.
2 Travelling from Puerto Rico to the US mainland is distinct from travelling within the fifty states in two main ways: first, all baggage must be inspected by the US Department of Agriculture at the airport; and second, passengers may be asked if they are US citizens by officers from the Immigration and Naturalization Service. For other practical purposes, travel between the Island and the mainland is considered an internal move within US territory. Still, some airline, train, and courier companies, as well as banks and retail businesses, classify Puerto Rico as an 'international' or 'overseas' destination.
3 The study reported in this essay was directed by Douglas S. Massey, of the University of Pennsylvania, and Jorge Durand, of the University of Guadalajara. The survey was part of the Latin American Migration Project, supported by the National Institute of Child Health and Human Development.
4 In 1996, Rafael Zapata conducted 65 interviews in Loíza. In 1998, Moira Pérez completed the sample of 100 households in the same area.

5 I am aware that using multiple movement as a proxy for circular migration may be problematic for some purposes – for instance, to calculate the velocity with which people travel back and forth between the Island and the mainland. However, I would argue that imposing an arbitrary time limit on the category of 'circular migrant', as much of the relevant literature has done before, is artificial and unnecessary. Hence, I prefer a minimal definition of circulation as the completion of two full migrant cycles, regardless of the spacing or duration of the trips.
6 The project's criteria for determining the number of trips included motive, duration, activity, and location of the household. Thus, if a person intended to work in the United States for several months and moved abroad with her household, that was counted as one trip.

References

Alicea, Marisa (1996) 'A chambered nautilus: Puerto Rican women's role in the social construction of a transnational community', paper presented at the workshop on 'Circular Migration Between Puerto Rico and the United States: A Transnational Approach,' Universidad del Sagrado Corazón, Santurce, Puerto Rico, September 24–5.

Alicea, Marisa (1990) 'Dual home bases: A reconceptualization of Puerto Rican migration', *Latino Studies Journal* 1(3): 78–98.

Alicea, Marisa (1989) *The Dual Base Phenomenon: A Reconceptualization of Puerto Rican Migration*, Ph.D. Dissertation, Northwestern University.

Ashton, Guy T. (1999) 'Professor's report on travel patterns fails to surprise', *The San Juan Star*, September 30, p. 78.

Ashton, Guy T. (1980) 'The return and re-return of long-term Puerto Rican migrants: A selective rural-urban sample', *Revista/Review Interamericana* 10(1): 27–45.

Autoridad de los Puertos, Oficina de Estudios Económicos (Puerto Rico) (1996) *Compendio estadístico*, San Juan: Autoridad de los Puertos.

Baerga, María del Carmen and Lanny Thompson (1990) 'Migration in a small semi-periphery: The movement of Puerto Ricans and Dominicans', *International Migration Review* 24(4): 656–83.

Basch, Linda, Nina Glick Schiller and Cristina Szanton-Blanc (1994) *Nations Unbound: Transnational Projects, Postcolonial Predicaments, and Deterritorialized Nation-States*, New York: Gordon and Breach.

Bonilla, Frank and Ricardo Campos (1986) *Industry and Idleness*, New York: Centro de Estudios Puertorriqueños, Hunter College.

Bonilla, Frank and Héctor Colón Jordán (1979) ' "amá, Borinquen Me Llama!" Puerto Rican return migration in the 70s', *Migration Today* 7(2): 1–6.

Conway, Dennis, Mark Ellis and Naragandat Shiwdhan (1990) 'Caribbean international circulation: Are Puerto Rican women tied-circulators?' *Geoforum* 21(1): 51–66.

Cordell, Dennis D., Joel W. Gregory and Victor Piché (1996) *Hoe and Wage: A Social History of a Circular Migration System in West Africa*, Boulder, Co.: Westview.

Cordero-Guzmán, Héctor (1989) 'The socio-demographic characteristics of return migrants to Puerto Rico and their participation in the labor market 1965–1980', Master's Thesis, University of Chicago.

Dietz, James (1986) *Economic History of Puerto Rico: Institutional Change and Capitalist Development*, Princeton, N.J.: Princeton University Press.

Duany, Jorge (2000) 'Nation on the move: The construction of cultural identities in Puerto Rico and the diaspora', *American Ethnologist* 27(1): 5–30.

Duany, Jorge (1994–95) 'Common threads or disparate agendas? Research trends on migration from and to Puerto Rico', *Centro* 7(1): 60–77.

Duany, Jorge (1994) *Quisqueya on the Hudson: The Transnational Identity of Dominicans in Washington Heights*, New York: Dominican Studies Institute, City University of New York.

Durand, Jorge (1994) *Más allá de la línea: patrones migratorios entre México y Estados Unidos*, Mexico City: Consejo Nacional para la Cultura y las Artes.

Ellis, Mark, Dennis Conway and Adrian J. Bailey (1996) *The Circular Migration of Puerto Rican Women: Towards a Gendered Explanation*, Working Paper No. 98–5, Population Institute for Research and Training, Indiana University.

Enchautegui, María E. (1991) *Subsequent Moves and the Dynamics of the Migration Decision: The Case of Return Migration to Puerto Rico*, Ann Arbor: Population Studies Center, University of Michigan.

Fitzpatrick, Joseph P. (1987) *Puerto Rican Americans: The Meaning of Migration to the Mainland* (2nd edn), Englewood Cliffs, N.J.: Prentice-Hall.

Flores, Juan (1993) *Divided Borders: Essays on Puerto Rican Identity*, Houston: Arte Público Press.

García Canclini, Néstor (1990) *Culturas híbridas: estrategias para entrar y salir de la modernidad*, Mexico City: Grijalbo.

Grosfoguel, Ramón (1994–95) 'Caribbean colonial immigrants in the metropoles: A research agenda', *Centro* 7(1): 82–95.

Gupta, Akhil and James Ferguson (eds) (1997) *Culture, Power, Place: Explorations in Critical Anthropology*, Durham, N.C.: Duke University Press.

Hernández, David and Janet Scheff (1997) 'Puerto Rican ethnicity and U.S. citizenship on the Puerto Rico-New York commute', paper presented at the XX International Congress of the Latin American Studies Association, Guadalajara, Mexico, April 17–19.

Hernández, David and Janet Scheff (1993) 'Rethinking migration: having roots in two worlds', paper presented at the XIX Annual Conference of the Caribbean Studies Association, Kingston and Ocho Ríos, Jamaica, May 24–29.

Hernández Alvarez, José (1967) *Return Migration to Puerto Rico*, Berkeley: Institute for International Studies, University of California.

Hernández Cruz, Juan (1994) *Corrientes migratorias en Puerto Rico/Migratory Trends in Puerto Rico*, San Germán, P.R.: Centro de Publicaciones, Universidad Interamericana de Puerto Rico.

Hernández Cruz, Juan (1985) 'Migración de retorno o circulación de obreros boricuas?' *Revista de Ciencias Sociales* 24(1–2): 81–112.

History Task Force, Centro de Estudios Puertorriqueños (1979) *Labor Migration Under Capitalism: The Puerto Rican Experience*, New York: Monthly Review Press.

Hoerder, Dirk (ed.) (1985) *Labor Migration in the Atlantic Economies: The European and North American Working Classes during the Period of Industrialization*, Westport, Ct.: Greenwood.

Kearney, Michael (1995) 'The local and the global: The anthropology of globalization and transnationalism', *Annual Review of Anthropology* 24: 547–65.

Kearney, Michael (1991) 'Borders and boundaries of the state and self at the end of empire', *Journal of Historical Sociology* 4(1): 52–74.

Laó, Agustín (1997) 'Islands at the crossroads: Puerto Ricanness traveling between the translocal nation and the global city', in Frances Negrón-Muntaner and Ramón Grosfoguel (eds) *Puerto Rican Jam: Essays on Culture and Politics*, Minneapolis: University of Minnesota Press, pp. 169–88.

Martínez, Oscar J. (1994) *Border People: Life and Society on the U.S.-Mexico Borderlands*, Tucson: University of Arizona Press.

Massey, Douglas S., Rafael Alarcón, Jorge Durand and Humberto González (1987) *Return to Aztlan: The Social Process of International Migration from Western Mexico*, Berkeley and Los Angeles: University of California Press.

Massey, Douglas S., Joaquín Arango, Graeme Hugo, Ali Kouaouci, Adela Pellegrino and J. Edward Taylor (1998) *Worlds in Motion: Understanding International Migration at the End of the Millenium*, Oxford: Clarendon Press.

Massey, Douglas S. and René Zenteno (1998) 'A Validation of the Ethnosurvey: The Case of Mexico-U.S. Migration', unpublished manuscript, Population Studies Center, University of Pennsylvania.

Meléndez, Edwin (1993a) *Los que se van, los que regresan: Puerto Rican Migration to and from the United States, 1982–1988*, Political Economy Working Paper Series no. 1, New York: Centro de Estudios Puertorriqueños, Hunter College.

Meléndez, Edwin (1993b) 'Understanding Latino poverty', *Sage Race Relations Abstracts* 18(2): 1–42.

Mexican Migration Project (1999) Population Studies Center, University of Pennsylvania. Online. Available HTTP: http//www.lexis.pop.upenn.edu/mexmig.

Muschkin, Clara G. (1993) 'Consequences of return migrant status for employment in Puerto Rico', *International Migration Review* 27(1): 70–102.

Olmeda, Luz H. (1997) 'Aspectos socioeconómicos de la migración en el 1994–95', in Junta de Planificación (ed.) *Informe económico al Gobernador*, San Juan: Junta de Planificación de Puerto Rico, pp. 6–12.

Olwig, Karen Fog and Kirsten Hastrup (eds) (1997) *Siting Culture: The Shifting Anthropological Object*, London: Routledge.

Olwig, Karen Fog and Ninna Nyberg Sørensen (1999) *Mobile Livelihoods: Life and Work in a Globalizing World*, book proposal, Routledge Press, London.

Ortiz, Vilma (1994) 'Circular migration and employment among Puerto Rican women', *Latino Studies Journal* 4(2): 56–70.

Pantojas-García, Emilio (1990) *Development Strategies as Ideologies: Puerto Rico's Export-Led Industrialization Experience*, Boulder, Co.: Lynne Rienner.

Pedraza, Silvia and Rubén G. Rumbaut (eds) (1996) *Origins and Destinies: Immigration, Race, and Ethnicity in America*, Belmont, Ca.: Wadsworth.

Portes, Alejandro and Rubén G. Rumbaut (1996) *Immigrant America: A Portrait* (2nd edn), Berkeley: University of California Press.

Rivera-Batiz, Francisco and Carlos E. Santiago (1996) *Island Paradox: Puerto Rico in the 1990s*, New York: Russell Sage Foundation.

Rivera-Batiz, Francisco and Carlos E. Santiago (1994) *Puerto Ricans in the United States: A Changing Reality*, Washington, D.C.: National Puerto Rican Coalition.

Rodríguez, Clara (1993) 'Puerto Rican circular migration revisited', *Latino Studies Journal* 4(2): 93–113.

Rodríguez, Clara (1989) *Puerto Ricans: Born in the U.S.A.*, Boston: Unwin Hyman.

Rodríguez, Clara (1988) 'Circulating migration', *Journal of Hispanic Policy* 4: 5–9.

Rosenblum, Gerald (1973) *Immigrant Workers: Their Impact on American Labor Radicalism*, New York: Basic Books.

Rouse, Roger (1995) 'Thinking through transnationalism: Notes on the cultural politics of class relations in the contemporary United States', *Public Culture* 7: 353–402.

Rouse, Roger (1991) 'Mexican migration and the social space of postmodernism', *Diaspora* 1(1): 8–23.

Sánchez, Luis Rafael (1994) *La guagua aérea*, Río Piedras, P.R.: Cultural.

Sánchez Korrol, Virginia (1994) *From Colonia to Community: The History of Puerto Ricans in New York City* (2nd edn), Berkeley: University of California Press.

Santiago, Carlos E (1993) 'The migratory impact of minimum wage legislation: Puerto Rico, 1970–1987', *International Migration Review* 27(4): 772–95.

Schiller, Nina Glick, Linda Basch and Cristina Blanc-Szanton (eds) (1992) *Towards a Transnational Perspective on Migration: Race, Class, Ethnicity, and Nationalism Reconsidered*, New York: New York Academy of Sciences.

Schiller, Nina Glick, Linda Basch and Cristina Szanton-Blanc (1995) 'From immigrant to transmigrant: Theorizing transnational migration', *Anthropological Quarterly* 68(1): 48–63.

Segal, Aaron (1996) 'Locating the swallows: Caribbean recycling migration', paper presented at the XXII Annual Conference of the Caribbean Studies Association, San Juan, Puerto Rico, May 27–31.

Smith, Michael Peter and Luis E. Guarnizo, (eds) (1998). *Transnationalism from Below*, Volume 6 of Comparative Urban and Community Research, New Brunswick, N.J.: Transaction.

Tienda, Marta (1989) 'Puerto Ricans and the underclass debate', *Annals of the American Academy of Political and Social Science* 501 (January): 105–19.

Tienda, Marta and William Díaz (1987) 'Puerto Rican circular migration', *The New York Times*, August 28: A31.

Torre, Carlos, Hugo Rodríguez-Vecchini and William Burgos (eds) (1994) *The Commuter Nation: Perspectives on Puerto Rican Migration*, Río Piedras, P.R.: Editorial de la Universidad de Puerto Rico.

Urciuoli, Bonnie (1996) *Exposing Prejudice: Puerto Rican Experiences of Language, Race, and Class*, Boulder, Co.: Westview.

U.S. Department of Commerce, Bureau of the Census (1993) *1990 Census of Population: Social and Economic Characteristics*, Washington, D.C.: U.S. Government Printing Office.

Zentella, Ana Celia (1997) *Growing Up Bilingual: Puerto Rican Children in New York*, Malden M.A.: Blackwell.

Part III

Livelihoods and the transnational return

9 Transnational livelihoods and identities in return migration to the Caribbean

The case of skilled returnees to Jamaica

Elizabeth Thomas-Hope

International migration is not just the movement of people between places, it is a relocation of the individual and, by extension the group, with respect to the global social, economic and political system. Thus migration requires a reshaping of livelihood and, thereby, a reformulation of identity. This is necessitated both by the outward migration and the return.

The return is a significant aspect of Caribbean migration, but one that only recently has caught the attention of academic researchers and policy makers in the region. In the countries of destination, most of the attention paid to Caribbean international migration has been with respect to the outward movement and especially to migrant adaptation to and assimilation in the receiving society, as well as with issues of ethnicity and race relations. In the countries of migrant origin in the Caribbean, emigration has been treated traditionally as a welcome opportunity for the outward movement of surplus labour, but since the 1960s and 1970s it began to attract attention in terms of the loss of talent or 'brain drain', and the impact of this aspect of migration upon Caribbean countries.

An important characteristic of Caribbean migration in the twentieth century has been the transnational networks that have been established. The transnational household is largely based on the extent and nature of displacement of migrants that occurred and linked to this the extent of counter-flows that developed outward movement of people is discussed in greater detail elsewhere (Pessar 1982; Thomas-Hope 1985; Basch *et al.* 1987). Aspects of the migration process that remain little understood chiefly relate to the migrants' return and the nature of the transnational household after the return. This paper evaluates the extent and ways in which the return becomes part of and reinforces the transnational household. This is examined through the livelihood strategies and identities of the return migrants that incorporate the countries of previous and current residence demonstrated through the social networks and economic links of the return migrants. The paper further highlights the fact that the returnees display the social behaviours and cultural values of the country of their previous residence, as a characteristic of their new transnational identities.

Caribbean return migration and the transnational community

Caribbean migration has always had an essentially transnational character. While the movements of people, information and goods were greatly restricted by the difficulty of communication and travel in the nineteenth and early twentieth centuries, there was always a significant return flow associated with the movements. Return flows of migrants from Panama and Central America were significant until the mid-twentieth century when the cycle was complete and there were no longer new arrivals. The migration to Europe in the 1950s and 1960s and the migrations chiefly since the 1960s to the United States and Canada, likewise have generated a significant return movement, particularly since the late 1970s. For most Caribbean people, migration has come to be regarded less as a means of permanent departure from the home country and more as a mechanism for extending the opportunities of work and education beyond the limitations of small island systems (Thomas-Hope 1992). The linkages that are maintained between members of households and families across national boundaries are critical for maintaining the opportunities to return periodically or permanently. It is common for migrants to return to their Caribbean country of origin for occasional or regular visits over a prolonged period of time after which some return to reside indefinitely while others continue to circulate.

Even with evidence of significant return and reciprocal moves of people between Caribbean countries and migration destinations in North America and Western Europe, the migration process itself has traditionally been regarded as a series of linear flows from points of origin to destination, with migration viewed solely in terms of population displacement. Yet, when Caribbean international migration is examined in its entirety, activities at places of migration origin and destination are seen to be intrinsically linked and the presence of migrants abroad, as also their pattern of return, seen to be part of the wider transnational system of outflow, interaction and feedback (Thomas-Hope 1986, 1988; Georges 1990; Schiller, Basch and Blanc 1995).

The variability that occurs in the return phase of migration is largely related to the principal purpose of the initial outward migration and its characteristics in terms of periodicity of movement and duration of stay abroad. In particular, the total displacement of persons from the community and/or household in the Caribbean when migration takes place is not typical, even when the time spent abroad extends over several years. More usually there is a significant element of circulation and the maintenance of linkages and involvement in activities to varying extents. This circulatory aspect of the migration is of particular relevance for the establishment and characteristics of the transnational household and, by extension, the transnational community.

Indeed, the characteristics of the return of migrants to Jamaica and throughout the Caribbean, are principally conditioned by the strength and persistence of the transnational linkages maintained between those household and family members abroad and those remaining in their home countries. Further, the strength of the transnational linkages themselves is largely conditioned by the livelihood strategies of the migrants and their households or wider family units. The more the activities of individuals in households and families extend to other locations, the stronger the network of international interactions.

The significance of circulation, whatever the time scale, lies in the pattern of reciprocal flow. Few studies of Caribbean migration have focussed upon these flows, especially where they have occurred as part of long-term migration, as opposed to the movements of short-stay, transient or guest worker movements. The circulatory flows of people, capital, goods, ideas and information in the long-stay or permanent migrant are those factors that maintain the transnational household, family and community (Thomas-Hope 1985, 1986, 1988; Basch *et al.*, 1987). The significance of the 'homeward orientation' has been identified and discussed elsewhere, including the fact that the mentality of return is accompanied by the many tangible aspects of flow and interaction that characterize the transnational household (Rubenstein 1982; Thomas-Hope 1999a,b).

Return migration and livelihood

Livelihood is not to be equated solely with work, whether this is waged or informal. Rather, livelihood is 'best understood in reference to sets of social processes that have economic and social consequences' (Barber 1996). As also articulated, 'livelihood comprises the capabilities, assets (stores, resources, claims and accesses) and activities required for a means of living' (Chambers and Conway 1992). In addition, concepts and perspectives about life, livelihood and work arise out of culturally specific and significant practices, perceptions and attitudes. Through a broad understanding of livelihood it becomes possible to see the interrelationships between livelihood and identity. Within the context of the mobility of people outwards from the Caribbean and later returning, the characteristics of migration condition the lives of those persons that are involved. Livelihoods are changed by virtue of the constraints and opportunities of the new multi-locational existence which is not only multi-national, but also involves a multi-cultural environment of work as also of social and domestic activities.

Livelihoods with respect to transnational persons involve working in one place and context, maintaining their families in another, socializing, investing, making purchases of goods and services, engaging in leisure pursuits, each at different points in the network and within the context of different accepted behaviours. Further, aspirations, dreams and goals are played out, or imagined, in the context of different points in the individual's transnational space. The individual can thus live in one place but focus upon another for anticipating or enjoying subsequent rewards. The livelihood of the individual becomes defined by the total space not just one segment of it that approximates, or is confined to, national boundaries, not even to one's country of citizenship or principal country of residence at any particular period of time.

Furthermore, the process has become increasingly complex as migration has created multiple bases in relation to which people move and interact with varying frequency and with respect to varying aspects of their lives. Citizenship options and choices emerge, alternative or new livelihood strategies evolve, the sense of national loyalty, political certainty, geographic parameters of action and boundaries of livelihood change. The experience involves lives and livelihoods that span at least two cultures with expectations and constraints of sometimes a very different nature, and of a work ethic and rewards of work where in some cases the contrast is very obvious, in other cases, almost imperceptible to the observer, but which is deeply significant to the migrants at the personal level and often influences their adjustment.

In the current phase of globalization, everyone is consciously or subconsciously affected in various ways by global movement and communication systems that increase the connectivity of places. Further, one cannot be part of the dynamic of a transnational space without responding at different levels to its demands – material, social and also psychological. In so doing the returnees become transnational persons.

The networks transmit both multi-lateral and bilateral interactions. The motivations for the perpetuation of the connections are variously political, economic and market-driven, social, domestic and emotional. The dynamic of this phenomenon is generated by interactions and linkages at all levels: regions and nations, organizations and institutions as well as communities, families, households and individuals. The impact at the levels of community and country occurs as they become part of the system of interaction as people, goods, money, and ideas, enter and depart from the community and nation. Households with members abroad relate in a more personal, though still somewhat removed way, to a world that extends beyond immediate national boundaries. They reflect the particular characteristics of the migrants as well as the role, the obligations and expectations of their migration and livelihoods change to accommodate them.

At the individual level, migrants are forced into a re-positioning of self in relation to the former place of residence, through which they experience a transition of consciousness, a transition in being, and in the very sense of self.

Return migration and identity

Factors that influence the ways in which migrants are incorporated into society at their destinations – whether in the movement outwards from their home country or on their return, influence not only their livelihoods but also their identities. The identity of a migrant group is partly influenced by the livelihood patterns and other factors such as their racial and linguistic characteristics in relation to the other minorities and in relation to the dominant social group. Of great significance also is the educational level of the majority that constitute the group and the labour market positions or niches which they occupy. There are other niches and positions upon which identities are generated: the migrants' position in the housing market, in the educational system and the commercial sector. These factors, in combination, serve to condition the choices available and thus the parameters of the livelihood patterns that the migrant group can establish and, in relation to those livelihoods, the identity of the group.

The group identity of migrants either at their initial destination or on their return, reflects the ways in which they are viewed from various perspectives. In part, migrant identities are established on the basis of the way they are perceived by the dominant group in the society to which they arrive, partly by other population sectors that also reside at the same location and partly by the migrants themselves.

The existence in Jamaica of sixteen associations of return residents covering all parishes of the island, as well as additional interest groups, is a clear indication of the shared sense of identity which exists among return migrants, and their need of support in adapting to conditions in Jamaica after having lived abroad for many years. Through the associations, returnees are able to provide mutual support in the problems encountered as they try to re-adapt to life in Jamaica. For example, they lobby for improvements through the media, they organize social events and they disseminate information on the benefits to which return migrants (especially from the United Kingdom) are entitled and how to go about obtaining them.

The strength of the identity of migrants of all types is largely based on the ease and extent of incorporation into the 'new' society. The greater the difference and the more difficult the incorporation, the more distinctly separate the identity. Where the differences are hardly or not at all apparent, the visibility of the group is negligible. So it is with the sample of individuals interviewed for this study. Their livelihoods and identities so effectively span two or more countries and cultures that they constitute a virtually non-identifiable group in two (or more) societies. This raises important theoretical questions concerning the livelihood patterns and construction of identities among the 'invisible group' of return migrants.

Here, the case of Jamaica is examined in relation to a population of professional persons who returned within the period 1995–8 and who were part of a Return of Talent Programme in Jamaica, sponsored by the International Organization for Migration (IOM). This is a highly educated group of migrants, returning at various stages of their careers. While they represent only one type of return migrant, they do provide an entry into understanding the nature of transnational livelihoods and identities in the context of the return.

Return migration of skilled nationals to Jamaica

Since 1993, the Government of Jamaica and other Caribbean governments have put in place a programme for encouraging the return of professional persons. In Jamaica, the programme has comprised two aspects. One has been a general Returning Residents Programme whereby the government endeavoured to encourage the return of nationals abroad by addressing their immediate needs associated with the return. This has been done by providing information, incentives on duty concessions for eligible persons, the streamlining of systems and procedures to facilitate the relocation process and encouragement to persons who wished to participate in the work force. An information guide was published and made available at the consular missions in London, New York, Toronto and Ottawa. The second focus has been to target high-level technical and managerial nationals to return to fill employment requirements in the public sector. To this end, the Government of Jamaica included in its National Indicative Programme under the 7th Protocol of the LOME IV Convention, a two-and-a-half year Return of Talent Programme. This was funded by the European Union with a sum of one million ECU and implemented by the International Organization for Migration (IOM) (Williams 1998).

The return of talent programme

This IOM programme was implemented in two phases. The first phase, from February 1 1994 to June 4 1997, facilitated the return to Jamaica of thirty-nine highly qualified professionals to fill vacant positions in the public sector. The major response came from Jamaican nationals residing in the United States, Canada, the United Kingdom, Guyana, the Bahamas, the Czech Republic and Belgium. Applications were also received from candidates in Switzerland, Saudi Arabia, Hungary and Lesotho. Phase two of the programme, June 5 1997 to June 4 1998, mandated the recruitment of twenty persons. This was against a background of 118 requests from the public sector for filling vacancies (IOM documents).

Financial incentives were offered through the programme by way of one-way air-fares for the candidate and immediate family members; up to fifty per cent of the cost of shipping household goods; a one-time re-entry subsidy; two-year's of full medical and accident insurance; a monthly salary subsidy; equipment including literature and machines required for the candidate's work. The aim was that, given the financial incentives, the persons recruited would remain in their assigned positions in the public sector for a minimum of the two years of the project, during which time the required transfer of knowledge and technology should have taken place. Thus the programme was at least in part based on the view that the permanent return of the skilled migrants was not essential to the success of the programme and that the later re-migration of some persons would be expected. Further, it reflected an awareness of the importance of flows of ideas and expertise through the migration and return migration process that is not necessarily conditional upon the duration of stay of the individual migrant.

Profile of the population in the return of talent programme

The sample population, interviewed over a three-month period at the end of 1999 and the beginning of 2000, was comprised of thirty-five persons from the total population of fifty-nine involved in the Return of Talent Programme. Attempts were made to contact and include in the study all persons who had participated in this programme. However, a number of persons could not be located as they had changed employment from that in which they had initially engaged and had left no forwarding address. A small number declined to participate.

Men comprised 62.9 per cent of the sample population and women 37.1 per cent. Because of the nature of selectivity of the Programme, more than two-thirds of the group were between ages 31 and 50 and the rest over 50 when they returned, having initially migrated between ages 25 and 35 either to take up employment or as students. Again, consistent with the nature of the employment gaps they were to fill, all had tertiary education, with 42.9 per cent in receipt of a Master degree, 20 per cent of a doctorate. In a number of cases (45.7 per cent), the returnees had received at least part of their tertiary or professional education in Jamaica. The majority (51.4 per cent) had returned to Jamaica from the United States of America; 14.3 per cent each from Canada and the United Kingdom; 17 per cent from locations in the Caribbean; one person from having lived and studied in Poland. Most persons interviewed had returned between 1995 and 1996, two persons had returned between 1993 and 1994 and six in 1997. Some persons in the group had already returned to Jamaica and were in the process of taking up employment prior to knowing about and later being accepted into the Return of Talent Programme. Others had made the decision to return and then took the opportunity of applying to the programme.

Livelihoods of the return migrants

Transnational livelihoods involve activities in the workforce and at the work-place, and are based upon the migrants maintaining the facility to move back and forth between countries without immigration restrictions and to transfer goods and capital from one place to another.

Participation in the workforce

Unlike many return migrants, those who participated in the Return of Talent Programme were all returning to the labour force and, in the first instance, to public sector employment. All but one of the returnees in the sample population were employed full-time; most were still in the public sector positions that they filled on their initial return, but a few had moved on to work in the private sector.

The population of returning migrants in this study included senior direc-tors, administrators and project officers in government ministries and agencies, university lecturers, engineers, architects and medical personnel.

Social networks

The return migrants' regular interaction with family in all cases involved at least two countries. Family members in Jamaica played a very important part in the lives of the group but so too did those family members (invariably adult children) in the country of their previous residence. The balance between social interactions with persons in Jamaica and with persons abroad varied but overall, regular interactions with friends similarly spanned at least two countries. Nearly one quarter of the people in the study interacted mostly with friends who were living abroad, and just over a quarter, mostly with friends in Jamaica. The rest of the population in the study indicated that they interacted more or less equally with friends in Jamaica as with those abroad. Only for a small percentage of the group (14.3 per cent), had their network of friends become 'almost entirely' Jamaica-based since returning; for others (17.1 per cent), 'quite a lot' of their friends were local.

In the return phase of the migration, persons retained contacts abroad but also re-established or re-enforced earlier contacts and friendships at home. To these were added some new contacts after returning, on balance increasing the Jamaica-based nature of social networks over those that existed during the migration phase but at the same time, without replacing the networks of persons abroad.

Nearly one-third of the returnees mostly interacted socially with persons whom they had known prior to migrating from Jamaica, but nearly half (49 per cent) of the returnees mostly interacted socially with persons who they had not already known but whom they had met since the return. There was, therefore, quite considerable continuity or re-connecting with the social network that had existed prior to migrating, but to an even greater extent was the establishment of new social connections since the return. In addition, some, though less than a half, of the present social contacts were developed while the migrants were living abroad.

The social networks were truly transnational in nature, comprised of a combination of persons whom the returnees had met prior to migrating, while living abroad and since returning. Overall, however, comparing these three components of the returnee social networks, the largest group of current contacts had been developed while the migrants were overseas.

Vacations and the purchase of goods

Only a quarter of the group had spent their vacation leave in Jamaica in the current year, the others (28.6 per cent) had travelled back to the United States and the rest to Canada, Britain and other parts of the Caribbean. This had been the general pattern for previous years since their return, reflecting the strong tendency to spend vacations in familiar places abroad and usually reinforcing social and family connections at those places. The spending of vacations in North America or in Britain is not a practice confined to returning migrants. However, it is a strong indication of the general transnational nature of Jamaican society, as a large percentage of vacations abroad are spent with family and friends.

The majority of returnees transported virtually all their household goods with them when they returned. Only a few returnees did most of their shopping for clothing in Jamaica and only 25.7 per cent purchased books and professional items in Jamaica. A larger percentage (34 per cent) mostly purchased household articles in Jamaica. Overall, therefore, the orientation in terms of the acquisition of goods remained largely external. The pattern of behaviour relating to the purchase of goods did demonstrate the transnational pattern and with an emphasis placed upon consumer activity in the overseas country rather than in the Caribbean.

Financial transfers and financial security

Contrary to the general expectation in the Caribbean of returning migrants, most of the returning professionals in this study did not remit or transfer substantial sums of money from their previous country of residence to Jamaica either prior to their return or subsequently. Only 20 per cent of the persons in the study indicated that they transferred what they regarded to be relatively large sums at the time of returning. Therefore, they tended to live on earnings from their current work in Jamaica, leaving savings previously generated abroad in an overseas country.

Despite the emphasis in consumer purchasing overseas, the pattern of investing was different. The vast majority of persons (82.9 per cent of the sample) currently tended to invest in Jamaica more than they did abroad. However, although any investment of the money earned in Jamaica remained in the country, at the same time, as indicated above, income earned abroad was left there and not repatriated to Jamaica. The financial security of maintaining income abroad was regarded to be of great importance to ensure security at that side of their migration trajectory. It would be very rare that a return migrant would close the potential for keeping investments or savings in the country of previous residence. However, there was a tendency to re-evaluate periodically their situation with respect to the transnational pattern of savings and investment and many particularly intended to do so when the time came for them to retire.

In terms of the climate for investment, the high interest rates available in Jamaica were balanced against the poor confidence in the stability of the banking sector. Besides, the rate of exchange further limited confidence in saving locally. For example, the Jamaican dollar against the United States dollar was JMD 23.01 to USD 1.00 in 1992 and fell each year to JMD 37.02 to USD1.00 in 1996 (Planning Institute of Jamaica 1997) and to approximately JMD 45 to USD1.00 in 2000.

Almost half the number of persons in the sample population would be entitled to social security payments from the country of their former residence abroad and or state pension when they reached retirement age, even if they remained in Jamaica until they retired. A small number would also be in receipt of company pensions from their previous place of work abroad upon retirement in Jamaica. The sense of security financially is largely supported by the external country to which they had previously migrated. This money would in due course be remitted to the migrant in Jamaica, provided that they had not re-migrated before retiring.

With respect to health insurance, the majority of persons or their dependants no longer had any health insurance in a country abroad and thus relied totally on health care in Jamaica. Nevertheless, a significant proportion, nearly one-third, still had access to health care facilities overseas and were very clear in the view that in the event of requiring these services, they would immediately return abroad to avail themselves of the medical facilities.

Lifestyles and standards of living

Return migrants of all types expected to obtain standards of living in Jamaica that were equal to, or higher, than those they had experienced abroad. This was usually achievable in Jamaica and one of the more positive aspects of the migrants' experiences related to the pleasant lifestyles that they enjoyed on the return. Likewise, conditions were generally conducive to good health primarily on account of favourable climatic conditions. High quality educational institutions were available for migrants wishing to pursue further educational or professional qualifications.

On the negative side of the balance was the high incidence of crime and the perceived threat to personal security. Personal security, as well as conditions of work, were the factors that were most significant in the returnees' re-adjustment to living in Jamaica. A major factor associated with the low level of perceived security was a diminution of the sense of freedom. Some returnees expressed their sense of being constrained in their movements, especially in engaging in leisure or social activities on their own. Thus, while the wish was to retain behaviours relating to the freedom to retain the practices relating to unrestricted movement, people generally had to modify their behaviour to adapt to local conditions. Other lifestyle changes were also reluctantly made in relation to behaviours relating to expectations of service in service departments. The return migrants tried to retain the patterns of business transactions and operations that they had previously experienced abroad. Within a short time of returning however, expectations and behaviours of this nature were significantly modified to conform to local patterns. Likewise, in the case of diet and culinary habits, there was a significant retention of those developed while living abroad while at the same time a partial return to former practice.

There was considerable variability in the extent of the change that the migrants had experienced in their habits and behaviours since their return as compared with those practised when they were abroad. Despite the changes that had occurred with respect to many aspects of their lives, such as types of food eaten and leisure activities, patterns of working, well over half of the returnees had largely retained their former lifestyle patterns, and the rest had partly done so. In all cases, therefore, the lifestyles of the returnees were all distinctly transnational in nature, varying only in the extent and precise characteristics of incorporation of the two or more cultures of their migration outward and return destinations.

The return migrants developed strategies at various levels for coping with the demands of more than one place and, to a greater or lesser extent, had to adjust and re-adjust their lifestyles on their return to Jamaica. Even then, their lifestyles as all other aspects of their lives, remained closely linked to the country abroad in which they had previously resided. The continuities and changes that occurred were reflected in the returnees' social networks, the locations they frequented for vacations and those chosen for shopping, and their spatial patterns of saving and investment. Overall, the livelihoods of the return migrants demonstrated a combination of two cultures but balanced in such a way that at the personal level, they could adjust in a practical and emotional sense to the culture of their new destination – albeit their former home. Therefore, the return not only had a significant impact upon the changes in livelihood of the migrants but also upon the migrants' sense of identity on their return.

Identity and the return migrants

The identity of professional persons who return to Jamaica is principally of relevance to the individual migrants themselves. They have been ascribed no group identity by society at large, partly because they demonstrate no visible signs of distinctiveness and partly because of the inclusiveness of such a grouping. A large proportion of professional persons in Jamaica have lived abroad, and thus have been migrants, at some stage of their lives. Nevertheless, at the personal level, a number of emotional challenges arise in the process of the migrant's re-adjustment to living in Jamaica generally and, specifically to the work environment, their commitment to and concepts of Jamaican citizenship and their sense of identity and of belonging.

Adjustment to living in Jamaica

The professional returnees in the Return of Talent Programme are not typically members of the Returning Migrants Associations. They largely had the information, or the contacts and the skills to acquire information as required. Besides, the Return of Talent Programme provided a point of contact and some relevant information and financial assistance to relocate and supplement their salaries for a two-year period for those engaged in the programme.

Only one-third of the group found it fairly or very difficult to re-adjust to living in Jamaica. The circumstances that chiefly facilitated the adjustment process were the personal support of family and friends. In addition, having the feeling that 'Jamaica is home' and the sense of identity associated with being 'home' was a major factor in overcoming the negative aspects of the re-adjustment – primarily what was described as the negative nature of the work ethic as well as the country's social problems. These caused the returnees to question the extent to which they were adjusted to life in Jamaica.

At the personal level the living conditions were regarded as being very favourable but two-thirds of the sample population recorded their dissatisfaction with the social aspects of life that they found in Jamaica in general. Of the other third, half had no complaints while half felt that although they were not particularly dissatisfied, there was room for improvement. There were more negative feelings about the economic aspects of Jamaica, though there were some also who had no complaints and others who felt that there was room for improvement. In terms of other aspects of life there was in general greater levels of satisfaction experienced.

Adjustment to the work environment

For Jamaicans working in North America and Europe, the return usually necessitated a significant loss of income and benefits at the outset. Furthermore, managerial and operational styles in Jamaica differed from those of North America and Europe. In particular, migrants returned with expectations of being able to maintain a speed and efficiency of working that they were subsequently unable to achieve. As a result, migrants who had been away from Jamaica for many years invariably became frustrated while, at the same time, in their struggle to change structures, non-migrant colleagues in some cases became resentful of them. Unless the returnees were able to adapt to the new working environment, the chances were that they would begin to consider re-migrating. However, even in the process of adapting there was a possibility that, with the passage of time, this process could itself bring about a reduced sense of commitment at the workplace in the return migrants themselves.

Although the work environment did not generally provide an incentive to return to Jamaica, the living conditions were usually regarded as being favourable. But most kept trying to maintain the work patterns and aspirations developed abroad. This produced a great source of frustration. It was as though their motivation to achieve and orientation towards identified goals could not be easily compromised or abandoned because it had become so intricately linked to their self-assessment of success versus failure, their *raison d'etre* and therefore their sense of themselves. The option of re-entering the work environment of the country of previous migration or elsewhere, was frequently considered by many in the group.

Transnational citizenship

It was evident that just as in the initial emigration, so in the return moves, the negative factors were generally minimized in the minds of those who wanted to move and had the opportunity of doing so. However, prior to returning, migrants ensured that they had established their residency or citizenship status in their country of migration before departing. This was their 'safety valve' should they decide to leave Jamaica again for short or long periods of time at some later date. Many returns were, therefore, tentative in nature. Above all, the returnees were clearly disposed towards further movement abroad of varying duration. Nearly three quarters of the population felt that they might, or definitely would be going abroad to live and work again before reaching retirement. Most would return to the country in which they had previously lived, though there were some who felt that they would not necessarily return to the previous place of residence. This showed a penchant for future mobility, even to new destinations.

All the returnees held a Jamaican passport, in the main because of their sense of, and commitment to, 'being Jamaican'. However, the majority (58 per cent) had dual citizenship and held a passport of another country as well as a Jamaican passport. An additional 23 per cent had residency entitlements in another country in addition to Jamaica.

Although most returnees (80 per cent) felt a strong Jamaican identity, there was some ambivalence among the remaining 20 per cent. Besides, the situation was complicated by the weaker commitment to Jamaica on the part of spouses; there was a clear commitment in fewer than half the cases in the study population. The commitment to Jamaica of the children of the returnees was weaker still. For transnational persons who return to their country of birth, the experience of belonging and yet not belonging is a profound and persistent aspect of their identity.

Sense of identity

The sense of 'being Jamaican' was of major importance to most persons and was associated with the significance placed upon 'belonging'. This surpassed the negative feelings that emerged during the process of re-adjustment. The intensely unsettling emotion resulted from the conflict of feelings experienced in both being connected to place as part of intrinsic reality of 'home', and at the same time the difficulty or inability encountered in the re-locating of self at home. The result is the keeping open of all options and thus the return is re-affirmed consciously and subconsciously as merely a stage in the process – not an end in itself.

Conclusion

The transnational livelihoods that developed among skilled Jamaican nationals following the return deeply influenced and were influenced by the sense of identity of the returnees themselves. Livelihoods extended across international borders and were reflected in the identities of the returnees that were in most cases conditioned by strong outward orientations and, at the same time, a deep sense of attachment to Jamaica as 'home'.

International migration affects Caribbean people of all social classes, ethnic groups and age groups as well as males and females but in different ways. At times unskilled workers have dominated the movement, at other times the highly educated, skilled workers and professionals, sometimes chiefly females, at other times, males, largely depending on the opportunities afforded to different groups by the immigration regulations at the migration destinations. At all times young adults account for a high percentage of the flows. While there are many experiences shared by all social groups and the establishment of transnational networks are common to all, nevertheless, the specific characteristics of each type of migrant significantly influences the livelihoods and identities of the families and individuals who are directly involved.

The case of skilled professional migrants who returned to Jamaica within their working lives and thus as part of their careers, demonstrated the very great extent to which their movement produced less a situation of displacement and more a reinforcement of the linkages that already existed between the two locations and societies. Livelihoods were in some cases more externally oriented than in others, but in all cases they incorporated activities and social processes of both worlds.

So globalized in scope were the livelihoods and livelihood strategies of these return migrants that they not only spanned more than one country but also depended on more than one country in countless ways. This was associated with identities that had no fixed nature and were always in transit; and a sense that there were future movements still to come. The fact that a total displacement of the migrants did not occur among the returning nationals in this study, but that there was a strong persistence of the role of places of previous migration destinations in the lives of the skilled returning nationals, demonstrated the transnational character of their livelihoods. As in the outward phase of the migrations discussed above, so in the return phase, work and a range of social processes incorporated more than one location that extended across international boundaries based on the migration process.

Identities were deeply rooted in the sense of being Jamaican and the idea of Jamaica as home. This was reflected in their attachment to place in terms of the physical environment, the pleasure expressed at their familiarity with the language of cultural discourse whatever the changes that have taken place, and the comfort levels they felt with respect to closeness to family and to the place of childhood memories. Further, there was a sense of legitimacy with respect to being in the country of their birth and awareness of the fact that nothing could take this away. But this sense of being where one 'ought to be' – in the place of belonging – conflicted in the minds of some of the returnees with the sense of disappointment they felt in not easily being able to re-adjust to many aspects of life and work in Jamaica. For many, this produced an ambivalence in their sense of personal identity. It led to the need to retain a transnational livelihood and with it, the continued freedom to negotiate in various ways, the multi-national network of contacts that had developed throughout their migration cycle. Transnationality so permeated personal identities that it became a mechanism of keeping open not simply the options of re-migration, but more importantly, the opportunities for individuals to return to Jamaica yet with livelihoods that continued to exist in a wider global environment.

References

Barber, Pauline Gardiner (1996) 'Sustainable livelihood and equity issues for ISLE: Notes towards a definition', Unpublished paper for the core course on Livelihood for the Island Sustainability, Livelihood and Equity (ISLE) Project, Ujung Pandang, Indonesia, 1–6 December.

Basch, Linda, Wiltshire-Brodber, Rosina Wiltshire and Winston Wiltshire (1987) *Caribbean Regional and International Migration: Transnational Dimensions*, Ottawa: International Development and Research Centre (IDRC).

Chambers, R. and Conway, Gordon R. (1992) *Sustainable Rural Livelihood: Practical; Concepts for the 21st Century*, Sussex: Institute of Development Studies.

Georges, Eugenia (1990) *The Making of a Transnational Community: Migration, Development and Cultural Change in the Dominican Republic*, New York: Columbia University Press.

Pessar, Patricia (1982) *Kinship relations of production in the migration process: The case of Dominican emigration to the United States*, The New York Research Program in Inter-American Affairs at the New York University, Occasional Papers No. 32.

Planning Institute of Jamaica (1997, 1998) *Economic and Social Survey Jamaica*, Kingston, Jamaica.

Rubenstein, Hymie (1982) *Return migration to the English-speaking Caribbean: Review and commentary*, in W. F. Stinner, K. de Albuquerque and R. S. Bryce-Laporte (eds) *Return Migration and Remittances: Developing a Caribbean Perspective*, Washington D.C.: Research Institute for Immigration and Ethnic Studies, Smithsonian Institution, pp. 3–34.

Schiller, Nina Glick, Basch, Linda and Szanton-Blanc, Cristina (1995) *From immigrant to transmigrant: Theorizing transnational migration, Anthropological Quarterly* 68: 48–63.

Thomas-Hope, Elizabeth (1985) 'Return migration and its implications for Caribbean development' in Robert Pastor (ed.) *Migration and Development in the Caribbean: The Unexplored Connection*, Boulder: Westview Press, pp. 157–77.

Thomas-Hope, Elizabeth (1986) 'Transients and settlers: Varieties of Caribbean migrants and the socio-economic implications of their return', *International Migration*, 24: 559–70.

Thomas-Hope, Elizabeth (1988) 'Caribbean skilled international migration and the transnational household', *Geoforum*, 19(4): 423–32.

Thomas-Hope, Elizabeth (1992) *Explanation in Caribbean Migration: Perception and the Image – Jamaica, Barbados and St. Vincent*, London: Macmillan.

Thomas-Hope, Elizabeth (1999a) 'Emigration dynamics in the Anglophone Caribbean', in Reginald Appleyard (ed.) *Emigration Dynamics in Developing Countries* Vol. III *Mexico, Central America and the Caribbean*, Aldershot: Avebury, pp. 232–84.

Thomas-Hope, Elizabeth (1999b) *Return migration to Jamaica and its development potential*, International Migration. 37(1): 183–208.

Williams, Elizabeth (1998) *Key Issues relating to migration in Jamaica* (unpublished paper), Kingston, Jamaica: International Organization for Migration.

10 The final move?

Displaced livelihoods and collective returns in Peru and Guatemala

Finn Stepputat

Displaced livelihoods and collective returns

This chapter compares two cases of spatial movement that usually fall into two separate fields of study. One is the return of refugees who, in returning, are by definition crossing an international border, in this case the border between Mexico and Guatemala. The other is the return of Peruvian highlanders who have left their rural villages and sought refuge from the widespread violence in their region in the nearest city. The two cases of movement are similar in the sense that both involve people who have been identified, labelled and assisted by national and international agencies as victims of violent conflict, as 'refugees' in the first case and 'internally displaced persons' (IDPs) in the second. We may categorize the two cases as 'forced migration', but the difference between voluntary and forced migration is not absolute.[1] While the forced/voluntary distinction may not be the most fertile point of departure for an analysis of the directions, dynamics and effects of particular movements, it is important in defining rights, entitlements and livelihood spaces. I will therefore analyse the two cases of movement as taking place partly within a 'transnational space' generated through the appropriation and application of the categories of refugees, IDPs and returnees – partly outside this space.

The post-structuralist critique of essentializing notions of refugees, migrants, IDPs, returnees and repatriated persons came to prominence during the 1990s. Researchers criticized the tendency to regard migrant and refugee lives as problematic in respect of their 'uprooting' and displacement, that is, the perception of displaced people as likely to suffer from trauma, identity problems, poverty and disorientation, and therefore as being in need of healing and assistance. The inherent celebration of rootedness and the problematization of uprooting were linked to the predominance of the territorial nation state and the 'national order of things' (Mallki 1992). Transnational studies were suggested as an alternative, non-national way of analysing mobility and belonging. This move led some commentators to an uncritical endorsement of the notion of mobility which failed to account for unequal access to it or the material constraints of mobile livelihoods (Massey 1994; Stepputat and Sørensen 1999; Hyndman 2000). While endorsing the transnational approach, I will explore an additional analytical path, one which de-essentializes categories of displaced people by coining and foregrounding the idea of 'displaced livelihoods' in the analysis of mobility, belonging and change.

The notion of a livelihood is seen as comprising not only specific ways of producing, exchanging and consuming, but also ideas about 'proper' lives and the negotiations over recognition, identity, entitlements and rights. However, livelihoods are sometimes disrupted by major political or economic transformations, such as liberal reforms, nationalization, market collapse or violent conflict. These transformations may sweep away entitlements, violate rights, crush vested hopes and investments in the future, undermine customary livelihood practices, dissolve collective identities, and inhibit social and spatial mobility. The term 'displaced livelihood' thus denotes the composite effects of a particular subset of disruptions, namely the disruption of spatial mobility. By focusing on displaced livelihoods rather than displaced people, the analysis does not a priori privilege those who have moved over those who have had their livelihoods destroyed by not being able to move, nor does it a priori problematize spatial displacement relative to the displacement of livelihoods. In addition, the notion elicits a historical analysis of mobile livelihood practices and struggles for the recuperation of mobility.

The collective practices and political identities that are articulated in such struggles constitute an important backdrop for the understanding of the individual and collective strategies of 'refugees' and 'IDPs'. In both the Guatemalan and Peruvian cases, the return movements are similar in the sense that they are both imagined and organized as collective enterprises by the participants in the process. One could argue that spatial movement is often organized collectively, since many people follow the same patterns of mobile livelihood and share information and experience in the process; but in the two present cases, the participants were represented by formal organizations, and the move was undertaken by everybody at the same time in logistically grandiose and highly visible operations. Many, in particular the agencies involved, imagine returns as a final move, the move to displacement and transience, the point zero from which development will proceed.

Finally, given the apparently predominating direction of migration from poorer to richer regions, from rural to urban areas, and from South to North, the two collective returns stand out as exceptions, as counter-currents that call for scrutiny and explanation because they are proceeding in the opposite direction. In the current international context in which migration issues receive a great deal of political attention, such counter-currents are encouraged in many different ways through migration policies, conflict management, humanitarian assistance and development aid. International agencies have presented return and repatriation as the best and most 'natural' solution to problems of displacement, but, as many scholars pointed out during the 1990s, we cannot take the will to return in the aftermath of armed conflict for granted. Likewise a range of concepts, such as reconstruction, reintegration, and reconciliation, convey the image of displaced persons and refugees going back to something familiar, while 'construction', 'innovation' and 'creativity' might be more appropriate concepts for the social processes at play (Gmelch 1980; Hammond 1999).

The following analysis will focus on: (1) The production of a transnational space through the international categories of refugees and IDPs respectively; (2) the histories of displaced livelihoods and rural movements in the Guatemalan and Peruvian highlands; (3) the framing of IDPs and refugees under the prevailing security regimes; and (4) the organization and aftermath of two cases of collective returns in Guatemala and Peru.[2]

Refugees and IDPs in transnational space

The field of refugees as a particular area of international and national intervention has been increasingly institutionalized since the Second World War. As a point of departure in interpreting repatriation and return movements, I understand the field of refugees as a transnational space in which different agents, operating across borders and engaging governments with reference to universal moral values, produce material effects. This space is defined by discourses, institutions and flows that produce the phenomenon of the refugee as a particular identity, as a problem to be solved and hence as a particular field of institutional intervention. While the field of refugees is generated on the basis of an international convention and the UN High Commissioner for Refugees, the field has become transnational in the sense that networks of non-governmental agencies, popular movements and people on the move manage the refugee concept in ways that go beyond the direct control of national governments.[3]

In this space, discourses and images circulate which construct refugees as victims and objects of assistance and solidarity, alongside (contradictory) images which construct them as intruders, dangerous sources of social, political and epidemiological pollution etc. Here we also see certain techniques for the administration and control of refugee populations, the distribution of humanitarian aid and the implementation of programmes for the formation of 'human capital' through training and education.

Using Henry LeFebvre's term, we may talk about the production of an abstract space (LeFebvre 1991), an institutionalized and apparently transparent space that permits the identification and localization of refugees as a visible and controllable social entity, the refugee camp being the archetype of this particular space (Mallki 1992). Thus the logic of the national order conditions the formation of a collective identity based on the category of the refugee. Of course, many other factors intervene in the production of particular collective refugee subjects, but the category defines the limits, rights and qualities that qualify refugees for assistance.

However, 'refugee' is a negotiable category that may be appropriated and interpreted in many forms and for many reasons. At the social level I will interpret the refugee category as open and unstable, a strategic space that forms the basis of temporary alliances between individuals and households, and facilitates the generation and accumulation of political and material resources. As such, the category of the refugee provides conditions for certain livelihoods by giving access to ID cards, licences, credits, utensils, technical advice and education, while other livelihoods, in particular mobile ones, are inhibited by the control exerted over refugee populations. Depending on the degree of control, people may enter and leave the category. But, as the case of the Guatemalan refugees shows, the category, and the collective subject formed on its basis, may also serve as a strategic alliance that permits groups of populations to cross international borders under conditions over which the refugees themselves may have some control.

Internally displaced persons

During the second half of the 1980s, the 'IDP' appeared as a concept at the international level, together with attempts to structure the protection of, and draw attention to, internally displaced people, not least in Central America. In the 1990s conjuncture of military and humanitarian interventions on the basis of criteria relating to human rights, political and technical development in the field of IDPs has been reinforced.[4]

One determining factor in this reinforcement is the increased political importance given to the issue of migration and the related attempts to control immigration to the richer countries. 'Cross-border operations', 'protected areas' and peacekeeping operations may be seen as attempts to contain violent conflict and the creation of refugees that would otherwise be caught up in refugee camps along the borders or reach the countries of the North. Together with repatriation programmes, the IDP is the institutional inventory that can bring about this 'internalisation' of refugees (Suhrke 1993) and extend the transnational humanitarian space still further.

Mobile livelihoods and rural movements in Peru and Guatemala

In the following, I will analyse two trajectories of mobility and livelihood that developed under conditions of violent conflict in central Peru and in the border areas between Guatemala and Mexico. In the Peruvian case, the actions of the Peruvian army and the Shining Path under the leadership of Abigail Guzman drove maybe 600,000 people away from the areas of conflict between 1982 and 1992. In the department of Huancavelica, many Quechua-speaking people responded to the violence by exploring possibilities in and around Huancayo, the commercial centre of the neighbouring province. Like those who went to Lima or to the tropical lowlands, they had the chance to join government schemes of collective return to their villages in Huancavelica during the second half of the 90s.

During the violent conflict between the Guatemalan army and the insurgent groups joined together in the URNG, more than 100,000 villagers in the border area sought refuge in southern Mexico. Many of them were Maya-speaking people from the highlands who had recently settled in the tropical lowlands. Some of the refugees were concentrated and assisted in camps and settlements in Mexico; others soon returned or were dispersed across the region. Between 1993 and 1999, they returned to Guatemala in comparatively large numbers following a negotiated agreement with the Guatemalan government in 1992.

The two conflicts share a number of similarities in terms of the changes in livelihood conditions that enabled armed groups to mobilize rural populations. While mobility between different ecological niches of production at different altitudes constituted an important element of rural livelihood in both regions, conditions in the emerging state changed in the nineteenth century: liberal land reforms and the developing plantation economies had the effect of reducing the highland villages' access to land and pasture at different altitudes. The indigenous communities also became involved in systems of (forced) labour migration to lowland plantations. In practice, indigenous highland communities were excluded from full citizenship.

Access to land as the basis for rural livelihood and recognition of the villagers as citizens became an issue in rural political movements in the twentieth century. Reformist military governments carried out land and political reforms in order to incorporate the indigenous population into the nation state politically as well as economically, but with little immediate success. In the Guatemalan case, reforms were halted and reversed after a military coup in 1954. In Peru, land reforms were carried out in 1968, but haciendas were substituted by co-operatives or large state farms, which many peasant communities regarded as just as dominating as the haciendas had been. When the Shining Path started to organize the indigenous population around 1980, they exploited these tensions between state farms and communities that were longing for increased access to land and pasture.

In Guatemala, land reform re-emerged as a critical issue for mobilization in the social, leftist movements of the 70s, when 'organization' became the basis for political struggle and for alternative visions of livelihoods, involving modern forms of co-operation. In both cases, guerrilla movements attempting to undermine the state dominated the political scene of the 80s. Guerrilla actions in both Peru and Guatemala were concentrated in regions with poor communications and the sparse presence of state institutions apart from the army, which arrived in order to carry out counterinsurgency operations. The armed actions and system of control imposed by both insurgency and counterinsurgency led hundreds of thousands of people to leave or stay away from the countryside in the areas of conflict.

Displaced livelihoods

The organization and representation of space is a central dimension of power, not least of the forms of power related to the territorial nation state.[5] Segregations, exclusions, ghettos, roads and roadblocks, grids and enclosures all provide methods of managing potentially dangerous differences and subversive movements, social as well as spatial, within the territorial limits of the nation state. Conditions of violent conflict, displacement and exile are no exception. In general, it seems justified to suggest that conditions of violent conflict reduce liberty of movement, as movement becomes an essential issue in security (Stepputat 1999). This is the case for both Peru and Guatemala.

Refugees in Mexico

By carrying out numerous massacres, organizing the population in civil patrols for self-defence and setting up numerous checkpoints, the Guatemalan army gave the rural population little choice. They could stay more or less fixed in the villages, or flee to safer areas within or outside the country. While many peasants took refuge on the plantations at the south coast, movement between the plantations and the highlands was rendered difficult by several factors: mobility required passes and hence formalized relations with the authorities; passage through the numerous checkpoints had to be negotiated in many instances; villagers were obliged to participate in the civil patrols on a regular basis or else pay a substitute if they left the village in order to engage in migrant labour; and those who fled the villages were afraid of being associated with the guerrillas if they tried to return to their villages upon flight.

Likewise, those who left the country were subjected to restrictions of movement or, if they chose to engage in illicit movement, to the increased danger of being arrested, harassed and repatriated by the state authorities. In Chiapas, Mexico, refugees were either recognized as such and located in camps and settlements with limited rights to movement, or else they sought to pass as Mexicans and conduct a life with limited and precarious access to health, education, markets, land and work (Salvadó 1988).

However, mobility was essential for survival, whether they had relief provisions or not. While land was in scarce supply in the areas of refuge, seasonal occupation was available, although at low wages, given the plentiful supply of Guatemalan farm hands. Coffee, corn, cattle and horticulture provided jobs in different parts of the borderlands at different times in the agricultural calendar. Young people, mainly male but increasingly including female refugees, sought better opportunities in the cities of southern Mexico or else left for USA, following paths opened up by the first groups of refugees, who had already reached different places in that country.[6] Men engaged in construction work in the cities, while women were mainly engaged in the domestic sector. Many others combined wage labour with retail commercial activities, a niche that was not occupied by the Mexicans (Hernandez *et al.* 1993).

When, in 1984, the Mexican government decided to relocate the Guatemalan refugees away from the border due to Guatemalan army incursions and fears of social unrest spilling over into Chiapas, the thrust of the international refugee regime was changing, from an emphasis on resettlement as the preferred solution to refugee situations in the 1970s, to 'local integration' in the early 1980s. While the Mexican government was inclined to offer only temporary asylum and to push for repatriation, refugee agencies sought to prevent the 'dependency syndrome' and to reduce overall expenditure by reorienting relief towards projects for 'self-sufficiency'. They invariably imagined the refugees as peasants-in-refuge (Lopez Rivera 1997) and regarded land as the basic precondition for self-sufficiency, in combination with income-generating projects and occasional wage labour in agriculture. The government limited permits to travel and work to the province of residence and attempted to control labour contracting. Physical control was abandoned after the first year, and soon public transport was connecting the refugee settlements with the major markets in the province.

The idea of the 'program for self-sufficiency' was to create a self-sufficient development where the refugees produced what they needed, including food, clothes and furniture, and where they would develop their production beyond their own immediate needs and start marketing their products in the surrounding area. Thus, the idea of the 'projects' was intimately tied to the settlement and based on the collective organization of cash-crop production, shops, workshops, marketing and training in new skills. Maintaining the settlements depended on the labour and material support of the refugees themselves.

The overall idea was shared by refugee leaders and the staffs of UNHCR and La Comisión Mexicana para Ayuda a Refugiados (COMAR). The programme promised to reduce the necessity for relief over time and hence the costs of United Nations High Commissioner for Refugees (UNHCR). It was compatible with the government policy of containing the refugees in manageable spaces and maintaining a coherent refugee community that was oriented towards a possible return to Guatemala. Finally, the programme linked up with the academic and political formation of Mexican and international staff, as well as the refugee leaders with respect to 'organization' and 'community development' as the bases of development and integration. The idea of community-based development invariably invoked (Mayan) traditions of collective labour, mutual trust and communal identity, even though the refugee 'community' was very heterogeneous with respect to place of origin, prior land relations, ethnic identity, organizational experience and political affiliations.

In order to make the collective project work in spite of the ever-increasing (and illegal) mobility of the refugees, settlement regulations dictated that nobody could leave the settlement for more than one month. Recycling age-old communal membership practices, everybody had to 'take turns', contribute to general work turnouts, undertake organizational tasks and support teachers and health promoters among the refugees. Therefore, members of the refugee community had to alternate between making money elsewhere and working in the settlement in order to maintain their entitlements there. However, the scheme was not able to counter refugee strategies. Family-based commerce outdid co-operative efforts to organize commercial relations, and although many people were afraid of leaving the safe environment of the settlement, individuals seeking out wage labour soon brought refugees far beyond the limits imposed on their mobility. Not having proper identity papers, the Guatemalans were given miserable conditions, and the obligation to return to the settlements within a month made it difficult to improve work relations over time. Adolescents, however, tended to stay more or less permanently away from the settlements, which then became a place to go to visit the family, see old friends, participate in communal *fiestas* and flaunt the things that money could buy, such as ghetto-blasters, leather boots, watches and BMX bikes.

In the settlements, a remarkably strong distinction was generated between the wage-based form of livelihood, involving work in distant (and for the refugees, prohibited) cities, and the place-bound 'peasant-refugee' form of livelihood, which included wage labour in local agriculture only. This distinction is the key to several conflicts and differences of a political, cultural and generational nature. For one thing, in accordance with the Mexican refugee regime, the leaders defined the quality of refugeehood in terms of spatial confinement: 'I thought this was going to be a camp of political refugees, confined to this place. Nevertheless, this has turned into a work camp, and it shouldn't be like this; we're political refugees, but people have forgotten that they're refugees, that they're only lodging here. Therefore, I've never left the camp for work. Instead, I prepare my *milpa* better, and my wife and the kids raise pigs and chickens. I think we should have worked more persistently in the projects, but people are not united.'[7]

The peasant-refugee livelihood was promoted by both refugee leaders and agency staff, and clearly involved a generational conflict. By losing land, the older men had also lost power over the young men, but they still controlled the system of distribution of projects through their relationship with the Mexican authorities and UNHCR. Although many young men were largely beyond control in far away places, they were criticized by the older generation for their lack of respect: 'In the city, they lose respect, they lose their qualities. They don't learn anything, but they forget how to make *milpa*, and how to make *tortillas*. They leave as Christians, but they return as delinquents (*ladrones*).'

While defining knowledge in a distinct and limited way, this representation of migrant labour leans on an idealization of the rural community *vis-à-vis* urban modernity, which also draws upon the historical resistance towards migrant labour on plantations. Urban modernity is considered to be insecure, immoral, corrupting and productive of barren wealth only. Adults regarded the BMX bike, for example, as being useless for practical purposes, unlike the tricycle, which was used to transport heavy goods. The city was symbolized by the tempting apple that led to the Fall of Man.[8]

The non-integration policy and anti-migratory livelihood practices were also the main agenda of 'the organizations', the four guerrilla movements present in the settlements, that focused their attention on nation state-centred politics back in Guatemala. In effect, an image of 'the real refugee' appeared in everyday discourse that combined active participation in the refugee community with the desire to return to Guatemala. The refugees should neither integrate too much into Mexican society, nor go back before conditions were safe. Rather, they should consider the future and prepare for their return.

Displaced in a Peruvian city

In stark contrast to the highly visible concentrations of Guatemalan refugees, the 'internally displaced' in the Peruvian city of Huancayo lived dispersed in and around the city during the 1980s and 1990s. For many years, the identity and concept of the *desplazados* (displaced) was not commonly known, and concerned people in Huancayo, mainly connected with the churches, were only remotely linked to transnational humanitarian spaces. Another factor that reduced the formation of an IDP identity was the Peruvian state's spatial strategy of containing displaced people. This was very different from the Mexican strategy. As in many other cases of internal displacement, the Peruvian state did not recognize displacement as a problem to be singled out and remedied publicly. Displacement was regarded a security issue and a matter for the intelligence services, police and army. In particular, poor neighbourhoods were raided and intensely monitored, and many people, mostly men, who arrived on the city's outskirts were identified and registered. If they appeared on the lists of people being accused of participating in subversive activities, they were arrested.

The attempts by churches and local NGOs to organize 'internally displaced people' as a group of victims suffered from difficult conditions of security and from the compulsion to survive physically in an area with high surpluses of labour. In comparison with the internationally funded relief reaching the Guatemalan refugees, the resources channelled through local NGOs to IDPs were very limited. However, these provisions did provide the material kernel of organization in the Huancayo area, where family and community networks were mobilized around 'committees', soup kitchens and workshops. According to former participants in the emergency programmes, they used food as a kind of bait in order to overcome the cautious attitudes of prospective IDPs.

Committees of 'migrants from the zones of emergency' were set up in the mid-1980s, organized in much the same way as the formally recognized 'peasant communities,' although they had no access to land. They were indeed de-territorialized peasant communities who kept their records, agendas and communal treasure, to which all members contributed, as well as their paraphernalia of official recognition: mainly the stamp and the paginated record book. However, membership was not confined to the territorial communities 'of origin'; some had broader, albeit regionally defined constituencies, such as the sons of Ayacucho and the Christian Community. The activities of most of them were centred around a soup kitchen, but several managed to attract funds and assistance for minor artisan or agricultural projects.

Encouraged and assisted by local NGOs, the committees were joined together into a central organization, Jatarai Ayllu, which organized cultural festivals and demonstrations together with other popular organizations when conditions of security permitted this degree of visibility. They also arranged mass weddings in order to obtain the identity papers that many of their members had lost. At its height, the organization could mobilize several thousand individuals. Leaders were trained in organization and planning in order to take over responsibility for activities in the longer term. Nevertheless, the NGOs had serious problems with this enterprise. The committees did not work very well in either economic or organizational terms. The workshops tended to become 'personalized', and the participants did not display any understanding of 'the collective character of this activity' (SEPAR 1990: 10). In other words, the workshops carried on as private enterprises as soon as they became viable and no longer depended on NGO support for credits, training etc. After an NGO meeting in Huancayo in 1989, the participants concluded that 'it is hard to guarantee continuity, basically because of the need for permanent subsidies, or *because of the inherent dispersion and instability of the migrants'* (ibid.: 18, my emphasis).

From the perspective of analysing mobile livelihoods, we may interpret the organization of the 'migrants from the zones of emergency' (later IDPs) as an attempt to fix them in manageable sites and structures. However, this attempt was jeopardized by the constant movement of the migrants, some moving because of the precarious conditions of security and housing, others because of wage labour elsewhere. They also engaged in a number of different economic and organizational activities within and outside the frameworks set up for them by the NGOs. In this respect, the relationship between the migrants and the popular/revolutionary movement was perceived as problematic by several of the NGOs: 'The multi-participation of migrants... could be an obstacle if they lose their identity as displaced, thereby jeopardizing their demanding attitude' (ibid.: 15–16).

Thus, from the NGOs' point of view, the stability and organization of the IDPs was necessary before they could become identified and recognized collectively as citizens of the state with special rights and entitlements as victims of the armed conflict. Since the IDP was a new concept and furthermore was deeply embedded in conflict-related representations, the government ignored the issue until international attention to the situation of IDPs in Peru increased in 1992–4.[9] By then, the government had organized a programme of assistance for the repopulation of rural Peru, the PAR. The NGOs engaged in the construction of region- and nation-wide organizations of IDPs in order to strengthen the power of both the IDPs and themselves, working as brokers between the latter and the international donors.

In the words of representatives of Jatarai Ayllu, the international attention produced an 'organization fever', with copies of Jatarai Ayllu being organized in many places around the country.[10] But it also produced the problem of policing the limits of the category, keeping people with 'illegitimate' claims from capturing resources for IDPs. IDP representatives, NGOs and the government agency set up for the 'repopulation' of rural Peru all engaged in this policing, fairly unsuccessfully as it happened (as described in Chapter 1). On the other hand, as organizations failed to produce substantial resources, the IDP organizations lost momentum from 1994–5. As of 1999 funds dried up, and the social 'base' was hard to identify and even harder to mobilize for practical purposes. In particular, young people were not represented in the organization. A small group of leaders remained, some of whom tried to make a political career out of their experience, their acquired leadership skills, and the claim to represent a segment of the Peruvian population.

Imagined return communities and the final move?

How, under these different sets of conditions, was 'return' imagined and organized by the returnees and the intervening agencies in the two cases?

Guatemala

In the camp environment, an abstract community of Guatemalan refugees found in the project a concrete expression of the 'organized and collective return' that was launched by the Permanent Commissions (CCPP). The CCPP was an organization of representatives who were elected in all the settlements and camps in 1987 as a reaction to the official programme of voluntary repatriation. Mistrusting the will of the civilian government to secure their lives in a thoroughly militarized Guatemala, the CCPP insisted on a collective return under certain conditions. The CCPP campaign included a thorough registration of the land that the refugees had left in Guatemala, the land that the CCPP would work to recuperate.

The 'organized and collective return' was a hegemonic project in the refugee camps in the sense that it came to define the parameters and oppositions of the debates that were being articulated among the refugees. The goal was to obtain access to direct negotiations with the Guatemalan government in order to achieve an agreement which would guarantee their right to return collectively (i.e. in larger groups than demanded by the government) and to organize and move freely, their exemption from military service for three years, and access to their land. While these demands were met in the final agreement of 8 October 1992, the CCPP did not succeed in removing the army from the return areas, a demand that challenged the sovereignty of the government.

During their first years in exile, the refugees had construed a common past through the institutionalization of certain narratives that were elicited and appreciated by journalists and solidarity groups. These narratives emphasized the struggle of the poor for dignity, autonomy, democracy and material improvement. They struggled against the rich and their army, who tried to break the back of the indigenous people and take over their land through the counterinsurgency programme that had caused the painful exodus from their beloved country, Guatemala.

With the conceptualization of the organized and collective return, the refugees began outlining a common future, another characteristic of the nation as an imagined community (Anderson 1991): 'We have to learn before returning to Guatemala. There, nobody will help us. We need our children to learn how to manage tractors, machinery . . . Here [in Mexico] it is possible to learn something, and with the projects there is no need to send our sons to build hotels'.[11] In sum, at the beginning of the 1990s, most of the refugees wanted to return or be repatriated to Guatemala. As a UNHCR spokesman said in 1996 in the midst of multiple returns: 'Here we facilitate returns, we do not [have to] promote returns' (Camacho and Aguilar 1997: 155). There is an implicit reference here to many other situations when UNHCR had the role of promoting repatriations, if not directly against the will of the refugees, then by pushing them hard in that direction, as dictated by the overall international refugee policy.[12]

The refugee category and the Mexican administration of this category contributed greatly to the formation of the organization for returnees by subjecting them to a number of formal restrictions in terms of movement, employment and land ownership. The frequent resettlements also had an effect. 'Here we always have to change our attitude [because of the unstable conditions]. To live on one's own land is different'. 'Outside of your home, a long way from your country, one has no rights. In Guatemala, wherever you go, no one can say that you're a stranger'. 'We are floating in the air, we have no land. We have to think about the future so the children will not be lost when we die. We have to position our family in our own land (*tierra*).'[13]

In the discourses of the Guatemalan refugees, their attachment to their ancestral land and the importance of corn production for their identity has frequently been highlighted as the reason why they fought so bravely for their return (e.g. Hanlon 1999). Many leaflets on the Guatemalan refugees and their return represent them as culturally bound to return, 'culture' being depicted as the traditional attachment to the land. But as the above statements indicate, the will to return had as much, even more to do with the question of how to provide the political conditions of livelihood practices. Thus, for them, livelihood encompassed the right to move, the right to own land and to settle freely, and the security of a place to stay until you yourself decide to move: in short, mobile livelihoods.

Furthermore, while land may be important as linking people to the ancestors, the connection with the future seemed to preoccupy the older generation as well: 'Here in Mexico life is happy, there is food, there is work, but we cannot make progress: you cannot plant even the smallest tree because here we are *posados* [lodged on the land of others]'. Planting trees is not only a long-term strategy for diversifying livelihoods by investing in, for example, fruit and coffee production and hence to 'make progress'; it is also an important symbol of land ownership as opposed to the conditions on the private estates, where tenants were not allowed to 'plant things with roots'. This was, however, an imagination that was specific to the older generation. The younger generation were not necessarily keen to pursue agriculture as their main activity.

Between 1993 and 1999 more than twenty returns took place, with 300 to 2500 participants in each, all heading towards return settlements on former haciendas that had been purchased with funds from the international aid organizations.

Comparing collective returns in Peru[14] *and Guatemala*

The bulk of collective returns in Peru were organized by PAR, the government agency (Programme for the Support of Repopulation), which had substantial international funding. PAR claimed to have assisted some 150,000 returnees from 1994 to 1998, but this figure was disputed by NGOs (USCR 1998), who also criticized the assistance for being inappropriate at times. The most obvious similarity between the Guatemalan and the Peruvian cases is the staging of public demonstrations. By organizing returns in a formal way and involving national or international authorities, the two return movements were inserted into a (trans-)national space that broadened the scope for alliances for the participants. This provided the necessary political space for negotiating livelihoods. In principle, at least, the returnees enhanced their own protection by being visible from afar. In the Guatemalan returns, UNHCR and the representatives of donors and transnational NGOs accompanied the process, together with government authorities.

The Peruvian returns, on the other hand, had much less international presence, if any. Several ministries, the mayors involved, the government's Human Rights office and the army were 'represented in the returns, together with the authorities in the department of return. The latter were present in order to 'take over responsibility for the returning citizens'. Journalists and photographers from the national media were invited to magnify the impact of the return of 'victims of terrorism'.[15] Thus, the public spectacle was designed not only to prove to the participants that they were being incorporated as full citizens but also as a national ritual of peace, reconstruction and repopulation, an expression of statecraft. This was 'the re-conquest of Peru's abandoned villages', as a general put it.[16]

While many procedures and items were standard, drawn from the vocabulary and guidelines of repatriations and resettlements across the world, the recruitment of returnees in Peru was different from the Guatemalan case. First, Peruvian returnee groups often did not emerge from within pre-existing IDP organizations unless local NGOs working with these organizations were in charge of the return; PAR, the state programme, did not co-operate with either NGOs or IDP organizations. The leaders who took the initiative in organizing a return had to localize and mobilize potential participants through networks of people from their district, who were living dispersed in neighbourhoods in and around Huancayo. Secondly, while the authorities in Guatemala accepted Guatemalan returnees by virtue of their refugee status, the Peruvian authorities undertook a screening of those listed in order to verify their claims to be displaced persons. In both cases, the returnees had to go through a major medical check-up before departure.

The negotiated accord between the returnees and the government, which in the Guatemalan case strengthened their position and entitlements considerably, constitutes the main difference between the two cases. Peruvian returnees did refer to 'the law of return', but this 'law' in its turn referred to the vague formulations in the constitution of PAR, the government programme. While returnees in both cases had access to relief provisions, the Guatemalan refugees were privileged, since the negotiated accords and international support gave them access to credits for land purchases. They were also assisted in organizing productive projects that would help them pay back the loans. The Peruvian returnees were not guaranteed any development projects, but they were assured that the presence of returnees in a community would improve their chances of being targeted by government assistance programmes, now that the authorities had visited them and knew about the condition their communities were in.

Another difference is fundamental for the ways in which collectivity and individuality were framed in the two cases. The Guatemalan refugees had not been able to maintain close relationships with their communities and thus uphold communal entitlements, not so much because of the international border – which represented a minor obstacle – but because of the organization of civil patrols in their home regions, where they would have been treated as subversives if identified. On the other hand, the negotiated return gave them the option of returning to segregated return settlements, where they formed co-operatives and organized production and settlements from scratch.

For the Peruvian returnees, return to their 'communities of origin' was the only option: there was no provision or official support for their negotiating access to land and pastures, which had often been taken over by fellow *comuneros* and adolescents, who had grown up since they left. In some cases, returnees repopulated abandoned villages, which, of course, provided a different set of dynamics to the situation,[17] but in the region under study, all villages of return had residents who had resisted, or at least maintained membership as *comuneros*, during the armed conflict.

Returnees and the others

Despite the fact that the situations of return in Guatemala and Peru were different in several respects, there were striking similarities when it comes to the ways in which the returnees imagined their return, their new links with the community of origin, and the differences between themselves and 'the others'. The others were either those who stayed, or those who returned independently before the moment of official return. In the Guatemalan case, the neighbours of the return settlement were often labelled 'the patrollers', while in Peru they were just known as *comuneros* or community members.

In any case, the returnees were very outspoken about the changes they had gone through while away. One of the Guatemalan returnees, Isabel, described the changes in this way: 'Well, I think that, thanks to the refuge, we turned out very nice, we learned to write and other things, we learned how to live in the world. If we were the same (as before) we wouldn't think of returns, we wouldn't think about doing nice things, we wouldn't know anything. If Isabel were still in the village, she would be the same. We have changed. We became experienced in Mexico.' It is as if she describes the birth of a modern subject, conscious of its own power to change, to transform not only herself but also the others and the environment, to make plans and projects, and to make them succeed. The official position of the returnees was to share the benefits of what they had learned while in exile, where the NGOs and other institutions had trained health and dental promoters, human rights promoters, and so forth.

Likewise, among the internally displaced in Peru who returned home, there was a sense of being able to contribute to the development of the community: 'We came to this place with one sole objective, to bring development. We did not come to murder, to mistreat, or to invade. As the (PAR) engineer says, the community that has returnees has support'. The returnees saw themselves as innovators with ideas about developing a more productive race of sheep by crossbreeding the small Andino sheep with the imported Hampshire sheep, they showed an interest in the latest technology of stock-raising 'from the most advanced countries', and they speculated about how to develop new crops and other products for export. In this sense, they no longer considered themselves just *campesinos*; rather, they saw themselves as following the neo-liberal trend in becoming farmers or even *empresarios* involved in international trade.

This self-identification with development is linked to their characterization of 'the others', of 'those who stayed', as less developed. Without going into details here, in both cases the returnees' stereotyping emphasizes the following traits: 'the others' are violent, uneducated, unable to organize properly, immobile, ignorant, destructive of resources and the ecological balance, and unable to change themselves or forge any change in the community. In short, the returnees have adopted the constructions of social mobility found in development discourses and combined them with their own constructions of geographical mobility. This makes it possible for them to imagine themselves as the leaders, brokers and innovators of the community with respect to their experience of movement (Stepputat and Sørensen 1999).

Moving on: Dismantling collective livelihoods

Given the different conditions for the formation of a collective subject 'in refuge' in Peru and Mexico, the forms and problems of resettlement differ. The Peruvian return was framed by the village or district community, with a high degree of continuity between past and present. The Guatemalan return, on the other hand, brought people from different regions, ethnic groups and municipalities together in one return settlement. But the dynamic of relations between the collectivity and individual livelihood practices is nevertheless a common and very explicit subject of debate among returnees in both cases.

'New hope' and old livelihood practices in Guatemala

When, in 1994, two hundred returnee families took over the former cattle ranch of Chaculá, close to the Mexican border, they discussed what name to give their new home. *Colonia Nueva Esperanza* was agreed on, since it symbolized the utopian enterprise of the collective return. The Mexican word for an urban neighbourhood, *colónia*, signalled the inclusive, multiethnic, urban character of the new settlement, and distinguished it from the monoethnic and rural 'village' community or *aldea*. The vision was to found a 'peasant settlement' with an urban layout, but with more space between the houses, for intensive agricultural use. Production-wise, the idea was to construct an industrialized 'peasant enterprise' for the co-operative exploitation of the land, cattle and forest. At the local level, the settlement was supposed to be a model of alternative modernity, with autonomous government, new forms of production and organization, promotion of Human Rights in a militarized area, and initiatives for regional organization for improvements at the level of infrastructure and services. A secondary (board) school, the first one outside the municipal capital, was planned, and leaders envisioned the founding of a 'peasant university' in the settlement.

The intricate organization of the co-operative and the settlement, the centralized control of the common property, the generous (but short-lived) international funding and the technical support were intended to enable the returnees to make a living without having to engage in labour migration. Migration was considered by the leadership, their advisors and the aid agencies to be inimical to the welfare of the population. While resounding with the older generation's 'peasant utopia', which developed in reaction to a century of enforced migrant labour on the lowland plantations, the younger generation had different ambitions and connections. In particular the young men were keen to explore possibilities in Mexico and the US.

Several years later, the popular name of the settlement was still Chaculá, and the 'new hope' had faded considerably. The co-operative enterprise was in deep trouble, not least because many members actively resisted the co-operative. After two years, 20 per cent of households had left the settlement for good, most of them returning to their former villages. Unpaid labour obligations had been reduced, and high degrees of absenteeism were forcing many aid projects – construction works, reforestation, shops, herding etc – to hire on the basis of salaries. The 'private' land that had been granted by the co-operative to individual households had grudgingly been extended from 0.4 to 2.8 hectares. This reduced the possibilities for large-scale collective enterprises, but individual households were eagerly pursuing individual corn and coffee production. Those who were able to recover their access to communal land in the former village community shared their labour between Chaculá and these villages. As relief provisions dwindled, many men returned to Mexico for temporary work, though this was the general condition of the rural population in the area of return.

The progressive relaxation of the central control of common resources was very similar to the process that the refugees had gone through in Mexico. The recovery of household autonomy seems to have coincided with the reductions in relief supplies in both cases, a process that forced households to secure and control livelihoods by any means possible. Refugees had certainly gained new capacities in the areas of negotiation, organization, book-keeping, project management and human rights, but these were not necessarily helpful in a region with poor communications and meagre resources, limited purchasing power and no employment opportunities. Most of the returnees did not manage specific knowledge of land, vegetation or the microclimate, nor did they have the technical skills necessary to set up industrialized forms of production.

One difference between the processes of individualization of the late 80s and the 90s was the position of women. As has been widely observed, the conditions of camp life may well give the women more control over household resources relative to men, due to the mode of relief provision. In the case of Guatemalan younger women in exile, they also had the opportunity to become literate and learn Spanish in the multiethnic environment of the camps. The communal tasks gave them a chance to become more familiar with public appearances and leadership.[18] This obviously challenged gender relations 'at the heart of the family'. To many women, 'learning to deal with the husband' was the major challenge in exile (Crosby 1999: 185). Back in Guatemala, however, women did not become members of the co-operative, and male leaders even harassed the women's organizations (Krznaric 1997).

Recovering community and land in Peru?

The transnational space of action and vision, generated through the internationally supported IDP concept, helped the Peruvian returnees re-establish themselves in the 'communities of origin'. The frequent reference to 'the Law of Return' illustrates the air of powerful authorization behind the returns, and, as government representatives and returnees argued, 'In Peru, people are free to settle wherever they want to'. If required, police officers accompanied the returnees and stayed with them for a few days, and the return officer made follow-up visits to see if provisions had reached the communities. In one case of acute conflict between returnees and *comuneros*, the government official mediated and drew up an act of reconciliation: 'This act is a transaction with the intervention of the State and the National Police, it is not just an ordinary act. It is an act about a return (which is) organized and supported by the State.'[19]

Thus, arrival and reception still took place within the purview of government institutions, and the ideology of community supported the idea of return and reintegration. According to the *comuneros*, the returnees were, after all, 'sons of the community', and they remarked, 'We shall all work as one single man'.[20] Hence, the returnees were welcome to find somewhere to live in the 'urban zone', but only if they could prove that they were 'truly sons' of the community, that is, by contributing to the progress of the place, would they become members of the community. Thus, beyond the arrival and the relief provisions, some of which benefited the entire community, improvements depended on negotiations with the community on one side and state institutions on the other.

Since the returnees did not have access to land or official backing to recover land or communal pasture, their bargaining position as a collective enterprise was limited in the (many) cases in which the returnees did not constitute the majority of the community. They depended on the strategy of *ganarse el cariño*, 'winning the love' of the community, as they expressed it.[21] In the cases observed, the returnees did not have immediate access to the commons. Often, their own agricultural land had been taken over by members of their own family. Given the cost and inconvenience of taking these cases to court, returnees would usually refrain from pursuing recovery.

As for the communal pasture, a *de facto* parcelling of plots had taken place since the early 80s, when most of the returnees left. Formerly, access to the common pasture was conditioned by presence in and membership of the peasant community. Several arrangements existed that gave newcomers or newly established households the possibility to raise their own herds of sheep, llamas and alpaca by taking care of the herds of well-to-do pastoralists in the community.[22] But as population and herds have grown, families have come to occupy well-defined tracts of pasture more permanently, with members of the community, whether resident in the village or the city, dividing the commons among themselves. However, the formal privatization of the commons was on the neo-liberal government's agenda during the 90s. Peasant communities were in the process of deciding for themselves whether to privatize or not, a process which was accelerated by the returns. In one returnee community, the highly unequal *de facto* distribution of the pasture opened up possible alliances between the returnees and poorer *comuneros* directed against the (rich) leaders who were pressing for privatization. The poorer section voted for the entry of the returnees.

To a large extent, the return is permeated by a myth, the myth that the state, the NGOs and 'the Nations' will provide some miraculous solution to their problems of generating a livelihood in the countryside. As one of the leaders of a return group asked us during the preparations: 'Can you give us advice as to what to do the day after our return?' The leader of a successful return operation recalled his experience after one year in a few words: 'We were wrong. The reality of the village shocked us.' Most returnees gave up after a few weeks and went back to the city and the migration circuits. A few single mothers had benefited from family obligations to allow new families to raise their own herds by herding the family's animals. Even those who had become *comuneros* depended mainly on continued mobile livelihood practices.

Thus, the collectivity of the return is only momentary. Returnee leaders may retain the group as their personal constituencies if they prove to be successful in negotiations over land, pasture or (income-generating) 'projects' for the returnees. But they are more likely to become integrated into the communal leadership or circuits of *residentes*, mainly urban-based 'sons of the community' with a political or exclusively symbolic relationship to the peasant community. The returnees in question did not see themselves as part of an 'abstract community of return' in Peru that would support their progress in practical terms.

Conclusions

Probably, more than any other disruptive event, the conditions of violent conflict tend to invigorate the control of territory and mobility on the part of local, national and insurgent authorities. Since spatial movement becomes a security issue within as much as across international borders, the stakes at play in regard to mobility are magnified. Therefore, mobility becomes more difficult, to a point where people may be either immobilized or effectively excluded from certain spaces, such as their own houses or land.[23] This spatial regime has severe consequences for people's livelihoods, whether they stay 'in place', 'take refuge' somewhere or they remain on the move and endure the risks involved. I suggest coining the notion of 'displaced livelihoods' to conceptualize the disruptions wrought upon existing livelihoods by the introduction of (new) delimitations in spatial mobility. The focus on spatial mobility justifies the use of a spatial metaphor – displacement – even in cases where people are immobilized. The 'displaced livelihood,' then, becomes a particular form of mobile livelihood, a form that is common but not exclusive to violent conflicts.

The cases of Peru and Guatemala/Mexico provide a plethora of examples of displaced livelihoods. Pastoralists cannot take their sheep to market without being heavily taxed on the way there. People cannot obtain access to non-local stables unless they can afford the outrageous charges for them. It becomes impossible, expensive or extremely risky to leave for migrant labour or regular education elsewhere – or to come back for the harvest or to re-secure local entitlements. Long-distance control of land and other localized resources becomes difficult or impossible. The households' combination of urban and rural livelihood practices is undercut, and new practices have to be developed. Even the spatial regimes of humanitarian assistance (to refugees, IDPs and returnees) tend to reproduce displaced livelihoods, either by denying the receivers the means and rights of mobility, or by regarding mobility as inappropriate and thereby de-legitimizing their claims to special victim status.

Although the concept of a 'displaced livelihood' does not distinguish between 'those who left' and 'those who stayed behind', the present chapter has focused on two cases of the displacement and collective return of people who are usually classified as belonging to different categories of victim, namely refugees and IDPs. The distinctive characteristic of the refugee camps in Mexico was the seclusion and all-encompassing organization of everyday life. Resources provided to the refugees were on a very different scale compared to those for the IDPs, including houses, land, schools, clinics, transportation, food and workshops, with a high degree of corporate, autonomous organization of everyday life. The UNHCR and the Mexican government shared a kind of negotiated sovereignty, the government being the '(step-)father' and the UN the incarnation of some higher justice to whom to appeal. Together they provided the framework within which refugee representatives controlled sanctions, type of organization and the distribution of resources. Still, households had a great deal of room for manoeuvre, and over time the authorities had to relax the corporate control of activities under pressure from collective insubordination.

In the case of Peru, those who fled the violence melted into the networks of marginal neighbourhoods, although those who looked or talked like people from the south (Ayacucho or Huancavelica) experienced discrimination. While many (especially men) were monitored individually, IDPs were not singled out as a particular subject of governance but were treated by the authorities as belonging to dangerous, marginal neighbourhoods. When people began to organize around soup kitchens on the basis of their experience of violence, displacement and/or discrimination, the organizations had little control over resources or the activities of individual members.

The NGOs that supported the organization of IDPs deplored the lack of stability and collectivity. According to other NGOs that argued against exclusive support for the 'displaced', '[s]ome NGOs used the Central American refugee experience to argue their case for them, and gave the *desplazados* the idea that they should have their own schools, their own hospitals, their own land, just like the refugees in their camps and the repatriated in their settlements'.[24] While this may be a caricature of their opponents, the refugee camp is but one version of 'asylums' and 'total institutions' that embody the double functions of 'care and control' in the name of a higher cause or reason. In the case of the IDPs, the framing – the modern and corporate ordering of their lives (Mitchell 1988) – did not take the form of a spatially segregated camp. Rather, the IDPs were to be framed in an organization with offices, workshops, leadership, secretaries and donor support, which could encompass and stabilize their livelihoods. In this way, they would stay in (one) place and be able to form a new political subject with national leverage.

The two returns may be compared by means of de Certeau's (1984) distinction between strategies and tactics, and in particular between strategic and tactical movement. The collective returns are strategic in the sense that they rely heavily on visualizing and textualizing techniques which render the move highly visible, controllable, and relatively well known to a broad national and international audience. One important enabling element in this strategic and collective movement is the existence of internationally defined categories of 'unstable' populations that have been given certain rights to be represented *vis-à-vis* national and international institutions. This, in principle, enhances security by mobilizing (inter)national conventions and institutions.

If we turn to the question of how these categories are filled in by the movers themselves, we may note that both situations of return rely on the mobilization of the resource of 'organization' in order to enhance security and change both the sites *and* forms of livelihood practices – in other words, to orchestrate new beginnings for people caught on the move. Encounters and negotiations of livelihood spaces in the sites of return take place within an institutional framework that is authorized from afar. Thus, the places of return are effectively placed on the maps of public institutions.

These strategic techniques, rendering movement visible and constructing 'proper' and stable places from where the environment can be controlled, have usually been considered part of the inventory of states. However, the returnees have appropriated these techniques and the inherent advantages of being seen and known by states and media. Having been either excluded in a camp or deprived of a proper place from where they can claim citizenship, the returnees seem to strive to become recognized as belonging to particular places. It is evident that their understanding of good lives comprises the right to move, as well as access to a proper place of belonging.

Nevertheless, the two cases display important differences. In the Guatemalan case, the collectivity of the return movement draws upon an abstract community, a politically defined, national subject, which became embodied in ethnically mixed settlements of returnees. In the Peruvian case, the collectivity draws primarily on place-bound communities, that is, on collectivities that are defined in terms of particular lineages and a particular place as the common frame of reference. On the other hand, 'internally displaced persons' as a collective and politically potent subject rapidly fades away. This difference is owed, I suggest, to the weaker status of the category of the IDPs relative to the refugee, which relates to issues of national sovereignty and the international governance of mobility. The spatial segregation of refugees in particular camps and settlements, and the strong international support for their return, seem to be the strongest reasons for the difference between the two cases. In both cases, however, the collectivity relies on a celebrated inventory of communitarian practices and ethics.

In contrast to the above description of strategic movement and containment, tactical movement implies individual, unruly or unspectacular movement. This is the kind of spatial mobility that defies control in the villages or camps, on the roads or in the cities, the mobility that questions the legitimacy of the beneficiaries of assistance and elicits the wrath of authorities. We may also contrast the visible, collective returns with tactical moves involving informal negotiations which are commonly used by people who incorporate new sites and spaces in their livelihood practices or move altogether from one site to another. This kind of movement is often sequential, that is, it comprises many moves back and forth in order to build up alliances and resources in new (or old) places without burning one's bridges. Alliances and access to resources are negotiated along lines of patron–client relationships, family ties, friendships or customary labour-exchange relations.

With regard to the strategic/tactical distinction, the final observation to make is the importance of the overlaps and interactions between these different domains of negotiated movement. It is a case not of 'either-or', but rather of 'both-and'. This is obvious in both cases, although the tactics are much more prevalent in the Peruvian case, due to the weakness of the institutional framework, rights and entitlements of IDPs. In the Guatemalan case, the tactics of individual households contribute to the undermining of the collectivity as defined by the 'organized and collective return'. In any case, neither places of refuge nor places of return imply any absolute fixity or immobile livelihood. Rather, they constitute points of departure for negotiating new sorts of mobile livelihood.

Acknowledgements

This article owes a great deal to an extremely stimulating and long-term research collaboration with Ninna Nyberg Sørensen in the Andes and at the CDR in Copenhagen. I have also benefited from the insightful comments of Karen Fog Olwig and participants at the regional LIVELY seminar in Santo Domingo.

Notes

1 Richmond 1993; van Hear 1998; Crisp 1999; Stepputat and Sørensen 1999.
2 The article is based on several periods of fieldwork in Mexico (1988, 1990, 1994), Guatemala (1993, 1994–5, 1996) and Peru (1998, 1999, 2000). Fieldwork in Peru was undertaken in co-operation with Ninna Nyberg Sørensen.
3 Appadurai (1993: 419) has described the global refugee regime as a permanent structure of an emerging post-national order, but this is highly debatable, since, for example, UNHCR may be seen as doing the job of (some) national government in order to uphold the national order of things (Mallki 1992; Hyndman 2000).
4 See for example Cohen 1998.
5 See Foucault 1977; de Certeau 1984; Mitchell 1988.
6 Hernandez *et al.* 1993; see also Burns 1993; Hagan 1994.
7 Interview, Campeche, October 1988.
8 There is a long history in Latin America of linking the image of the devil to wage labour on plantations, down the mines and the like (Taussig 1980).
9 Among others, ICVA (the International Committee of Voluntary Agencies) and the representative of the UN Secretary General, Francis Deng, visited Peru in this period.
10 Interviewed in April 1999.
11 Interview with representative, Campeche, November 1988.

12 Chimni 1999. In the late 1980s, many refugees in Mexico perceived a push to return since HCR was continuously forced to reduce their budgets.
13 Excerpts from interviews undertaken in Chiapas in 1994.
14 See Sørensen, this volume, for further details of Peruvian returns. In this chapter, the emphasis is on the similarities and differences between the two cases.
15 The newspapers represented were sympathetic to the Fujimori government.
16 Quotes from the return to San Martin, Acobambilla in 1999.
17 See, for example, Wilson 1997; Coronel 1999; Gamarra 1999.
18 See North and Simmons 1999; Torres 1999; Crosby 1999.
19 Field notes, May 1999.
20 These expressions were repeated on several occasions in different communities.
21 See also Carla Tamagna, this volume.
22 See, for example, Smith 1989.
23 See also Stepputat and Sørensen 1999.
24 Field notes, April 1999.

References

Anderson, Benedict (1991) *Imagined Communities*, London and New York: Verso.

Appadurai, Arjun (1993) 'Patriotism and its futures', *Public Culture* 4(1): 411–29.

Burns, Allan F. (1993) *Maya in Exile. Guatemalans in Florida*, Philadelphia: Temple University Press.

Camacho Nassar, C. and C. Aguilar Stwolinsky (1997) *Memoria de la Esperanza: El retorno de los refugiados guatemaltecos*, Guatemala: CEAR.

Chimni, B. S. (1999) 'From resettlement to involuntary repatriation: Towards a critical history of durable solutions to refugee problems', Geneva: UNHCR (Working Paper No. 2).

Cohen, Roberta (1998) 'Recent trends in protection and assistance for internally displaced people', in J. Hampton (ed.) *Internally Displaced People: A Global Survey*, pp. 1–9. London: Earthscan Publications.

Coronel, José (1999) 'Movilidad Campesina: Efectos de la Violencia Politica en Ayacucho,' in Fiona Wilson (ed.) *Violencia y Espacio Social: Estudios Sobre Conflicto y Recuperación*. Lima: IEP.

Crisp, Jeff (1999) 'Policy challenges of the new diasporas', Geneva: UNHCR (Working Paper No. 7).

Crosby, Alison (1999) 'To whom shall the nation belong? The gender and ethnic dimension of refugee return and the struggle for peace in Guatemala', in L. L. North and A. B. Simmons (eds), *Journeys of Fear: Refugee Return and National Transformation in Guatemala*, Montreal and Kingston: McGill-Queen's University.

de Certeau, Michel (1984) *The Practice of Everyday Life*, Berkeley and Los Angeles: University of California Press.

Foucault, Michel (1977) *Discipline and Punish: The Birth of the Prison*, London: Allan Lane.

Gamarra, Jeffrey (1999) 'Lo Público y Privado: Un análisis del Espacio Social en Comunidades de Retornantes en Ayacucho', in Fiona Wilson (ed.), *Violencia y Espacio Social: Estudios sobre conflicto y recuperación*, Lima: IEP.

Gmelch, G. (1980) 'Return migration', Annual *Review of Anthropology* 9: 135–59.

Hagan, Jaqueline M. (1994) *Deciding to be Legal: A Maya Community in Houston*, Philadelphia: Temple University Press.

Hanlon, C. Nolin (1999) 'Guatemalan refugees and returnees: Place and Maya identity', in L. L. North and A. B. Simmons (eds), *Journeys of Fear: Refugee Return and National Transformation in Guatemala*, Montreal and Kingston: McGill-Queen's University.

Hammond (1999) 'Examining the discourse of repatriation: Towards a more proactive theory of return migration', in R. Black and K. Koser (eds), *The End of the Refugee Cycle? Refugee Repatriation and Reconstruction*, Oxford: Berghahn.

Hernandez Castillo, R. A. *et al.* (1993) *La Experiencia de Refugio en Chiapas: Nuevas Relaciones en la Frontera sur de Mexico*, Mexico D.F.: Academia Mexicana de Derechos Humanas.

Hyndman, Jennifer (2000) *Managing Displacement. Refugees and the Politics of Humanitarianism*, Minneapolis: University of Minnesota Press.

Krznaric, Roman (1997) 'Guatemalan returnees and the dilemma of political mobilization', Journal of Refugee Studies 10 (1).

Lefebvre, H. (1991) *The Production of Space*, Oxford: Blackwell Publishers.

Lopez Rivera, Oscar A. (1997) *De la Agonía a la Esperanza Cautiva*, Guatemala: C. E. G.

Mallkii, Liisa (1992) 'National geographic: The rooting of peoples and the territorialization of national identity among scholars and refugees', *Cultural Anthropology* 7(1): 24–44.

Massey, D. (1994) *Space, Place and Gender*, Cambridge: Polity Press.

Mitchell, Timothy (1988) *Colonizing Egypt*, Cambridge: Cambridge University Press.

North, Liisa L. and Alan B. Simmons (eds) (1999) *Journeys of Fear: Refugee Return and National Transformation in Guatemala*, Montreal and Kingston: McGill-Queen's University.

Richmond, A. H. (1993) 'Reactive migration: Sociological perspectives on refugee movements', *Journal of Refugee Studies* 6(1): 5–24.

Salvadó, L. R. (1988) *The Other Refugees: A Study of Nonrecognized Guatemalan Refugees in Chiapas, Mexico*, Washington D.C.: CIPRA, Geargetown University.

SEPAR (1990) *I. Encuentro de Intercambio de Experiencias: Alternativas para Migrantes de Zonas de Emergencia*, Huancayo: SEPAR.

Smith, Gavin (1989) *Livelihood and Resistance: Peasants and the Politics of Land in Peru*, Berkeley and Los Angeles: University of California Press.

Stepputat, Finn (1999) 'Politics of displacement', *Journal of Historical Sociology* 12(1): 54–80.

Stepputat, Finn and Ninna Nyberg Sørensen (1999) 'Negotiating movement', in Ninna Nyberg Sørensen (ed.), *Narrating Mobility, Boundaries and Belonging*, Copenhagen: Centre for Development Research: Working Paper No. 99.7.

Suhrke Astri (1993) 'A crisis diminished: refugees in the developing world', *International Journal* 48(2): 215–39.

Taussig, Michael (1980) *The Devil and Commodity Fetishism in South America*, Chapell Hill: University of North Carolina Press.

Torres, M. Gabriela (1999) 'The unexpected consequences of violence: Rethinking gender roles and ethnicity', in L. L. North and A. B. Simmons (eds) *Journeys of Fear: Refugee Return and National Transformation in Guatemala*, Montreal and Kingston: McGill-Queen's University.

U.S. Committee for Refugees (USCR) (1998) *World Refugee Survey 1998*, Washington D.C.

van Hear, Nicholas (1998) *New Diasporas: The Mass Exodus, Dispersal and Regrouping of Migrant Communities*, London: UCL Press.

Wilson, Fiona (1997) 'Recuperation in the Peruvian Andes', *European Journal of Development Research* 9(1): 231–45.

Index